05/07

Org
Beho

Organizational Behaviour
Lecturers' Resource Manual

John Martin
The University of Hull

INTERNATIONAL
THOMSON
BUSINESS PRESS

INTERNATIONAL THOMSON BUSINESS PRESS
I ⓉP® An International Thomson Publishing Company

London • Bonn • Boston • Johannesburg • Madrid • Melbourne • Mexico City • New York • Paris
Singapore • Tokyo • Toronto • Albany, NY • Belmont, CA • Cincinnati, OH • Detroit, MI

**Organizational Behaviour
Lecturers' Resource Manual**

Copyright © 1999 John Martin

First published 1999 by International Thomson Business Press
I(T)P® A division of International Thomson Publishing Inc.
The ITP logo is a trademark under licence

British Library Cataloguing-in-Publication Data
A catalogue record for this book is available from the British Library

First edition 1999

Produced by Gray Publishing, Tunbridge Wells, Kent
Printed in the UK by Antony Rowe Ltd., Chippenham, Wiltshire

ISBN 1-86152-163-4

International Thomson Business Press
Berkshire House
168–173 High Holborn
London WC1V 7AA
UK

http://www.itbp.com

Contents

The *Lecturers' Resource Manual* contains a chapter for each chapter in *Organizational Behaviour*. Each chapter contains an identical range of features to support teaching activity related to that topic. They are:

■ Chapter outline.
■ Learning objectives.
■ Teaching notes and chapter summary.
■ Discussion questions: outline answers for selected questions from the main text.
■ Either one of the Management in Action panels included as a case study, or a discussion topic, with student tasks identified.

Each section of the *Lecturers' Resource Manual* is included with the intention of supporting and enhancing the teaching of that particular topic and of encouraging integration of the material for students. For example, the teaching notes are not intended just as lecture guides, but to serve as a ready reference and refresher for lecturers on the content. The inclusion of a Management in Action panel as a case study is designed to demonstrate how the material included in *Organizational Behaviour* can be used creatively in tutorials and workshops. Finally, the outline answers are not intended to offer definitive solutions, but to illustrate some of the richness, breadth and depth that might be expected from students as they actually begin to understand and think about the material studied.

Introduction

The *Lecturers' Resource Manual* is designed to facilitate the use of *Organizational Behaviour* by making it easier for lecturers to adapt it to their own teaching requirements, and to be able to guide students in their study of the subject. It is one of a number of support elements available to both lecturers and students as part of the teaching package. Other elements in the learning support process include (within the book):

- Key readings. These are all taken from the same source book to facilitate student access. They are extracts from many of the leading thinkers and writers associated with the chapter topics. They are included to provide breadth, depth and a degree of critical reflection for students.
- Further readings. These reflect a diverse, interesting and relevant collection of sources that offer supportive, explanatory, applied or contradictory perspectives on the chapter material.
- Research questions. These are included to provide students with elaboration opportunity within a research context. Some of them are intended as scholarship based activities and others as applied or field research. The purpose being to allow students to develop competencies in research and to gain insights into the pleasures, difficulties and complexity of the process.
- Discussion questions. These are designed to offer students an opportunity to practice their understanding of the subject matter. They could be used as the basis of essay work, or of class discussion and debate.
- Management in Action panels. These are included in the book as an indication of how the real world relates to the chapter topics and to reflect the richness and complexity involved. They can also be used as the basis of case study activity and an example of how this could be achieved is included in many of the chapters in this *Lecturers' Resource Manual*. Many of the Management in Action panels lend

themselves to some form of analysis and discussion and this is demonstrated through the material included in this guide.

Support materials available through the Internet are:

- Short answer questions. These could be used as the basis of class tests or more formal assessment. They could also be used in tutorial situations as the basis of class/group discussion and consensus building, before the answer is revealed by the lecturer.
- Case studies. These are relatively short cases that are not included in *Organizational Behaviour*. They could be used for class/group work or as the basis of assessment through presentation or report.
- Related web locations. These are intended to offer students and lecturers access to a broad range of material that can assist with explanation, elaboration and contextualizing the material.
- Book list. This is intended to indicate books and other sources that are either already included in *Organizational Behaviour* and other sources as they become available. It represents a means of keeping the text fresh and up-to-date.
- Video material. This should provide an indication of some of the video material that can be used by lecturers in support of their teaching.
- Course outlines. These are simply suggestions for how *Organizational Behaviour* can be accommodated around different patterns of course design.
- Transferring from other texts. This section provides some guidance on how *Organizational Behaviour* can replace a number of the other texts in the field.
- Author feedback. This aspect of the web is intended to provide a mechanism through which students and lecturers can interact to the benefit of their own development and understanding of the subject. It also provides a means of updating other users with interesting ideas and examples along with contributing to the development of subsequent editions.

CHAPTER 1

Management and organizations

Chapter outline

This chapter introduces the concepts of organization and management. This is followed by consideration of research in the social sciences, how it differs from the natural sciences and the concept of an organization as a social construction. Management is then introduced as a specific category of activity within an organization. Organizational behaviour and other perspectives are also introduced. The chapter concludes with managerial perspectives on these topics.

Learning objectives

After studying this chapter and working through the associated Management in Action panels, discussion questions and research activities, students should be able to:

- Understand the evolution of organizations as social structures intended to contribute to human society.
- Describe the distinction between research in the natural and social sciences.
- Explain the particular difficulties involved in studying and developing theories in the area of management.
- Outline some of the ways in which organizations change and evolve over time.
- Assess the relative merits of the differing theoretical traditions in the study of organizations.
- Appreciate that the concept 'organization' incorporates many different forms.
- Discuss the nature of management and its relationship to the organization within which it is practised.
- Detail how the study of organizational behaviour can contribute to an understanding of management.

Teaching notes and chapter summary

Introduction

- Organizations are an inescapable feature of modern social experience.

- Organizations impact on all aspects of the human experience.
- Management is also inextricably linked to the functioning of organizations.

A first look at organizations

- Organization usually refers to those public and private sector bodies that provide goods and services.
- There are many bodies that bear strong similarity to commercial organizations but which are undeniably different in function or purpose.
- Is a trade union an organization in the same sense of the term as a university?
- No two commercial organizations are the same.
- Some of the major variables that influence the profile of organizations:
  - Size.
  - Age.
  - Industry.
  - Technology.
  - Management style.
  - Structure.
  - Scope of operations.
  - Management preference.
  - Profitability.
  - Culture.
  - Location.

Definitions of an organization include:
A 'Organizations are collections of people working together in a coordinated and structured fashion to achieve one or more goals,' Barney and Griffin (1992, p 5).
B 'Organizations are social arrangements for the controlled performance of collective goals,' Huczynski and Buchanan (1991, p 7).
C Organizations are ... 'consciously created arrangements to achieve goals by collective means,' Thompson and McHugh (1995, p 3).

- There is no single definition that tightly defines the term organization.

A first look at management

- Managers organize and control the organizations that employ them.
- In a small company they may own the organization.
- Management must ensure that the objectives of the beneficial owners are achieved.
- They are required to operationalize the objectives of the beneficial owners.
- It is from that perspective that their decision-making function and power originates.
- With delayering managers began to experience high levels of stress and job insecurity.
- Managers are employees expected to act *in loco-parentis* for the owner.
- The major differences in management activity are:
  - Level.
  - Job.
  - Industry.
  - Preference.
- Management reflects a complex process carried out in a complex organizational environment.

Natural and social science research

- To understand organizations and management, explanations should stand up to critical evaluation and replication.
- The natural sciences have developed mechanisms over many centuries that are able to meet that need.
- It is not possible to isolate the key variables and replicate organizational functioning in the laboratory.
- Study of these phenomena therefore rest firmly within the social science arena.
- Management theory has emerged over the last 100 years.
- Experience of the world is dependent upon three activities:
  - Detect.
  - Interpret.
  - Predict.
- Reality is a social construction experienced within the mind of each individual. Figure 1.3 illustrates this point.
- Interpretation of explanations offered by a researcher requires consideration of their perspective.
- Figure 1.4 illustrates this by showing that it is never possible to fully understand another's perspective.
- The scientific process is described in Figure 1.5.
- Another important feature of social science research is the level at which it is being carried out:
  - Individual.
  - Group.
  - Managerial.
  - Organizational.
  - Societal.
- Social science research also contains ethical dimensions.

The evolution of organizations

- Organizations have always existed in one form or another.
- They began with the development of collective activity as a means of improving the chances of survival.
- This is still evident today in the many small family businesses.
- Organization not based upon family was used by the Sumerians 3500 years BC.
- By 300 BC the Romans had a significant banking and insurance industry.
- With the fall of the Roman Empire large organizations disappeared.
- During the Middle Ages the Guild became a significant force in organizational activity.
- The emergence of the factory system during the Industrial Revolution again changed the nature of organizations.
- Factory production required different types of job to be designed for both workers and management.
- The bureaucratic approach emerged to run large-scale administrative organizations.
- This was necessary in the days before computer technology.
- Bureaucracy became expensive to run, slow to respond and unable to meet the needs of customers.
- Over recent years alternative structural forms have evolved.
- Organizations can be classified in relation to profit or non-profit activities.
- The discussion has emphasized a Western perspective.
- In the Asian world there were parallel developments from different traditions.

Challenges facing organizations

- The world is constantly changing through evolution and revolution.
- The pace of change is occurring at an ever more rapid rate.
- A catch-phrase over recent years has been an exhortation to innovate or die.
- Johnson and Scholes identify the following environmental influences surrounding an organization:
  - Political/legal.
  - Economic.
  - Social/cultural.
  - Technological.
- These represent a very rational view of change.

■ In addition political reasons lead managers to seek change.

■ Equally managers enhance their career prospects by pursuing change.

People within organizations

■ Organizations do not exist in any real sense of the word.

■ It is the people within them that breathe life into them.

■ Earlier the manager was described as acting on behalf of an absentee owner.

■ This is an agency perspective – the manager acting as an agent of the owner.

■ Cyert and March were writing about coalitions as early as 1964.

■ Rhenman wrote about stakeholders in the running of organizations at about the same time.

■ Figure 1.7 illustrates some of the primary stakeholder groups.

■ Stakeholder groups are people and so provide a basis for analysis.

■ The predictable consistency of computer technology makes it an attractive option in work activities.

■ People cannot match the relentless consistency of performance achieved by robots.

■ Human beings do have some advantages over computer technology:
  – Adaptability.
  – Flexibility.
  – They can show initiative.

■ It is people that create and operate organizations.

■ It is yet more people who regulate the organization in terms of safety, taxation, financial matters and fraud.

■ Even more people are the suppliers and customers of the organization.

■ Within the organization careers are worked out and living standards are determined.

■ Individuals seek to advance their own position and status at the expense of others.

■ Human behaviour influences the perception and understanding of organizations themselves.

■ Metaphors are employed by people to understand the characteristics and functions attributed to organizations.

The study of organizations

■ The study of organizations takes many different forms:
  – Management disciplines (marketing, finance, etc.).
  – Sociologists, psychologists.
  – Economists, lawyers.
  – Critical thinkers from various traditions.

■ The assumptions in the mainstream and critical traditions are identified in Table 1.1.

■ The critical tradition requires approaches to the study of organizations to be:
  – Reflexive.
  – Embedded.
  – Multi-dimensional.
  – Dialectical and contradictory.
  – Socially transforming.

Why organizations need managers

■ Managers:
  – Plan.
  – Organize.
  – Control the acquisition, disposal and application of resources in pursuit of the owner's goals.

■ That view reflects the classical model described by Fayol in 1916.

■ From that perspective management is a very rational process.

■ There are fundamental differences between the jobs of managers and other employees.

■ The impact of their activities on other employees sets them apart.

■ It is management that decide who to recruit and who to dismiss.

■ Managers are able to direct, channel and change the organizational experience for employees.

Why managers need organizations

■ A joke suggests that there are only two skills in management:
  – To create enough problems to justify one's job.
  – But not to create more problems than make for a comfortable life.

■ Some of the factors that create a reciprocal need between managers and organizations include:
  – Career.
  – Status and power.
  – Work preference.
  – Professionalization.
  – Self-interest.
  – Lifestyle.
  – Expectation.

The study of management

■ Prior to the twentieth century management literature tended to be the writings of individuals on their own perspectives.

■ Babbage (1832), a mathematician by training, attempted to offer ideas on how to improve the efficiency of operational activity.

■ One of the first teachers of management topics was Andrew Ure who taught in Glasgow in the early seventeenth century.

■ The beginning of the twentieth century saw the study of management feature in its own right.

■ Table 1.2 identifies a number of the mainstream perspectives to management theory.

■ Alvesson and Willmott describe the critical perspective on the study of management as incorporating the following:
  – Management as social practice.
  – Tensions exist in management practice.
  – Critical studies are themselves embedded.
  – Critical studies seek to illuminate and transform power relations.
  – Critical theory contains an emancipatory intent.
  – Critical analysis is concerned with the critique of ideology.
  – Critical theory implies more than a reconstruction of mainstream perspectives.

■ The study of management is a complex process and there are many different perspectives.

The emergence of organizational behaviour

■ Organizational behaviour is a mainstream perspective on management.

■ It has strong links with the human relations school.

■ The study of organizational behaviour involves two distinct features:
  – Interdisciplinary.
  – Explanatory.

■ The study of organizational behaviour can be most easily reflected in a diagram, see Figure 1.8.

Management and organizations: a management perspective

■ Management can be described in terms of three main functions:
  – Direction.
  – Resources.
  – People.

■ There are four variables in management activity:
  – Role.
  – Skill.
  – Globalization.
  – Ethics.

■ Some large multi-nationals are larger in financial terms than many countries.

■ This provides considerable influence and power.

■ Organizational behaviour can assist with the development of appropriate competencies.

■ With increasing knowledge and understanding comes an increased ability to control.

■ From a management perspective running an organization is about the following dimensions:
  – Personal.
  – Interpersonal.
  – Social.

  – Power.
  – Political.

■ The technical aspects of taking decisions and running an organization are at best ranked equal with these factors.

Conclusions

■ The concepts of both organization and management have been introduced.

■ Also introduced were some of the research approaches adopted to the study of these issues.

■ It set out to provide a background to the study of management and organizations from an organizational behaviour perspective.

Discussion questions: outline answers for selected questions

3. 'It is not possible to generate robust social science theories because there are so many variables at work. It requires the development of a totally new science.' To what extent would you agree with this statement and why?

   This question seeks to ensure that students recognize the relative complexity of the social as compared with the natural sciences. Laboratory studies do have a part to play in identifying causal relationships between variables in the social sciences, but there are significant limitations in being able to transpose such findings into the 'real' world. The questions speak of a new science and students might find the opportunity to use their creative powers to imagine just what such a science might be like and how it would differ from those that exist today. Equally some form of conclusion from their analysis would be expected and the stronger students should be able to justify their own opinions in this.

4. 'There is no such thing as a typical organization or management job therefore it is pointless attempting to theorize about them.' To what extent would you agree with this view? Justify your answer.

   It is common to find that the terms organization and management are treated as being homogeneous concepts. Yet any cursory glance at either soon identifies the variety contained within them. This question seeks to draw out from students just how much they recognize this and how they are able to reconcile this against the homogeneous perspective of much theory. The stronger students will probably draw on their own experience to illustrate the variety found within these terms. Equally the stronger students should be able to justify the study of both through the richness of available theory, the evolution of knowledge as a process and the value of guidelines rather than prescriptions. Some might even identify the commercial advantages that can be secured by managers who are able to judge which models are appropriate in particular circumstances.

5. 'Managers need organizations.' To what extent do you agree with this view and why?

This question seeks to encourage students to explore the reciprocal needs between managers and organizations. It is not possible for large organizations to be run without managers. But equally this question seeks to provide the opportunity for debate about the extent and consequences for organizations of the existence of a category of worker known as a manager. Do managers run organizations based on self-interest and if so to what extent and what are the consequences for the other stakeholder groups? These are just some of the issues that could be expected to be addressed in a good answer. The stronger student might even go on to explore the role of management education in this scenario.

8. Why do you think that individual human beings seek out jobs as managers?

This question will produce a crop of standard answers in terms of money, status, satisfaction and perhaps even expectation. However, among the stronger students it might encourage consideration of psychological reasons for job choice, the need for power and control, the social structures that equate standard of living and status with vertical position in the hierarchy among other perspectives.

Case study

The inclusion of a case study in this chapter is intended to provide lecturers with the opportunity to use this method of teaching which requires students to analyse a situation and form a judgement about their preferred solution. Groups of students could be encouraged to challenge each other on their solutions in order to deepen their understanding of the material and of the need to fully justify courses of action. This process should also provide lecturers with the opportunity to demonstrate that very rarely is only one solution available and that alternative routes might be equally (or more) valuable depending upon the forces acting on the situation and subsequent events.

In this instance the case study is taken directly from the text itself.

Management in Action 1.1: Implementing Japanese management methods

This report describes what happened when a Japanese company decided to begin operations in Wales. Clearly the Japanese management found that 'things' were different to what they had become accustomed to back home. Changes were needed to allow the company to achieve its objectives.

Student tasks

In groups imagine that you have worked as a manager in your home country for 15 years, all of that time in the same company, which makes high quality bedroom furniture. The company is expanding its international manufacturing operations and having built up a sizeable export trade with other countries, your company has decided to open a factory in a country called Martinland, which is many thousands of miles away, but would be a useful base from which to serve a number of regional markets. You have been appointed as the chief executive of the new operation and told that you are to be responsible for the planning, construction, commissioning and running of the new factory.

1. How would you go about planning such a major work assignment?
2. How and on what basis would you determine your team to undertake the project?
3. How would you find out about the planned location and what it would be like to work there?
4. To what extent do you think that an understanding of organizational behaviour might help with the project?

Prepare a brief (not more than 15 minute) presentation on the questions posed and present them to the rest of the class. Be prepared to answer questions from your classmates and also to defend your answers to each question.

CHAPTER 2

Perception and attitude formation

Chapter outline

In this chapter we consider the concepts of perception and attitude. We begin by describing perception as a process and then review each of the stages in detail. This is followed by the introduction of attitudes as a basis of behaviour, also demonstrating the links with perception. An introduction to the topic of impression management follows, together with the organizational implications of perception. The chapter concludes with a review of the management perspectives on perception and attitude formation.

Learning objectives

After studying the chapter and working through the associated exercises, Management in Action panels, discussion questions and research activities, students should be able to:

■ Describe the processes of perception and attitude formation.
■ Detail the perceptual framework model.
■ Explain the links between perception, attitude and subsequent behaviour in an organizational context.
■ Understand what it is about perception and attitude formation that makes it difficult for managers to utilize them in managing people.
■ Discuss the practical and ethical dilemmas facing managers in their attempts to shape perceptions and attitudes.
■ Appreciate the links between perception, attitudes and other management activities.
■ Outline the impression and image management concepts and their relationship with perception and attitude formation.
■ Assess the significance of the behaviour of others being subject to interpretation through the perceptual filters within managers.

Teaching notes and chapter summary

Introduction

■ Perception is a process of:
  – simplification, and
  – classification
  in order to make stimuli meaningful.
■ Perception is usually subconscious.
■ The five main senses in which perception occurs:
  – Vision.
  – Sound.
  – Taste.
  – Touch.
  – Smell.
■ There is a sixth sense, an awareness of spatial relationships.
■ Perception provides a basis for action.
■ Attitudes are formed as a result of experience and socialization.
■ Some attitudes are deeply held and difficult to change, others change with experience.

Perception as a process

■ Survival requires a differentiation between trivial and important events.
■ The young woman or an old woman picture (Figure 2.1) suggests that individuals interpret the 'raw material' available.

A model of perception

■ Figure 2.2 in the text demonstrates the process.

Receipt of a stimulus

■ Each of the senses has its own mechanisms for the registration of stimuli.
■ Perceptions from our senses can play tricks, magicians rely on this to amaze.

Selection of stimuli for attention

■ The selection of which stimulus to pay attention to is a function of three main elements:
  A The circumstances.
  B Factors external to the individual including:
    – Repetition.
    – Size.
    – Contrast.
    – Novelty.
    – Intensity.
    – Motion.
    – Familiarity.
  C Factors internal to the individual, including:
    – Personality.
    – Learning and past experience.
    – Motivation.
    – Objectives.

Organization of stimuli into meaningful patterns

■ The process of grouping the stimuli into meaningful patterns is one that develops with experience.
■ The most important aspects of this process appear to be:
    – The figure-ground principle.
    – The principle of continuity.
    – The principle of proximity.
    – The principle of closure.
    – The principle of similarity.

Interpretation of the significance of the stimulus

Judging the significance of a stimulus is a subjective process and goes beyond the information provided.

A Perceptual errors

■ Mistakes in the process of making sense of perceptual information include:
    – The halo effect.
    – The horns effect.
■ Stereotyping.
    – Perceptual defence.
    – Expectancy.
    – Projection.

B Attributions

■ Kelley's view of the criteria used to identify covariance include:
    – Distinctiveness.
    – Consensus.
    – Consistency.
■ Attribution theory does not identify the actual cause of behaviour.
■ It provides the perceiver's view of the cause of the behaviour.

Response behaviour

■ Individuals react to the perceptual world depending upon needs at the time, including:
    – Pressure to achieve a particular objective.
    – Interest in the task in hand.
    – Distraction opportunity.
    – Consequences of failure to achieve the end result.
    – Physiological state.
■ The actual behavioural responses can fall into one of two main categories:
    – Internal behaviour shapers.
    – Observable behaviour.

The learning loop

■ Feedback encourages individuals learn from experience.
■ The effect of learning on the perceptual process can be demonstrated through a number of illusions (Figures 2.3–2.5, 2.8–2.10 and 2.12).

Person perception

■ Person perception is important in a work setting.
■ Warr (Figure 2.13) offers a model of person perception based on five components:
    – The person and context information base.
    – Input selector.
    – The perceiver's state.
    – The processing centre.
    – The response level.
■ A simplified form is a three-factor process (Figure 2.14):
    – The characteristics of the perceiver.
    – The characteristics of the perceived.
    – The situational variables.
■ This has strong links with attribution theory.

The basis of attitudes

■ Attitudes are linked with many other aspects of behaviour.
■ They are relatively stable dispositions to behave in particular ways towards objects, institutions, situations, ideas or other people.
■ They are considered to develop as a result of experience.
■ Some attitudes are deeply held and difficult to change, whilst others are more superficial and easy to drop or amend.
■ Rosenberg suggests that to change an attitude it is necessary to change the underlying feelings or beliefs.
■ This approach relies on a model of attitudes based on the three components from Figure 2.15:
    – Cognitive component.
    – Affective component.
    – Behavioural component.

- Salancik and Pfeffer suggest that attitudes develop from encountered social frameworks and experiences (Figure 2.16).
- The two approaches are not mutually exclusive.

Attitudes and behaviour

- Katz suggests that attitudes serve four main functions:
  - Adjustment.
  - Ego-defensive.
  - Value-expressive.
  - Knowledge.
- Festinger developed cognitive dissonance to explain behaviour where conflicts existed between components:
  - There may be dissonant or 'non-fitting' relations among cognitive elements.
  - Dissonance gives rise to pressures to avoid further increases in it and to actively seek reductions.
  - Manifestations of these pressures include behaviour changes, changes of cognition, and circumspect exposure to new information.

Impression management

- Impression management is familiar to all actors and politicians.
- Within an organization there are several aspects associated with impression management, including:
  - Marketing.
  - Career strategies.
  - Public image.
  - Managerial.

Perception, attitudes and organizations

- Organizations have many aspects of perception and attitudes to contend with:
  - The attitudes and perceptions of actual customers.
  - The attitudes and perceptions of potential customers.
  - The attitudes and perceptions of the wider community.
  - The attitudes and behaviours of employees.
  - Supplier attitudes and perceptions.
  - The organization's competitors.
  - Regulators.
  - Owners.

Perception, attitudes and control

- Managers have to achieve objectives through other people.
- In order to control behaviour within the organization, managers have either to:
  - demand, or
  - persuade individuals to undertake what is required of them.

- In either case each party perceives the actions of others and responds according to that understanding.

Perception and attitude formation: a management perspective

- Managers must manage in a dynamic situation.
- Perceptions are a constant source of information in that process.
- Perception is a truly personal experience.
- Employees and managers are not likely to interpret the facts in the same way, or even in a consistent way across time.
- Managers attempt to operate in a three-dimensional world in this context (Figure 2.18):
  - Time.
  - Locus.
  - Direction.
- Managers attempt to extract the maximum utility from these concepts in manipulating the perceptions and attitudes of others.
- Figure 2.19 shows that managers receive a great many stimuli from a variety of sources.
- The result is a response set that directs subsequent action in the running of the organization.
- It is the role that managers play that make their perceptions of particular importance.
- That is not to suggest that employees have no influence on the process, simply to state that the ultimate influence rests with managers.
- Perceptual selectivity directs individuals to give credence to information provided from sources that are regarded as more authoritative.
- This phenomenon also influences how men perceive women.
- Deaux and Emswiller demonstrated that men interpreted competence in women as the result of luck rather than skill.
- Ragins and Sundstrom suggested that women managers were perceived to have higher levels of expert power than men.
- Direct attempts to influence attitudes and perceptions are not usual.
- It can be detected indirectly through control and authority, including:
  - Conflict determination and resolution.
  - Culture.
  - Communications.
  - Management style.
  - Work organization, job design and satisfaction.
  - Participative management.
  - Power and control.
  - Reward structures.
- Perception can lead to discriminatory behaviour.

Conclusions

- Perception and attitude formation are key aspects of management.
- They also raise ethical issues.
- They are dynamic processes and of value in helping to simplify complexity.
- They also make people vulnerable to mistakes in classification.
- The challenge facing managers is to make positive use of these concepts whilst not becoming cynical and manipulative.
- Perception is one of the fundamental ways in which attitudes are formed.

Discussion questions: outline answers for selected questions

2. Describe the perception process.

   This question expects students to be able to describe the various models used in the text, perhaps even drawing the models. The stronger answers should also make some attempt to interpret some of the elements in the process, giving examples to illustrate the points being made and also recognizing that all of the senses are involved. An extremely good answer would incorporate an attempt to make some links between perception and attitude formation as well as the potential consequences of perceptual errors, etc.

4. Do attitudes depend on perceptions, or the other way around?

   This question seeks to make students think about the relationship between attitudes and perceptions. It is a difficult question to answer, and in practice there is no definitive answer, as the processes are mutually dependent. Weaker students may 'dive' straight into this question without giving it any real thought and quickly run into difficulties. The stronger student may well bring into the discussion issues associated with human development and the mutually dependent and reinforcing nature of the process.

5. Provide an explanation for the phrase, 'Beauty is in the eye of the beholder.'

   This question should present students with a comparatively easy opportunity to describe the perceptual process and to explain the individuality of it. They should be able to explain some of the factors and forces that influence perceptions and justify why these might differ between individuals. Given that this text is associated with organizational behaviour the stronger students should be able to illustrate their answer by using examples from that context.

8. Can managers influence the attitudes and perceptions of their subordinates? How could they set about doing so?

   This question will be quite difficult for those students with limited organizational experience. A good answer should not only provide examples of the techniques that could be applied by managers, but also an attempt at a theoretical justification for their use. An excellent answer might be expected to also make some evaluation of the techniques adopted by managers in terms of industrial relations, motivation, trust and ethics.

Case study

The inclusion of a case study in this chapter is intended to provide lecturers with the opportunity to use this method of teaching which requires students to analyse a situation and form a judgement about their preferred solution. Groups of students could be encouraged to challenge each other on their solutions in order to deepen their understanding of the material and of the need to fully justify courses of action. This process should also provide lecturers with the opportunity to demonstrate that very rarely is only one solution available and that alternative routes might be equally (or more) valuable depending upon the forces acting on the situation and subsequent events.

In this instance the case study is taken directly from the text itself.

Management in Action 2.1: Attitudes and perceptions in times of change

Student tasks

In groups imagine that you are the Personnel Director of the company described in the case:

1. The time is before the problems have happened and you are planning your future personnel department size and strategy. What would you do to strengthen your department and enable it to play an effective role in the changes facing the company? For example would you recruit additional staff at a senior level from outside the company?
2. Given that you have become aware of the problems indicated in the case beginning to emerge, how would you react?
3. Given that the problems could not be solved early in the process and that they escalated to the significance indicated, how would you then deal with them?
4. Were the problems and difficulties experienced the inevitable consequences of perception and attitudes in an organizational situation which contained a degree of risk for the individuals concerned?

5. What lessons do you draw from this case in relation to perception and attitude formation in an organizational context?

Prepare a brief (not more than 15 minute) presentation on the questions posed and present them to the rest of the class. Be prepared to answer questions from your classmates and also to defend your answers to each of the questions.

CHAPTER 3

Personality

Chapter outline

This chapter introduces the concept of personality. We begin with a description of what personality is and how it is defined. This leads into a consideration of how personality has been measured, along with a review of the major theories. The development and application of psychometric tests is also integrated into the discussion. The use of personality is then analysed in the context of an organization, followed by a review of the management perspectives.

Learning objectives

After studying this chapter and working through the associated Management in Action panels, discussion questions and research exercises students should be able to:

- Outline the concept of personality.
- Describe the major theoretical approaches to the study of personality.
- Appreciate the links between personality and other aspects of individual difference.
- Understand the strengths and weaknesses of each of the major theories of personality.
- Detail the relevance of personality for other levels of analysis within an organizational setting.
- Discuss the basic process involved in the development of a psychometric test.
- Explain the distinction between psychometric tests and the projective approach to personality measurement.
- Assess the significance of personality as a basis for taking decisions relating to people within organizations.

Teaching notes and chapter summary

Introduction

- The concept of personality can be traced back to the early Greeks.

- Personality is about individual difference.
- Each human being has the potential to behave in similar ways, yet they do not.
- Individuals find themselves attracted to some people and repelled by others.
- Some of the reasons for this are based on the perception and attitude factors discussed in Chapter 2.
- Personality is a concept that eludes precise definition.
- Hall and Lindzey (1970) suggest that definitions reflect the theoretical perspective adopted, rather than conceptual insights.
- It is not possible to observe a psychological phenomenon.
- Consider how people are described as differing from each other:
  - Physical description. Height, weight, build, hair length and colour.
  - Emotional description. Gushing, withdrawn, nervous or manipulative.
  - Sociability description. Friendly, generous, giving, likeable or 'nice'.
- Not all are aspects of personality.

The study of personality

- Personality represents those personal characteristics that result in consistent patterns of behaviour (Burger, 1986).
- This rather loose definition leaves many issues unresolved.
- Also ignored is any reference to the source of personality.
- Figure 3.1 reflects the relationship between the nature and nurture aspects of personality:
  A Genetic influences.
  B Environmental influences include:
    - Family.
    - Culture.
    - Experience.

- Nomothetic theories of personality are based upon the identification and measurement of characteristics:
  - psychometric tests are used to measure the existence of certain characteristics.
- Idiographic approaches take into account the uniqueness of each individual:
  - Personality reflects the dynamic interaction between the individual and the environment.
- A third approach combines elements of both idiographic and nomothetic approaches.

Nomothetic perspectives

- The nomothetic approach concentrates on the identification and measurement of the common characteristics of personality.
- This allows the measurement and comparison of personality profiles for individuals.
- The best known were developed by:
  - Eysenck.
  - Cattell.

Eysenck and the study of personality types

- Eysenck describes the historical four temperaments of personality as:
  - Sanguine.
  - Phlegmatic.
  - Melancholic.
  - Choleric.
- Eysenck's research involved the rating of individuals and the completion of questionnaires by subjects in Great Britain, the USA and Europe.
- Factor analysis identified the underlying dimensions of personality:
  - Extroversion – introversion.
  - Neuroticism – stability.
- Figure 3.2 reflects the relationship between Eysenck's personality dimensions and the temperaments.

Assessment of the theory

- Eysenck claims that personality is linked to physiological functioning.
- For example, neuroticism is positively linked with the autonomic nervous system that controls body temperature, heartbeat, etc.
- There have been many criticisms of the work of Eysenck including:
  - The role that nature and genetics is said to play.
  - Also, a theory based on two dimensions is overly simplistic.
- His work is based on a considerable amount of detailed research.
- Eysenck does not claim that there are only two dimensions simply that they account for most of the published research.

Cattell and personality characteristics

- Cattell developed the 16 Personality Factor Questionnaire – 16PF.
- His research process:
  - Trait elements were identified.
  - Initial research.
  - Analysis 50 clusters were identified – surface traits.
  - Identification of source traits – factor analysis of the surface traits produced 16 personality factors.
- Cattell used three sources of information:
  - L-Data.
  - Q-Data.
  - T-Data.
- The 16 factors used by Cattell are shown in Figure 3.3.
- The results are converted to a score on a scale of one to ten by comparison with population norms.
- The individual factor scores are plotted as a profile of the individual's personality – Figure 3.4.
- Cattell identified eight second-order factors from the 16 factors.

Assessment of the theory

- The approach depends very much on the first step in the process.
- If all trait elements were identified then the rest must follow.
- The basis of the approach is that a verbal label exists to describe all behaviour.
- The links between what is observable, the words used as description and associated psychological structures are not clear.

Idiographic perspectives

- The idiographic perspective emphasizes the development of the self-concept.
- Idiographic theorists argue that:

  To understand personality it is necessary to understand how the individual relates to the world in which they live and the individual qualities that make each person different.

- Cooley introduced the concept of the looking-glass self.
- We see ourselves as others see us through the responses that we generate from others.
- Through interaction with others we come to understand who we are and learn to adapt our personality accordingly.
- Mead used the generalized other to reflect the two components of the self:
  - I. Being the unique, spontaneous and conscious aspects.
  - ME. Being the internalized norms and values learned through experience.

- The generalized other is the understanding that the individual develops of the expectations of society.
- It also provides for evolution in society through the adaptation of social norms.
- Rogers proposed that the main objective of personality is a desire to fully realize one's potential.
- His view of the linkages between the components are illustrated in Figure 3.5.
- One implication of this model is that the personality will be subject to change.

Other perspectives: Freud, Jung, Murray and Kelly

Freud and psychoanalysis

- Sigmund Freud lived from 1856 until 1939.
- He trained as a physician and then specialized as a neurologist.
- Most of his life was spent in Vienna.
- He began work with Joseph Breuer using hypnosis in the treatment of hysteria.
- Freud substituted free association in the treatment of patients.
- This was the critical step in the development of psychoanalysis.
- Free association begins with an item of emotional significance for an individual.
- The individual then allows their thoughts to flow until they break off the chain of association.
- This is then repeated for other items of significance.
- The resistance points became the focus for Freud's research.
- Freud used dreams as a source of ideas to begin the process of free association.
- According to Freud, there are three levels of mental activity:
  - Unconscious.
  - Pre-conscious.
  - Conscious.
- In addition the mind consisted of three areas:
  - Id.
  - Ego.
  - Super-ego.
- Behaviour is a balance between the three components of the mind.
- The intention of psychotherapy is to restore the balance between the three components.
- Freud described a process of personality development from birth through to early adult life:
  - Oral – from birth to about the age of two.
  - Anal – from about two years until four years of age.
  - Phallic – reflects the development in the awareness of genital significance.
- Through the id, ego and super-ego adults manage their interaction with the environment.

- Defence mechanisms protect the individual from unresolved internal conflict:
  - Sublimation.
  - Repression.
  - Denial.
  - Projection.
  - Reaction–formation.
  - Regression.
  - Isolation.
  - Undoing.

Assessment of the theory

- Freud's approach to personality is a complex model.
- Eysenck sets out the major objections to the theory:
  - Lack of data and statistical analysis.
  - Sample base.
  - Inadequate definition of terms used.
  - Lack of testability.
- Other arguments against his work include:
  - The use of circular arguments to support it.
  - By emphasizing childhood it ignored subsequent development.
- The model does offer an attempt to create a grand theory.
- Parts of the theory have been subjected to testing with some success.
- Freud's work led to other research on the complexity of personality.

Jung and the cognitive approach

- Jung was a close associate of Freud but they parted company in 1913.
- Jung developed an approach to personality based on Freudian theory, but which postulated three levels of personality:
  - A conscious level.
  - An unconscious level.
  - A collective unconscious.
- Personality differences were reflected by a number of dimensions including extroversion and introversion.
- Another was cognitive style, reflecting four approaches to information gathering and evaluation:
  - Sensing.
  - Intuiting.
  - Thinking.
  - Feeling.
- This is reflected in Figure 3.6.
- The main personality characteristics are shown in Table 3.1.

Assessment of the theory

- The theory is more easily tested than that of Freud.
- The Myers–Briggs Personality Indicator (MBTI) is based on Jung's view of personality.
- Eysenck claims that extroversion and introversion already existed.

Murray and personology

- Murray attempted to reflect the whole individual in a model.
- He preferred the term personology to psychology as the 'science of men taken as gross units'.
- Murray worked intensively with a small number of subjects.
- He identified a total of 44 variables including:
  - Needs – 20 manifest and eight latent needs.
  - Presses – the external determinants of behaviour.
  - Internal states – four internal states that are capable of influencing behaviour.
  - General traits – 12 of these, including anxiety, emotionality and creativity.
- He tested his subjects on 24 test applications in a single 36-hour period using:
  - Autobiographies.
  - Interviews.
  - Experiments.
  - Projective tests.

Assessment of the theory

- Murray drew on Freud and Jung but used a range of measurement to support his work.
- Eysenck claims that there is no validity for the projective technique.
- Murray was not the first person to use the projective technique.
- Leonardo Da Vinci recorded that paint smudges tended to be interpreted differently.
- The Rorschach test was named after the Swiss psychiatrist who developed the approach (Figure 3.8).
- Murray required subjects to create a story from an ambiguous picture.

Kelly's personal construct theory

- Kelly suggested that humans are essentially predictive in their approach to behaviour.
- A construct in this context is a bi-polar continuum of extremes.
- These are arranged into a framework as the personal construct system.
- For Kelly the personality is the framework for experimenting with the world.
- Individuals develop predictions for future events based on patterns in past events.
- Individuals differ in the networks of constructs developed.
- Constructs have a limited range of application.
- Construct systems are dynamic.
- This approach implies that the model accounts for individual difference.
- Kelly developed the Repertory Grid as a means of identifying and measuring constructs.
- The process is as follows:
  - The individual is asked to identify an important way in which two significant people are similar but differ from a third.

- This process is repeated until about 30 separate features are identified.
- A matrix is formed with the significant names along the top and the constructs identified listed down the side.
- A binary number would be entered in each cell based on the subject's assessment of named persons against the construct.
- The completed matrix can then be factor analysed to identify the similarities and differences between the constructs identified (Figure 3.9).

Assessment of the theory

- The repertory grid allows the identification of how the individual interacts with the world.
- It is grounded in a broad interpretation of personality.
- The model is also relevant to an understanding of perception and attitudes.
- This notion of experimenting with the world has led to criticism.
- The theory takes the whole person into account.
- The theory does not prejudge the form of personality.

Personality measurement

- Several ways in which personality can be measured have been introduced – the 16PF.
- Psychometrics – the process of mental measurement.
- There are two main reasons that psychometric tests are used:
  - Research into behaviour and an understanding of people.
  - To enable decisions relating to people to be made.
- There are three ways in which tests can measure personality:
  - Comparison of performance against a standard.
  - Norm-referenced measurement.
  - Criterion-referenced measurement.
- A test is claimed to be valid if it measures what it claims to measure.
- In addition a test needs to be reliable in producing the same answer over time.
- There are different forms of validity and reliability:
  - Face validity.
  - Predictive validity.
  - Construct validity.
  - Test/retest reliability.
  - Alternative form reliability.
  - Split half reliability.
- Test development can be summarized as follows:
  - Step 1. The initial idea perhaps a practical or theoretical need.
  - Step 2. The development of appropriate test items.
  - Step 3. The final forms of the test are developed and the administration arrangements designed.
  - Step 4. The standardization and norming process.
  - Step 5. The reliability and validity testing.

- At this point the test becomes available for use.
- The test might be subjected to criticism from other test designers, academics or users.

Personality: the organizational perspective

- The organizational value of personality is about suitability – to management.
- Organizational objectives require individuals with the approved characteristics
- Personality can be utilized as a control process.
- Another effect is the growth of an industry around personality measurement.

Personality: a management perspective

- Successful managers are claimed to have particular personality characteristics.
- Personality testing influences recruitment, development and promotion opportunities.
- The concept of personality is inseparable from the opportunities that it provides.
- The specification of desired characteristics is a process of social engineering.
- There are links between extroversion and jobs which require a high level of interpersonal activity.
- Research found little evidence of a long term relationship between test results and work performance.
- Assessment centres are used for selection and development purposes

Conclusions

- The concept of personality is a difficult one for managers.
- It operates at many different levels within the organization and has a number of different theoretical roots.
- Over 5000 different tests are available.
- Personality reflects how people get on with each other and features such as intelligence.
- Attempt at definition and links with work activities create difficulties.

Discussion questions: outline answers for selected questions.

2. To what extent does personality explain individual differences between people?

   This question seeks to encourage students to debate the nature of personality and individual difference. Frequently the two terms are used interchangeably. However to accept this assumes that all expressions of behaviour are a facet of personality. Clearly there are instances when this might well be true, for example murders carried out by someone with particular psychological problems.

However there are many other aspects of behaviour in which the links might be much less certain. For example some forms of body language are culturally specific or can be deliberately changed to give a particular effect. The question provides the opportunity to explore these issues and reach a general conclusion that the student can sustain by argument and belief.

4. Would it be desirable for all the employees within an organization to have the same personality? Why, or why not?

   This question brings the issue of personality into the organization and management. It can be argued that many of the recent initiatives in human resource management have been attempts to create a high degree of uniformity among employees in terms of their behaviour and personality characteristics. This is often justified in the name of consistency in customer relations, company image and improved efficiency. However, there is a counter argument. This argues that similarity and conformity can work against good decision making and that diversity is something to be encouraged. The Janis group think material from a later chapter serves as an illustration (although there were other forces at work in that context). The essential essence of this question is that there are strengths and weaknesses of either perspective in relation to this question and students would be expected to review this and form a judgement.

6. In what ways might personality and perception be linked?

   There are several perspectives to this question. Given that personality is a psychological construct 'belonging' to one person and that perception operates within another person, this question could be addressed from what would amount to a philosophical point of view. Equally, it could be tackled in relation to the existence of any causal links between the two. It could also examine any influence relationships that might exist. For example an examination of the extent to which personality might influence the perceptions made by individuals, or whether perception can influence personality. Whichever approach is adopted the student would be expected to provide a credible review of the evidence for their point of view and the implications of it. They would also be expected to examine any contradictory perspectives.

10. 'Any organization needs "different" people within it in order to optimize performance and effectiveness through the unique contribution of each individual.' Discuss.

This question is very similar to Question 4 above. It seeks to draw out a discussion on the relative merit of uniformity as against diversity in people. This time however the question has a more specific focus in organizational impact and personal contribution. As such it would expect a review of how diversity might impact on organizational performance through the differing contributions made by individuals.

Case study

The inclusion of a case study is intended to provide an opportunity to use this method of teaching, thereby allowing students to develop their own thinking in a safe environment in which they gain experience of defending their ideas within their peer group. The approach should also allow lecturers to demonstrate that very rarely is there a situation in which only one solution is possible.

In this instance the case study is taken from the text itself.

Management in Action 3.1: Down with super egos

Student tasks

In groups, imagine that you are a manager faced with a small number of 'super ego' people within your organization. How would you set about dealing with the situation if:

1. The Super-ego is your boss?
2. The Super-ego is one of your subordinates?
3. The Super-ego is a colleague?
4. The Super-ego is someone within the company whom your staff must deal with and it creates problems for them in doing their work?
5. The Super-ego is a customer?
6. The Super-ego is a supplier?

Prepare a brief (not more than 15 minute) presentation on the questions posed and present your proposals to the rest of the class. Be prepared to answer questions from your classmates and to defend your ideas for each question.

CHAPTER 4

Training and development

Chapter summary

This chapter begins with an introduction to the concepts of training and development. This is followed by a review of a number of learning theories that underpin much of the training activity within organizations. This leads naturally into a review of training and development from an organizational perspective. Following this will be a consideration of the application of the concepts within organizations from a management perspective.

Learning objectives

After studying this chapter and working through the associated Management in Action panels, discussion questions and research activities student should be able to:

■ Outline and differentiate between the concepts of training, development and education.
■ Describe the major theoretical approaches to the study of learning.
■ Understand the concept of a learning organization.
■ Appreciate the links between training and development and individual difference.
■ Discuss the strategic perspective on training and development.
■ Detail the relevance of training and development for the management and other groups within an organization.
■ Assess the organizational implications of training and development.
■ Explain the benefits that can be obtained from the use of technology in training.

Teaching notes and chapter summary

Introduction

■ Training and development are major activities within society and organizations.

■ Children spend a considerable number of years in the formal school system.
■ Organizations require flexibility and so find themselves in a position of having to constantly train and retrain employees.

Training and development

■ The *Oxford Dictionary* defines these three concepts in the following way:
   – Develop. To unfold more fully, to bring out all that is potentially contained within.
   – Educate. To bring up so as to form habits, manners, intellectual and physical aptitudes.
   – Train. To instruct and discipline in or for some particular art, profession, occupation or practice; to make proficient by such instruction and practice.
■ Education is a general process representing the basic preparation for adult life in the specific environment.
■ Socialization or induction process for new employees to a company would be an equivalent process.
■ Training is a job-specific form of education.
■ Development is a less specific activity which relates to potential. It is about the future and does not necessarily relate to the job that an individual presently undertakes.
■ Development as an activity has traditionally been reserved for managers. However, it is being increasingly used to describe the full range of training and development activity.
■ Development is often associated with the notion of human resource development, in which individual, career and organizational development are brought together.

Training and learning

■ Each of the terms education, training and development assume that learning takes place.
■ Learning can be defined as the relatively permanent

change in behaviour or potential behaviour that results from direct or indirect experience. The major elements in this definition are:
- Learning implies change.
- Learning implies sustained change.
- Learning influences behaviour.
- Learning results from experience.

■ The learning process is outlined in Figure 4.1.
■ Also indicated in the model are:
- External factors.
- Internal factors.
- Learning experience.
■ There are three main approaches to learning:
- Behaviourist theories.
- Cognitive theories.
- Social learning theories.

Behaviourist theories of learning

Pavlov and classical conditioning

■ Pavlov noticed that whenever his laboratory dogs were given food they salivated.
■ He gave this the term an unconditioned response.
■ The second step was to link this with a conditioned stimulus (a bell).
■ This was done by ringing the bell when food was presented.
■ Eventually the dogs would salivate when the bell was rung.
■ This was the third step, the conditioned response.
■ This series of steps can be shown as a diagram (Figure 4.2).
■ The conditioned response is a relatively simple reaction when compared with the behaviour of humans.
■ The conditioned response quickly died away if it was not frequently reinforced.
■ The work of Pavlov was running in parallel, although independently, with a number of American theorists.
■ Watson coined the term behaviourism to describe the emphasis on observable behaviour.
■ Watson believed that learning in the environment was responsible for almost all development, ability and personality in the growing child.
■ Thorndike built on the stimulus–response model through his studies of the ability of cats to escape from puzzle boxes.
■ From this he concluded that the cats learned by trial-and-error learning.
■ The behaviour so far described was at the unlearned reflex level.

Skinner and instrumental conditioning

■ Skinner is associated with the instrumental approach.
■ A hungry rat can be conditioned to press a lever to obtain food.

■ Respondent behaviour was said to be under the direct control of a stimulus.
■ Operant behaviour was seen in terms of spontaneity with no direct or obvious cause.
■ A stimulus controlling operant behaviour is referred to as a discriminative stimulus.
■ The behaviour is instrumental in producing an effect.
■ It is for the same reason that the term instrumental conditioning is used.
■ The best known experiments in this area involve laboratory rats being placed in a Skinner box (Figure 4.3).
■ Reinforcement is used to shape the behaviour pattern desired.
■ There are four variations to reinforcement schedules:
- Fixed ratio.
- Variable ratio.
- Fixed interval.
- Variable interval.
■ Partial reinforcement schedules produce sustained and rapid response rates.
■ This is positive reinforcement. There are also:
- Negative reinforcers.
- Omission.
- Punishment.
■ The relationship between these is reflected in Figure 4.4.
■ The process of instrumental conditioning has a wider application than the classical approach.
■ Instrumental conditioning can explain much of human behaviour has been established over many years.
■ The difficulty arises in being able to explain how reinforcement operates in every day exposure to multiple and random experience.
■ Conditioning cannot explain all the thought and behaviour patterns observed in people.
■ Individuals have objectives, also the purpose behind many of their behaviours do not easily fit into a conditioned model.
■ Figure 4.5 is a representation of the behavioural modification process which uses these ideas.

Cognitive approaches

■ These suggest that an individual develops internal frameworks that allow them to more effectively interact with the environment.
■ Kohler describes an experiment in which a chimpanzee demonstrated insight as a learning process.
■ Sultan was placed in a cage and given a short stick.
■ A piece of fruit was placed outside the cage and beyond the range of the short stick.
■ A longer stick was also placed outside the cage, but within range of the short stick.
■ After a number of false starts, he paused for a lengthy period and just looked around him.

- Suddenly, he jumped up, used the short stick to pull the long stick into range and thereby obtain the fruit.
- This suggested that the chimpanzee was using cognitive processes to create insights into the problem and how it could be solved.
- A simplified way of thinking about this is shown is Figure 4.6.
- A more recent approach is based on information processing.
- The three primary characteristics of skilled performance are:
  - Organization.
  - Goal directedness.
  - Utilization of feedback.
- Feedback enables the individual to more effectively achieve the goal being sought.
- It is rare in behaviour that a simple chain of events is the major determinant of activity.
- One way that the concept of feedback has been combined with the hierarchical notion of response habits is in the application of a TOTE unit (Figure 4.8).
- The linking of feedback into a hierarchical framework is important for understanding how learning fits into a cognitive model.
- It is also vital for the practice of human resource management within organizations.
- For example, appraisal systems rely on the provision of feedback on individual performance as a means of identifying training needs, development and career opportunities, as well as salary or bonus levels.

Social learning approach

- Infants are socialized into a family unit, young people are socialized into various social groups.
- In organizations the process is frequently referred to as an induction process.
- Socialization can also be regarded as a programmed period of experience.
- The best known example is Kolb's learning cycle.
- Kolb views the learning process as circular and perpetual:
  - Concrete experience.
  - Reflective observation.
  - Abstract conceptualization and generalization.
  - Experimentation in new situations.
- Social learning emphasizes the individual in the learning process.
- It places the responsibility for learning on the ability of the individual to establish links between behaviour and experience.
- External forces can only facilitate and encourage the process.
- The concept of continuous development implied by social learning suggests a five stage process:
  - Integration of learning and work.
  - Self-directed learning.
  - Emphasis on process rather than techniques.
  - Continuous development as an attitude.
  - Continuous development for organizations as well as individuals.

Training

- Most training is based around the notion of the learning curve (Figure 4.10).

The training process

- Training should be used on the basis of meeting an identified need.
- Training needs can be identified from a number of sources.
- Training programmes should be planned around the following issues:
  - Training objectives.
  - Training content.
  - Duration.

Training methods

- These include:
  - Demonstration.
  - Coaching.
  - Discovery training.
  - Job rotation, secondments and special assignments.
  - Action learning.
  - Job instruction.
  - Lecture.
  - Talks and discussion.
  - Case studies.
  - Role play and simulation.
  - Computer-based and programmed learning.
  - Distance learning.

Training evaluation

- Evaluating the benefits of training is a difficult process that attempts to measure the transfer of training to the organizational context.
- Trainees might enjoy the training event, yet gain little job-related benefit from it.
- Conversely, trainees may not enjoy the experience and yet find the job relevance high.
- There may also be change initiatives active at the same time.
- According to Hamblin evaluation takes place at a number of levels:
  - Reaction.
  - Learning.
  - Job behaviour.
  - Organization.
  - Ultimate value.
- Three features are apparent in these evaluation levels:
  - Measurement.
  - Time.
  - Hindsight.

Development

- The term employee development is increasingly finding favour.
- It is a process that allows potential to be realized.
- It places a high level of responsibility on the individual.
- Because of the longer time frame in development the return is not likely to become apparent for many years.
- For these reasons organizations are tending to make use of the concept of development centres.
- The learning organization is about the facilitation of the learning of all employees and the constant transformation of the organization in response to that new knowledge and ability.
- Mumford suggests that the main characteristics include:
  - Encouragement for managers to accept responsibility for the identification of their own training needs.
  - Encouragement for managers to set challenging learning goals for themselves.
  - The provision for all employees of regular performance reviews and feedback on learning achieved.
  - Encouragement for managers to identify learning opportunities in jobs and to provide new experiences from which employees and managers can learn.
  - Encouragement of a questioning attitude to the accepted ways of doing things within the organization.
  - The acceptance that when learning, some mistakes are inevitable, but that individuals should learn from them.
  - Encouragement of on-the-job training and other learning activities.
- It is part of the strategic human resource management perspective adopted by many organizations today.

Training and development: an organizational perspective

- Training and development impact on all aspects of the employment of people, from the induction of new employees to the development of future generations of directors.
- The workforce is male dominated at a senior level and there have been a number of initiatives to broaden the access of women to these positions.
- It is the various groups and teams within the organization that achieve objectives.
- Therefore, it is a necessary part of organizational life to be able to work as part of a team.
- Training in group formation and dynamics can provide a basis for shaping the behaviour of groups and so influencing the level of effectiveness achieved.

- Much of the purchasing, marketing and lobbying activity within organizations are based on training and development concepts and principles.
- The challenge facing managers and organizations is how to make cost-effective use of training and development.
- There is always costs associated with these activities and the benefits are not always easy to identify, or quick to materialize.
- Human beings are naturally adaptive and creative.
- If no training or development were to take place individuals would 'muddle through'.
- It is easy to imagine that more training and development activity would solve all management's problems.
- The challenge is one of finding the appropriate level of activity commensurate with organizational requirements.

Training and development: a management perspective

- There is a permanent background of need for training activity.
- There is also career progression for individuals.
- The failure of many organizations to meet these requirements has been a source of criticism.
- Management face a dilemma in the need to balance the costs and benefits.
- Over recent years there have been many initiatives to improve the impact and level of training and development.
- For the training specialist these are not just interesting issues for debate.
- Managers are under pressure for cost-effective output in the short term yet need to divert employee time to training activities.
- Organizations also need to be convinced of the value of the activity.
- It is a fact of commercial life that when economic stringency is necessary training activity is often the first to suffer cutbacks.
- Therefore managers ignore the value of it at their peril.
- Training and development have many applications:
  - Induction of new employees.
  - Initial job training.
  - Subsequent job training.
  - Training on transfer or promotion.
  - Training for special groups.
  - Development.
  - Professional development.
  - Specialist career development.
  - Manager's career development.
  - Development for directors and senior managers.
  - Job termination training.
  - Special initiative training and development.

■ Training and development gains significance from the inclusion of a strategic perspective to human resource management (Figure 4.11).

Conclusions

■ Training and development is an activity that continues for much of life.
■ Human behaviour is influenced in many ways by experiences.
■ Organizations need trained people in order to achieve objectives and they need to develop the talents of individuals in order to make provision for the future.
■ The strategic human resource approach practiced by many organizations today places a high priority on the development of employees in order to capture the benefits of the learning organization.

Discussion questions: outline answers for selected questions

3. 'Each individual should accept responsibility for their own training and development. It is not up to organizations to provide more than essential job-related training.' Discuss.

   This question seeks to draw out from students the broader aspects associated with training and development. There are several aspects to an answer for this question:
   A The responsibility for training and development activity.
   B Issues of career development and ownership of the process.
   C The delineation of 'essential job training'.
   D Equally there are elements associated with cost and benefits of training, the role of government and professional bodies that might find an expression in a first class answer to this question.

4. 'Training and development are nothing more than elaborate mechanisms for ensuring worker compliance with management's wishes.' Discuss.

   This is another question which seeks to draw out the broader perspectives on training and development. For example, it could be argued that compliance with management wishes is what capitalist organizations are all about in the search for profit. Therefore training is all about achieving that objective. Equally it could be argued that it is management that are responsible for planning, controlling, etc. and therefore they need to be assured that employees will follow that direction effectively. However there is also the political perspective that suggests that control contains significant overtones of social, political and status manipulation. The stronger answers will attempt to bring in this broader perspective and move beyond the managerial and rational explanation.

6. How would you recommend to your lecturers that they keep attendance at lectures high and ensure that work was handed in on time? Justify your views.

   This is a practical and applied question. Also it might also provide some interesting insights into the motivations (or otherwise) of students. If lecturers are lucky they might even obtain some good ideas on course design and presentation. It is a creative question which should demonstrate links between theory and practice.

7. 'Successful management requires considerable experience, it cannot be taught in a classroom.' Discuss this statement and identify the implications for management training and development.

   This seeks to draw out from students their understanding of what management is and how training and development can play a part in the development of appropriate skills. Given the nature of this book it is likely that students answering this question will be taking management or business related degrees. It is highly likely that such students will tend to stress the need to have a theoretical perspective on the topics as part of their preparation for a management career. However, the stronger answers might also begin to address issues associated with the transferability of skills from classroom to workplace and the development of skills not immediately business or management oriented, yet which have value in management jobs. Examples that come to mind are skills and abilities learned on history or maths degrees and the extent to which the skills acquired by such students are valued by recruiters of trainee managers. From the perspective of management as a leadership and relationship activity the need for practice and experience cannot be ignored and this should also be balanced in the answer. For post-experience and MBA-type students the dash for qualifications as a prerequisite for promotion might also feature in the discussion.

9. What should a manager do if a training programme designed to improve employee performance fails to have any effect?

   This question seeks to draw out a discussion on the need to monitor training activity and to begin the whole process by identifying training needs. If the needs are not adequately identified then any programme will be likely to underachieve against its objectives. Clearly, in the situation described some form of remedial action would be needed as well as a review of company practice to attempt to prevent such eventualities happening in the future.

Case study

The inclusion of case study in this chapter is intended to

provide lecturers with the opportunity to use this method of teaching which requires students to analyse a situation and form a judgement about their preferred solution. Groups of students could be encouraged to challenge each other on their solutions in order to deepen their understanding of the material and of the need to fully justify courses of action. The process should also provide lecturers with the opportunity to demonstrate that very rarely is only one solution available and that alternative routes might be equally (or more) valuable depending upon the forces acting upon the situation and subsequent events.

In this instance the case study is taken directly from the text itself.

Management in Action 4.2: The domestic supervisor and conditioning

Student tasks

In groups of about four people imagine that you have just been appointed as a domestic supervisor of a university hall of residence as described in the case study.

Your tasks are to:

1. Review the actions of the new domestic supervisor and form a judgement on their likely value in achieving the required objectives.
2. To what extent do the actions employed reflect a training approach or the exercise of basic management skill?
3. What actions would you take if the conditioning approach did not appear to be working with the existing staff?
4. Develop a strategy that you would adopt had you just been appointed domestic supervisor.
5. What lessons are apparent from this case about the relationship between management and training?

Prepare a brief (not more than 15 minute) presentation on the questions posed and present them to the rest of the class. Be prepared to answer questions from your classmates and also to defend your answers to each question.

CHAPTER 5

Motivation

Chapter outline

In this chapter we consider the topics of motivation and reward. We begin the discussion with a description of the major theories in this field. This is followed by an organizational review along with an introduction to the management perspectives relevant to the topic. The social context within which work is carried out means that there is a continual reappraisal of the role of work in people's lives. It is against this backdrop that managers must achieve objectives by motivating and rewarding employees.

Learning objectives

After studying this chapter and working through the associated Management in Action panels, discussion questions and research exercises students should be able to:

- Describe the major motivation theories.
- Outline the relationship between motivation and employee reward.
- Explain why motivation is a concept of considerable significance to managers.
- Understand what makes the study of motivation difficult.
- Discuss the dilemmas facing managers in applying motivation theory to a work setting.
- Appreciate the links between motivation and activities such as pay determination, employee participation and job design.
- Detail the various ways in which motivation theories can be classified.
- Assess the significance of classifying motivation theories.

Teaching notes and chapter summary

Introduction

- The term motivation is a familiar concept in business and team sports.

- The *Pocket English Dictionary* defines motive as 'What impels a person to action, e.g. fear, ambition, or love.'
- This however, is only part of the richness of the concept as it would be used in organizational behaviour terms.
- Psychologists have long recognized the distinction between drives and motives.
- Drives reflect the physiological/biological needs of the body.
- Motives reflect learned patterns of behaviour.
- Traction, the feeling among workers of being pulled along by the rhythm of a particular activity is a related term.
- This infers that highly repetitive jobs may contain motivational properties.

Early approaches to motivation

- In the pre-industrial era, communities were motivated by the need to survive and the perishable nature of much of the means of doing so.
- Slavery, bonded or enforced labour meant that individuals could be forced to perform tasks on behalf of others.
- There are examples of the pace of work being set at the Arsenal of Venice in the 1400s and of monks estimating the time to build churches and cathedrals.
- At the beginning of the twentieth century FW Taylor developed scientific management.
- It identified the one best way to do a job and motivated employees through linking wages to output.
- His initial attempts were successful (Table 5.1).
- The level of production increased considerably, but the wages of employees changed little (Table 5.2).
- Taylor's success was short lived and he was dismissed from the company in 1901 as the result of growing hostility.

- Chester Barnard suggests that motivation a balancing process:

> The net satisfactions which induce a man to contribute his efforts to an organization result from the positive advantages as against the disadvantages which are entailed.

The theories of motivation

- There is no one theory that can embrace the entire range of circumstances.
- Things that motivate today may not work tomorrow.
- Content theories identify the motives that produce behaviour.
- Process theories emphasize those mechanisms that encourage behaviour in context.
- Figure 5.1 provides an overview of these approaches.
- An intrinsic motivator is one that originates inside the individual.
- An extrinsic motivator is one that originates outside of the individual.

Content theories

Maslow's hierarchy of needs

- Maslow produced the idea that a hierarchy of needs could explain purposeful behaviour.
- The basis is that all individuals have innate needs or wants which they seek to satisfy.
- In addition these have an inbuilt prioritizing system.
- Figure 5.2 shows the model.
- The five levels are:
  - Physiological needs.
  - Safety needs.
  - Social needs.
  - Esteem needs.
  - Self-actualization needs.
- Maslow suggests that the hierarchy is not a rigid framework.
- The hierarchy displays the following properties:
  - A need once satisfied is no longer a motivator.
  - A need cannot be effective as a motivator until those before it have been satisfied.
  - If deprived of the source of satisfaction from a lower-order need it will again become a motivator.
  - There is a innate desire to work up the hierarchy.
  - Self-actualization cannot be exhausted.

Assessment of the theory

- Maslow did not specifically describe his theory as applicable to work situations.
- There are a number of difficulties in applying his theory in an organizational context:
  - Not everyone is motivated by things that go on inside the organization.

- The amount of satisfaction needed before a higher level need is activated is unknown.
  - The theory cannot explain all behaviour.
  - It is a theory based upon the USA in the 1940s.
  - Organizational events can be aimed at satisfaction of more than one level in the hierarchy.
  - Individuals will place different values on each need.
- Maslow's theory has been very influential over the years in assisting managers to motivate employees.
- It encourages managers to get the basics right.
- It forces managers to examine motivation from the employee perspective.

Alderfer's ERG theory

- Alderfer describes a three level hierarchy:
  - Existence needs.
  - Relatedness needs.
  - Growth needs.

Assessment of the theory

- Alderfer did not merely simplified the Maslow material.
- He suggests that individuals move through the hierarchy as each becomes satisfied.
- More than one need could be functioning at the same time, individuals may also regress back down the hierarchy.
- Alderfer also postulated a frustration–regression mechanism.
- Managers should address all three levels of need, but if one cannot be met then additional effort will need to be put into providing for the others as they will increase in significance.

McClelland's acquired needs theory

- This develops a different set of needs as the basis of motivational:
  - Achievement – nAch.
  - Affiliation – nAff.
  - Power – nPow.
- These can be seen as elements within the higher order needs described by Maslow.
- Needs are acquired through the social process of interacting with the environment.
- Everyone has these three needs although there is a tendency for only one to be dominant.
- Questionnaires similar to Figure 5.3 are able to identify individual needs.

Assessment of the theory

- Table 5.3 provides a work preference and job example for each category of need.
- One difficulty with such tables is the generalized nature of the preferences and examples.
- Also, if needs provide a basis for job suitability, how can this be linked with the fluid nature of the needs themselves?

Herzberg's two-factor theory

- The research involved interviews with 203 accountants and engineers from organizations around Pittsburgh.
- He used a critical incidents approach asking questions about what felt good or bad about work.
- A content analysis identified the factors which were fundamentally different to those that led to dissatisfaction.
- The hygiene factors were those that, if absent, caused dissatisfaction:
  - Salary.
  - Working conditions.
  - Job security.
  - Level and quality of supervision.
  - Company policies and administrative procedures.
  - Interpersonal relationships at work.
- Motivating factors were those that could encourage the individual to improve their work performance:
  - Recognition.
  - Sense of achievement.
  - Responsibility.
  - Nature of the work itself.
  - Growth.
  - Advancement.
- It is possible to compare this theory and those of Maslow, Alderfer and McClelland (Figure 5.4).
- The significance of Herzberg's model is that the two factors are not opposite ends of a continuum.
- Lack of positive levels in the hygiene factors does not lead to demotivation, but to dissatisfaction.
- High levels in the hygiene factors does not lead to motivation, but to non-dissatisfaction.
- High levels among the motivation factors will lead to positive motivation.
- Low levels of motivating influences will reduce the overall level of motivation, but not create dissatisfaction.
- It would create feelings of non-satisfaction.
- There is a middle ground between these two factors (Figure 5.5).
- There is a need to concentrate on two sets of factors at once.

Assessment of the theory

- There have been a number of criticisms of Herzberg's work:
  - The results are research dependent.
  - The results are capable of different interpretations.
  - It does not provide for individual difference.
  - It is restricted to manual or unskilled workers.

Process theories

Vroom's expectancy model

- The basis of expectancy models is that motivation is a function of the desirability of the outcome of behaviour.
- This is also referred to as a path–goal theory (Figure 5.6).
- Individual behaviour will be moulded by what is seen as the available rewards on offer and their importance to the individual.
- The model contains three key elements:
  - Valance.
  - Instrumentality.
  - Expectancy.
- The model can be described in an equation:

$$M = \Sigma(E \times V).$$

The Porter and Lawler extension   *Vroom's expectancy model*

- Porter and Lawler develop the model by attempting to link motivation and performance.
- In their model they draw attention to the range of variables such as the individual's view of work (Figure 5.7).

Assessment of the theories

- According to the expectancy model, individuals always seek to optimize the return on their investment of effort.
- The theory implies that managers must seek ways of strengthening the links between effort, performance and reward.
- Managers need to be able to identify the employee calculus.
- Because of the many components and the changeable nature of it this would become impossible.
- Hollenback used matrix algebra to deal with the number and combination of variables.

Adams equity theory

- People develop strong feelings about the relative fairness in the treatment that they receive at work.
- When reaching a conclusion on fairness, individuals need a point of reference.
- The main source being the perceived treatment of other people.
- Social exchange theory suggests that individuals operate social interactions as a form of trading.
- Every employee is paid a wage and this provides opportunity for comparison.
- Industrial relations specialists are well aware of equity in pay comparisons.
- Figure 5.8 reflects the operation of equity theory.

Assessment of the theory

■ Much of the research on equity theory has concentrated on its application to pay and rewards.
■ Dornstein examined the basis of comparison in people's judgements about the fairness of received pay and found that it changed depending upon a number of factors.
■ Organizations need to give close attention to equity when designing pay structures, merit awards and promotion.

Locke's goal theory

■ Locke suggested that intention plays a significant part in formulating their behaviour patterns.
■ This can be used to motivate.
■ It is from this perspective that many performance appraisal systems attempt to shape behaviour.
■ A model of goal theory is shown as Figure 5.9.
■ Within the model there are a number of issues that can significantly influence the outcome:
  – The more specific the goal the more likely it is to be achieved.
  – The completion requirement (finish date) should be specific.
  – Difficult to achieve goals are more likely to be achieved than easy to achieve goals.

Assessment of the theory

■ There have been a number of studies of goal setting approaches to motivation.
■ Generally the results have been supportive of the approach.
■ Individual difference, personality, previous education and training are among the factors that could have an effect on the model.
■ These remain to be researched in any depth.
■ The approach is widely used as the basis of performance appraisal systems, particularly where projects, tangible results or change was a feature.
■ Some jobs are not amenable to goal setting.
■ With an increasingly turbulent operating environment it is increasingly difficult for individuals to maintain performance targeted at specific goals.

Attribution theory and motivation

■ Attribution theory suggests that motivation is a response by the individual to a self-perception of their behaviour.
■ Individuals decide whether their behaviour is responding to internal or external influences.
■ On the basis of this decision, the individual will prefer to be intrinsically or extrinsically motivated.
■ The result of this affects the form of motivation that will be effective for that individual.
■ Wiersma concluded that the links between extrinsic and intrinsic motivation were complex and could work against each other.

■ It is argued that intrinsic motivation provides the best approach to obtaining a totally effective employee.
■ However, many motivation strategies use extrinsic principles to motivate employees.
■ The criticism of such approaches is that they purchase output, generating at best an instrumental or compliance response.

Additional perspectives on motivation

McGregor's theory X and theory Y

■ McGregor introduced underlying assumptions concerning human nature when he proposed theory X and theory Y.
■ His claim was that managers hold beliefs that classify employees into either a theory X or theory Y.
■ Consequently, managers operate policies and practices based on one or other of these sets of assumption (Figure 5.10).

Ouchi's theory Z

■ Ouchi investigated the ways that Japanese and American managers managed their subordinates.
■ In doing so he identified a number of cultural differences between the two:
  – American organizations.
    – Short-term employment.
    – Explicit control processes.
    – Individual decision making.
    – Individual responsibility.
    – Segmented concern.
    – Quick promotion.
    – Specialized careers.
  – Japanese organizations.
    – Lifetime employment.
    – Implicit control processes.
    – Collective decision making.
    – Collective responsibility.
    – Holistic concern.
    – Slow promotion.
    – Generalist careers.
■ From these profiles it is possible to identify a number of implications for motivational practice.

Hofstede and cultural influences on motivation

■ Hofstede introduced national culture into the debate about motivation.
■ In his research he used the following framework to study the differences between 40 countries:
  – Power distance.
  – Uncertainty avoidance.
  – Individualism–collectivism.
  – Masculinity.
■ Each of the theories of motivation reflect a particular set of cultural norms.

- They could be expected to be most effective in situations reflecting that particular cultural orientation.
- This introduces the notion that motivation theories may not be mutually exclusive.
- Trompenaars offers seven different dimensions of national culture which could impact on motivation.

Maccoby's social theory

- A more recent approach is that of Maccoby.
- He argues that the social and work environments have changed over recent years.
- The effect has invalidated the underlying value of traditional approaches to motivation.
- He argues that a new motivation theory is needed including concepts of trust, caring, meaning, self-knowledge and dignity.
- Emerging is a new type of worker, interested in self-development combined with a fair share of profit.

Motivation, reward and productivity

- The management of performance is a major issue for managers.
- One way of achieving this is through a controlled performance.
- Looked at as a model of motivation and rewards (Figure 5.11), it contains the following elements:
  - Work environment.
  - Ability.
  - Clarity of objectives.
  - Motivation to perform.
  - Job performance.
  - Intrinsic rewards.
  - Productivity.
  - Extrinsic rewards
  - Corporate objectives.

Motivation: an organizational perspective

- Motivation is an individual-level phenomenon.
- Content theories adopt a needs and wants perspective and process theories concentrate on the decision making that guides behaviour.
- Motivation is based on internal cognitive processes that are not available for direct inspection.
- Complexity is added because of:
  - Managerial assumptions.
  - Situational context.
  - Personal preference.
  - Instrumentality.
  - Bio-social basis of behaviour.
- Society determines many of aspects of life classified as needs.
- A Marxist analysis would question the basis of motivation grounded on needs that are socially constructed.

- Motivation theories have become surrogates for the search for meaning according to Seivers.
- Garrahan and Stewart review recent motivational practices, such as teamworking, quality circles and company culture.
- The negative impact on individuals can be identified.

Motivation: a management perspective

- Motivation can be seen as a means to achieve management's goals.
- Experience in the workplace and outside it influences the motivation level of people within it.
- Motivation is fluid, subject to variation in the individual.
- This makes managing motivation difficult.
- Managers face major difficulties in attempting to motivate employees.
- Not all theories offer a realistic option for motivating employees.
- Managers do not have freedom to change company policy to personalize motivational.
- Motivation is an individual level response but managers must operate with groups.
- Cafeteria or flexible benefits was developed to address this.
- Most theories originate from a Western culture and may not be valid in other settings.
- The options available with which to influence levels of motivation include:
  - Pay levels and structures.
  - Incentive schemes.
  - Organizational factors.
  - Performance appraisal.
  - Management style.
  - Feedback, praise and punishment.
  - Management by example.
  - Company policies.
- Managers do not have the opportunity to adjust all of the levers available, for the following reasons:
  - Availability.
  - Freedom of action.
  - Personal preference.
  - Variability.
  - Group norms.

Conclusion

- Motivation is an individual level response and yet managers must operate at a group level.
- Company policies and procedures have to be applied consistently if inequity is to be avoided.
- Motivation offer some opportunity to enhance work for individuals.
- Motivation is a social and a political concept as well as a psychological one.

Discussion questions and outline answers for selected questions

3. If you were a manager, would you prefer to have a team extrinsically or intrinsically motivated? Why?

   This question seeks to encourage students to recognize the distinction between extrinsic and intrinsic motivation. It should draw out as a starting point the 'internal–external' locus of behaviour and the 'benefits' associated with internalization. However the stronger students might also begin to recognize the relationships between theory and practice in this area. Issues of power, manipulation and control might also be expected to emerge.

4. Motivation is best achieved through offering employees a monetary reward for working harder. Discuss this statement.

   This question addresses the age old problem of money and motivation. In many ways it is a very difficult question to answer well. Some of the theories make specific provision for the basic needs and so it would be possible to provide a standard and bland answer on these lines. However, to go beyond that level requires some skill and considerable understanding of the complex relationship between money, work, private life, socially based needs which are constantly subjected to change, etc.

7. What is motivation? Describe two theories of motivation and suggest where you think they might be most useful, justify your answer.

   This question seeks to get students to draw out of the analysis that specific theories offer a partial reflection of motivation and might be applicable in some situations but not others.

9. It would be impossible for an organization to fully motivate all employees all of the time. Discuss.

   This question attempts to allow students the opportunity to demonstrate that motivation is a dynamic process within a dynamic environment. Every individual has slightly different needs and these change over time. because organizations must maintain a high degree of internal consistency in HR policy and treatment of employees it is difficult to find ways of motivating individuals effectively. Schemes are inevitably aimed at groups or employees in a general sense. Therefore it can be argued that a sub-optimal level of motivation is the best that can be achieved in most cases. The question seeks the student understanding and interpretation of this.

Case study

The inclusion of a case study in this chapter is intended to provide lecturers with the opportunity to use this method of teaching which requires students to analyse a situation and form a judgement about their preferred solution. Groups of students could be encouraged to challenge each other on their solutions in order to deepen their understanding of the material and of the need to fully justify courses of action. This process should also provide lecturers with the opportunity to demonstrate that very rarely is only one solution available and that alternative routes might be equally (or more) valuable depending upon the forces acting on the situation and subsequent events.

In this instance the case study is taken directly from the text itself.

Management in Action 5.7: An encouraging start to employee motivation

This report describes what happened when one company attempted to implement a motivation through involvement process. It was not a complete success and not everyone was prepared to become involved.

Student tasks

In groups imagine that you have been appointed as a management consultant to the company by Williamson. Your brief is to review what went wrong (if anything) and what the management should do now to move the involvement process forward. You have also been asked to consider the use of involvement as a motivational device and to specifically consider how to motivate employees who do not wish to become empowered and managers who see it as a threat.

You should prepare a management presentation of no more than 15 minutes duration addressing these issues. You should also be prepared to answer questions and justify your proposals at the end of your presentation.

CHAPTER 6

Group formation and structure

Chapter outline

This chapter begins with a consideration of the concept of a group. It then goes on to review the ways that groups are used within an organization and the distinctions between formal and informal groups. A short review of research into group working will be introduced before outlining a number of approaches to the study of how groups are formed and structured. This will be set into a critical review of the ideas discussed along with some indication of their relevance to management and organizations.

Learning objectives

After studying this chapter and working through the associated Management in Action panels, research activities and discussion questions, students should be able to:

- Outline the concept of a group as distinct from a collection of individuals.
- Understand the differences between formal and informal groups.
- Describe the Hawthorne studies and their significance in understanding the nature of groups.
- Discuss the different approaches to the study of how groups form and are structured.
- Appreciate the links between the group level of analysis within organizational behaviour and the individual and organizational levels.
- Detail some of the links between group formation and structure and job design, organization design and motivation.
- Explain the difficulties facing managers in attempting to manage both formal and informal groups.
- Assess the organizational implications of group activity.

Teaching notes and chapter summary

Introduction

- Groups form a significant part of the everyday experience of people.
- There are three types of group based on purpose:
  - Organizational.
  - Self-interest.
  - Affinity.
- Would a collection of human beings constitute a group?
- Shaw suggests that a group consists of two or more people who interact with each other in such a way that each influences and is influenced by the others.
- Schein suggests that a group can be any number of people who interact with each other, are psychologically aware of each other and think of themselves as a group.
- Both of these definitions have a number of features in common:
  - More than one person involved.
  - Interaction must take place.
  - Purpose, or intention.
  - Awareness.

Groups and organizations

- Organizations are made up of many groups.
- As a result of this segmentation it is necessary to provide integration mechanisms, for example production planning.
- Some of the more obvious form of groups are:
  - Hierarchical.
  - Specialism groupings.
  - Activity groupings.
  - Boundary spanning.
  - Professional.
- Likert developed the 'linking-pin' notion of groups (Figure 6.1).

■ Handy argues that individuals use groups for a number of purposes including social, affiliation needs and gaining support for their objectives.

■ The formation of formal groups is a process of selection and socialization.

Formal and informal groups

■ It is possible to differentiate formal from other groups by purpose.

■ Linking the work of Dubin and Argyle formal groups are involved in the following:
  – Teams.
  – Tasks.
  – Technology.
  – Decisions.
  – Management.

■ Informal groups exist within all organizations.

■ Within most formal groups there exist a number of informal ones.

■ Informal groups serve a number of positive and negative functions.

■ The role of networks in excluding women from management positions was demonstrated by Cooper and Davidson.

■ There is a danger of friendship groups working against the interests of management.

■ Such groups can form the basis of resistance to change.

■ It is at this point that friendship groups become interest groups.

■ The existence of informal groups is something that is frequently seen as a matter of concern by managers.

■ The grapevine can be a useful means of communication according to Dalton.

■ Katz suggests that informal groups can assist the integration of employees into the organization, blurring the distinction between work and non-work activities.

■ Informal groups form because the individuals wish to band together.

■ Standard operating procedures provide guidance on what should be done.

■ People in their working relationships, actually make this happen.

■ Employee commitment can be interpreted as attempts to tap into informal groups.

■ There are two reasons why groups are a significant factor for employers and employees:
  – Groups are necessary to achieve the organization's objectives.
  – Most humans prefer to associate with other people.

■ The main reasons that groups form include:
  – The need to have more than one person to undertake the work.
  – The need to incorporate the expertise of a number of people in order to achieve the end result.

  – The need for organizations to match complexity in the environment.
  – The opportunity to allow employees to minimize the worst aspects of their work by sharing it out.
  – Groups provide for the social needs of individuals.
  – Groups provide a basis for socialization into the norms of behaviour within the organization.
  – Group membership also provides the individual with a measure of protection from outside threat.
  – Groups also emerge as a result of the nature of the work to be undertaken within an organization.

Research approaches

■ Triplett observed that racing cyclists performed better when accompanied by a pacemaker.

■ The gain was approximately 20%.

■ This became known as social facilitation.

■ The audience effect refers to the enhancement in performance through the presence of others.

The British experience

■ During World War I the British government established a committee to study the relationship between working conditions, fatigue and output.

■ It became the Industrial Fatigue Research Board.

■ Among the conclusions drawn was that social conditions within which work was done had significant consequences.

■ Boredom was also less likely when people worked in groups.

The Hawthorne studies

■ The Western Electric Company began a series of investigations at its Hawthorne works in 1924.

■ In 1927 researchers from the Harvard Business School became involved.

■ Mayo was an Australian by birth and spent time during World War I working with disabled military personnel.

■ The studies within the Hawthorne works can be separated into four stages:
  – The illumination experiments.
  – The relay assembly test room study.
  – The interview programme.
  – The bank wiring observation room study.

■ Looking briefly at each in turn.

The illumination experiments

■ The intention of these experiments was to identify the relationship between levels of light and output.

■ The level of illumination was systematically varied and output monitored.

■ The results of the experiments were inconclusive.

■ Output increased even when the level of light was very poor.

- The highest level of output was recorded when the group returned to their normal working conditions.

The relay assembly test room study

- This work involved female workers assembling components to make relay switches.
- The work was highly repetitive and boring.
- Six women were selected from among the regular workforce.
- The research lasted two years and a number of variables were systematically varied, see Table 6.3.
- Output increased under each of the experimental manipulations.
- Output even increased when the experiment was ended and normal arrangements returned.
- The main reasons put forward as an explanation included:
  - The special status accruing to the women.
  - The influence of being consulted and kept informed by the experimenter.
  - Morale.
  - Management during the experiment was different.
  - The group was self-selected.

The interview programme

- More than 20,000 interviews were conducted.
- They were designed to identify employee attitudes and feelings.
- It quickly became apparent that workers wanted to talk about other aspects of their work.
- This allowed interviewees to discuss things that they considered important.
- Employee views about management in general, the company, even society as a whole were obtained.
- Indications about networks of informal groups was obtained.
- These were the primary means by which supervisors and leading employees controlled the productive activities and behaviour.
- The existence of informal groups led to the final stage in the research programme.

The bank wiring observation room study

- This consisted of the direct observation of 14 men.
- The men were organized into three teams.
- In addition, there were two inspectors.
- Observation identified two informal groups (Figure 6.2).
- These informal groups developed their own group norms.
- Much of the activity of the informal groups to control the behaviour of members.
- The groups became adept at being able to 'manage' management by meeting their expectations.
- By 'meeting' that expectation, employees retained effective control.

- The norms consisted of a number of rules:
  - Chisler.
  - Rate-buster.
  - Squealer.
- Another rule was that inspectors or supervisors should become part of the informal group.
- Group norms were enforced through a number of sanctions.

Key findings

- Informal groups inevitably form within formally designated groupings.
- Informal groups will not always match the groupings designated by management.
- Individuals at work are not simply motivated by pay and other tangible benefits.
- Informal groups will attempt a form of bottom-up management in order to influence their working environment.
- The rewards that an individual gains from membership of an informal group may be more significant and meaningful to that individual than any benefit that can be obtained from management.
- Informal groups may seek to frustrate management's intentions and objectives.
- The groups to which an individual belong will have a significant influence on their behaviour and attitudes towards work.
- First-line managers and supervisors are subjected to strong and competing pressures for their affiliations from those above and below.
- Management has little or no influence on the establishment and form or membership of informal groups within the organization.
- Informal groups can engage in competitive activities that are against the interests of the organization as a whole.
- The Hawthorne studies began a move towards the humanization of work.
- The Human Relations Movement was interested in how to adopt a social dimension to work organization and motivation.
- Another way of thinking about the humanization of work is an attempt by managers to maintain control within a changing social environment.

Group formation and development

- Informal groups come into existence for a number of reasons:
  - The nature and form of the formal organization.
  - The need for human beings to form relationships of their own choosing.
  - The voluntary nature of many informal groups offsets the involuntary nature of many formal groups.
  - The approach adopted by managers to the running of the organization.
  - The need to run the organization.

Group formation

- Homans proposed that any group existed within an environment of three elements:
  - Culture.
  - Physical.
  - Technological.
- This environment imposed a range of activities and interactions on the individuals and groups within the system.
- Homans suggested two features of the external and internal systems:
  - The external and internal systems are mutually dependent.
  - The two systems and the environment are mutually dependent.

Group development

- Groups do not automatically become effective at meeting their objectives and satisfying the needs of the individuals concerned.
- It is impossible to present a single comprehensive theory of how groups develop.
- Bass and Ryterband identify a four-stage model of group development:
  - Initial development of trust and membership.
  - Beginning of communication and decision making.
  - Performance improvement.
  - Ongoing maintenance and control.
- Tuckman and Jensen added a stage to the basic model:
  - Stage 1. Forming.
  - Stage 2. Storming.
  - Stage 3. Norming.
  - Stage 4. Performing.
  - Stage 5. Adjourning.
- A group may not successfully negotiate itself through the stages described.
- Unresolved difficulties will result in subsequent problems.
- Group norms are the means of regulating the behaviour of members.
- Norms become internalized and institutionalized in the accepted patterns of behaviour.
- Feldman suggests that groups will adopt a satisficing approach to regulating individual behaviour, unless:
  - Group survival is at risk.
  - Lack of clarity in the expected behaviour of group members is creating problems.
  - By taking action the group can avoid bringing into the open things that it would be embarrassing or difficult to resolve.
  - The central values held by the group are being threatened.

Group structure

- In formal groups the structure of the group may be dictated by the situation.

- Individuals have no direct say in who will be appointed and what role they will perform.
- Many groups within an organization are comprised of representatives of other groups or departments.
- These representatives will be subject to report back and direction from their sponsoring groups.
- There are a number of ways of considering group structure (Huczynski and Buchanan):
  - Status.
  - Power.
  - Liking.
  - Role.
  - Leadership.
- Belbin identifies nine team roles that it is suggested determine the performance of a group (Table 6.4).

Group formation and structure: a management perspective

- Groups are of particular significance to managers including:
  - The process of management involves the management of groups.
  - Managers must be part of some of the groups that they manage.
  - Managers are part of a management group in addition to any others.
  - There are moves to empowering employees.
- It is not uncommon for individuals to seek out personal or career benefits from group membership.
- Promotion opportunities can be enhanced by membership of the 'right' committees and being active in successful projects.
- Management is a political process.
- The significance of formal groups is self-evident in the compartmentalization of activity.
- Informal groups are also an inherent part of organizational life.

Managers need to develop an understanding of the importance of groups within an organization

- Within an organization the groups that exist are constantly subject to change:
  - New people join a department.
  - Existing members leave or are transferred to other duties.
  - Existing groups are reformulated as the tasks for which they were established change.
  - New groups are created as new tasks emerge.
- It is within a constantly changing milieu that managers must provide a framework of consistency and stability.
- It is in an attempt to provide stability that groups have a significant part to play.
- The relationships formed within a group can help to provide strength in times of difficulty.

■ Managers find themselves in a number of different groups.

■ Managers often ignore the formation and structural aspects of teams.

■ Informal groups are frequently ignored.

■ The challenge for managers is to provide the formal groupings that will allow the necessary activities to be undertaken whilst retaining some influence over informal groups.

■ It could be argued that the existence of informal groups is a function of management's attempt to control.

■ It can also be suggested that the informal group is a mechanism for achieving social meaning in a context where activity is dictated by others.

■ Perhaps therefore, the challenge facing managers is how to direct the energies of groups in the interests of the organization.

■ The use of group working can provide an appearance of lack of management control.

Conclusions

■ This chapter has considered the significance of groups.

■ It is clear that both formal and informal groups are significant in terms of organizational activity.

■ The existence of groups is closely associated with the need for control.

■ It could be argued that informal groups are a natural reaction to that situation.

Discussion questions: outline answers for selected questions.

2. Groups within organizations are different to groups in other contexts. Discuss this statement.

   This question seeks to draw out from students the differences and similarities between organizational groups and other situations in which they occur. Whilst there are many similarities between groups whatever their situational context organizations by the very nature of their function introduce a number of complexities to them. For example, very few senior management teams have much influence over the selection of colleagues. Indeed the same can be said of most workgroups. Therefore people are 'forced' by circumstances to work with other people with all that is implied by that. There are also so many teams or groups to which any individual belongs within an organization that the effective balancing of team roles would be difficult if not impossible. The need to achieve particular types of objectives is another force acting within organizations and which influences the form, use and behaviour of groups.

3. Is the distinction between the concept of formal and informal groups a useful one?

   This question is deliberately vague. It does not specify a context and so either the student should specify the boundaries chosen or adopt a deliberately wide basis for the answer. The question could be answered in many different ways. From a manager's perspective it could be taken that informal groups do not form part of the formal organization and are therefore a bad thing because they have the potential to disturb the ability to control. This approach would be essentially a bureaucratic perspective, in which everything must be controlled and accounted for if the organization is to be effective. The opposite view, that they offer the potential for improved effectiveness, could be made by someone who believes in 'ends, not means'. The essential argument being that people do not need to be closely controlled and 'structured' in order to do what is necessary in support of organizational objectives. In this question there is no right answer, the mark depends on how well the student argues for their particular case.

5. The bank wiring room observations demonstrate that employees can effectively manage managers without them being aware of it. Give and justify your own views on this statement.

   This question seeks the student's view on upwards management. Invariably the literature concentrates on management as a top-down process. However any experience of working in an organization soon provides exposure to the upwards variety. Essentially the bank wiring room employees provided managers with what they expected to see. Managers assumed therefore that everything was under control and looked no closer. It is but one example of a very common approach in any organization. Many employees at all levels (including managers) attempt to manage their own space and work activity through freeing up space between themselves and their boss. As one very experienced manager once said to me the only way to be really effective as a manager is, 'To believe nothing of what you were told and only half of what you saw.' A very good answer might also begin to explore issues of power and control in relation to this question.

9. Are groups within an organization an attempt to provide managers with the means of social control?

   This question seeks to draw out the student's views on the topics. For example it could be argued that by forming groups managers are attempting to reduce the variability that exists within an organization. Consequently control activity can be directed at groups rather than individuals. This is a variant of the argument often used by managers in support of the recognition of trade unions. Dealing with one group, representing the interests of all workers is easier than dealing with every individual. Taking the discussion further it is possible for managers to attempt to socialize groups within the organization to the same frame of reference and values as managers. This in turn makes it easier to manage through association. Group dynamics (the next chapter) provides a mechanism by which groups would then police their own members.

It would of course be possible to argue the opposite perspective. In so doing it would be necessary for students to address some of the issues indicated above.

Case study

The inclusion of a case study in this chapter is intended to provide lecturers with the opportunity to use this method of teaching which requires students to analyse a situation and form a judgement about their preferred solution. Groups of student could be encouraged to challenge each other on their solutions in order to deepen their understanding of the material and of the need to fully justify courses of action. This process should also provide lecturers with the opportunity to demonstrate that very rarely is only one solution available and that alternative routes might be equally (or more) valuable depending upon the forces acting upon the situation and subsequent events.

Exercise background

This exercise is based around four elements:

1. The Tuckman and Jensen five-stage model of group formation (forming, storming, norming, performing and adjourning) introduced on pp 187–8 of the text.

2. The team roles identified by Belbin and introduced on pp 189–90.
3. The Management in Action panel 6.6 on how to build teams on p 190.
4. Tutorial groups, work groups, study groups and case study teams as used in most courses.

Student tasks

In groups, review the use of groups in the learning process within your university, college or course. Are they intended to encourage and promote the understanding of material that you are studying and to develop analytical, technical, personal, communication and interpersonal skills and competencies?

In the context of a learning experience, what if any preparation was required of the groups in question before or during the process? Was the preparation required restricted to the task in hand, case study analysis and academic preparation? Was there any suggestion that a group formation or structure process might be necessary or desirable?

In the light of the items 1–3 from the list above. Consider:

■ The implications for the performance and effectiveness as learning processes of tutorial and other study-based groups of not adopting formal formation and structural procedures.
■ Identify how the effectiveness of tutorial and other study groups could be improved through the application of team-building techniques as indicated above. Remember that most students are members of many different study-based groups and so your proposals must take this into account.

Prepare a brief presentation (not more than 15 minutes) on the tasks above and present your ideas to the rest of the class. Be prepared to answer questions from your classmates and also to defend your ideas.

CHAPTER 7

Group dynamics and effectiveness

Chapter outline

This chapter begins with a consideration of the behavioural and control issues surrounding group activity. We then move on to consider the dynamics of the interaction within and between groups. Organizational requirements for effectiveness in group activity and the associated decision making are the next areas for consideration. This is followed by a critical review of the material and an introduction to the managerial and organizational context.

Learning objectives

After studying this chapter and working through the associated Management in Action panels, discussion questions and research activities, students should be able to:

■ Outline the nature of the dynamic processes that occur within and between groups.

■ Describe the concept of effectiveness as applied to group activities.

■ Explain how decisions are made in groups and the difficulties that can be encountered in reaching agreement.

■ Understand how control can be operated within groups.

■ Discuss the similarities and differences between models of how groups can be made more effective.

■ Appreciate the complex relationships that exists between the groups to which individuals belong.

■ Detail some of the links between groups and communications, negotiation, group formation and organizational design.

■ Assess the management implications of groups.

Teaching notes and chapter summary

Introduction

■ All groups function within a broader environment, involving:
  - The need for communication and interaction between members.
  - The need for communication and interaction with other groups.
  - The need to achieve objectives.
  - The need to control activities.
  - The provision of a means through which to meet the social needs and aspirations of members.
  - The need to take account of the social and political dimensions.

■ There are different patterns of communication (Figure 7.1).

■ Moreno developed the sociogram as a means of charting preferences and interactions between members (Figure 7.2).

■ Another approach was Bales interaction analysis (Table 7.1).

■ Bales' work indicates two significant aspects:
  - The task and the solution being sought.
  - The group atmosphere and member feelings.

■ There is also a political dimension to behaviour in groups.

■ A well-balanced group will display these functions in proportion to purpose, individuals and context.

Control within groups

■ Groups have the ability to influence the behaviour of members as demonstrated by Sheriff (Figure 7.3).

■ Socialization is a process of learning how 'things' are done.

■ Groups ensure that new members conform to the established task and maintenance requirements.

■ Factional activity and conflict are also possibilities.

■ Frequently, the positions adopted by groups (or members) become public and therefore difficult to overcome.

Decisions within groups

■ Many groups have a decision-making aspect.
■ Belbin's team roles provide a basis for group decision making.
■ Kretch *et al.* describe a more comprehensive model of group working including decision making (Figure 7.4).

Dynamics within groups

■ Groups must come to terms with their own internal functioning before they can effectively address the tasks facing them.
■ Freud was among the first to address these issues providing the basis of group dynamics.
■ Freud's work draws attention to the emotional power in group activity.
■ He also points to the existence of conscious and unconscious behaviours within groups.
■ Bion developed a psychotherapy model that relied upon group dynamics to create changes in individual behaviour.
■ Bion concluded that much group experience was the result of conflict between three aspects of group life:
  – The individual and their needs.
  – The group mentality.
  – The group culture.
■ The conflicts experienced between these three features produce a second level of grouping within the primary one.
■ These second level groupings (basic assumption groups) act to resolve tension for individuals.
■ These can be dealt with through:
  – Fight and flight responses.
  – Dependency.
  – Pairing.
■ Another way of describing the dynamic processes within a group is shown in Figure 7.5.
■ Margerison and McCann developed the team management wheel to reflect work preferences and group activity (Figure 7.6).
■ Hoffman provides a framework clustered around three categories:
  – Task roles.
  – Relationship roles.
  – Individual roles.
■ The main difference between Hoffman and Belbin and Margerison and McCann is that Hoffman is describing what can exist rather than what should exist.

Dynamics between groups

■ Groups invariably function in a world of groups (Figure 7.7).

■ The influences operating between groups can be shown as a diagram (Figure 7.8).
■ This model assumes that there are several intervening variables that interact on the relationships that exist between groups.

Group effectiveness

■ What makes an effective group?
■ Figure 7.4 suggests that there are two different outputs from group activity:
  – The achievement of objectives in a productive way.
  – Member satisfaction level with the experience.
■ Effectiveness should be measured against both of these criteria.
■ This raises the question of dependency between the two criteria.
■ Is it possible for a group to be 'effective' in achieving its objectives if the individuals are not 'satisfied'?
■ McGregor uses unity of purpose to explain the way that some managerial groups perform effectively.
■ He describes what differentiates effective from ineffective groups (Table 7.2).
■ The Belbin and Margerison and McCann models define the requirements for a balanced team if success is to be achieved.

Belbin's team roles

■ Belbin's team roles are:
  – The plant.
  – The resource investigator.
  – The co-ordinator.
  – The shaper.
  – The monitor evaluator.
  – The teamworker.
  – The implementer.
  – The completer.
  – The specialist.
■ Belbin describes that unsuccessful teams display the following characteristics:
  – There was only a tenuous link between the level of morale among and degree of success.
  – Mental ability proved to be a critical factor in that without someone of high ability failure was relatively certain.
  – Organization culture produces a preponderance of particular personality traits with a negative impact on group decision making.
  – Unless a balance of team roles is achieved the group is likely to be ineffective in operation.
  – Belbin identified about 30% of managers without a defined team role, the inclusion of such individuals de-stabilizes an otherwise effective group.
  – Corporate influences.
  – Role reversal.

■ Winning teams display the following characteristics:
 – An individual in the chair who could make use of the role to ensure an effective process.
 – A strong plant.
 – A good range of mental ability.
 – Wide team role coverage within the group.
 – A match between team roles and personal attributes.
 – The ability of the team to compensate for role imbalances.

Margerison and McCann's team management

■ Margerison and McCann use the analogy of a wheel to describe their team management system (Figure 7.6).

■ Figure 7.9 reflects the relationship between the team management wheel and other approaches.

■ The model is based on the team management index which measures work preferences on four dimensions:
 – Relationships.
 – Information.
 – Decisions.
 – Organization.

■ The preferences imply the following characteristics:
 – Creator–Innovators. These individuals are independent and likely to challenge the present ways of doing things. They can develop new ideas.
 – Explorer–Promoters. Individuals who generate new ideas and sell them to other people. They develop other people's ideas and push them towards implementation.
 – Assessor–Developers. Individuals good at linking the creative and operational sides of a team. They are good at taking an idea in principle and making it work in practice.
 – Thruster–Organizers. The people who can get things done. They can organize resources and people to achieve results.
 – Concluder–Producers. These people can ensure that results are achieved and the output will be 'up to standard'.
 – Controller–Inspectors. These individuals ensure that information is available to the group and that it is correct.
 – Upholder–Maintainers. Good at providing support and stability to a team. They support and advise rather than lead.
 – Reporter–Advisers. The data collection and interpretation specialists. They are the seekers out of 'truth' along with the collectors of information.
 – Linker. This activity is not seen as a preference as such, but as a skill that can be developed by any manager. This activity is central to team activity in that it performs a connecting role in ensuring that the team operates in an effective manner.

■ Different situations require different combinations of roles from the wheel.

■ What is termed a 'high-performing team', should:
 – Accept that Linkers are key team members.
 – Have high expectations and set high targets.
 – Gain high levels of job satisfaction.
 – Experience high levels of co-operation.
 – Provide team managers who lead by example.
 – Develop teams that have a balance of roles matched to skills.
 – Experience high degrees of autonomy.
 – Learn quickly from mistakes.
 – Develop teams that are 'customer' oriented.
 – Display good problem solving skills and review performance.
 – Are motivated to perform.

■ The reasons that teams fail, according to Margerison and McCann, include:
 – A lack of balance across the team roles.
 – A lack of effective linking between the roles.
 – A lack of effective relationship management within the team.
 – A lack of effective information management within the team.
 – The existence of impoverished decision-making processes.
 – The tendency to want to take decisions too early in the process.

Decision making within groups

■ One feature of decision making within groups is the degree to which the group can ensure consistency between members.

■ Asch describes an experiment in which subjects were asked to decide upon the length of a number of lines (Figure 7.10).

■ Most subjects (about 80%) displayed agreement with the rest of the group.

■ Asch suggested three reasons why subjects would adjust their opinions:
 – Perceptual movement.
 – Judgement movement.
 – Action movement.

■ Milgram considered response orientation based upon the influence of an authority figure.

■ Failure to give a correct response resulted in an electric shock being administered.

■ After each electric shock the voltage was increased for the next test.

■ The experimenter in this process was in fact the subject for the experiment, although they were not aware of it at the time.

■ The supposed subject was strapped into a chair and electrodes were fixed to their body but the electrodes were not wired up to the electric shock generator.

■ When the 'experimenter' began to show signs of resistance they were encouraged to go on by Milgram or other confederates.

■ Most of the 'experimenters' continued to the point where harm would have been done to the 'subject'.

■ Milgram concluded that the power of an authority figure was able to pressure individuals to exhibit extreme behaviour.

■ Whyte argues that in most cases a groups tend to mediocrity:

> In your capacity as a group member you feel a strong impulse to seek common ground with the others. Not just out of timidity but out of respect for the sense of the meeting you tend to soft-pedal that which would go against the grain. And that, unfortunately, can include unorthodox ideas.

■ Stoner suggested that groups take decisions that involved greater risk than an individual.

■ This became known as the *risky shift* phenomenon.

■ A number of explanations have been put forward for this, including:
 – Responsibility diffusion. Nordhoy re-examined the original data and found that perhaps, the phenomenon produces an exaggeration effect, rather than a one way shift in risk taking.
 – Cultural values.
 – Rational decision making.
 – Majority decision making.
 – Polarization. Moscovici and Zavalloni suggest that groups function in a way which tends to move individual attitudes towards extreme positions.

■ Janis reviewed a number of foreign policy decisions involving the American government and coined the phrase Groupthink.

■ His research included studying the Bay of Pigs disaster in Cuba and the Vietnam war.

■ He concluded that such effects were the result of concentrating on harmony and morale to the exclusion of other perspectives.

■ Janis identified a number of symptoms of Groupthink:
 – Invulnerability.
 – Rationalization.
 – Morality.
 – Values.
 – Pressure.
 – Self-censorship.
 – Unanimity.
 – Mindguards.

■ Janis also suggested a number of mechanisms to avoid groupthink, including:
 – encouragement for individuals to voice any doubts.
 – the use of sub-groups to serve as a cross check on ideas and analysis.
 – encouraging self-criticism among the group.
 – ensuring that junior members are allowed to speak first.

Group dynamics and effectiveness: a critical analysis

■ The Hawthorne studies are the basis of much thinking about groups.

■ It has been suggested that the studies were 'rigged'.

■ Employees were required to participate in them and the researchers became counsellors in collecting information and directing employee dissatisfactions.

■ The design of the research and interpretation of the evidence was a function of researcher attitudes, beliefs and values. However, the same point could be made of many research endeavours.

■ In analysing the data available, a researcher is looking for patterns, associations and trends.

■ Other studies, for example, those of Asch illustrate the ability of groups to produce conformity.

■ Yet the same experiment in the UK did not produce a compliance effect. This suggests that such effects could be a function of culture and social conditions.

■ In a study of informal work practices Bensman and Gerver studied an aircraft factory. Company policy stated that if wing parts were not in alignment disassembly and complete rebuilding should follow. The 'informal' practice was to use a hard steel screw to force the components together. Anyone found in possession of such screws was liable to instant dismissal. However, all employees carried one 'for emergencies'. Supervisors and inspectors knew of the practice and would turn a 'blind eye' as long as it was not used too frequently.

■ By allowing specific infringements of the rules, a balance of power was maintained through tolerance of focused deviancy.

■ Many groups are influential in organizational life.

■ The gathering of information about these groups is an issue of concern to managers.

■ It was reported that during the 1985 British miners strike the government and managers employed agents to collect information from the various trade union areas. This led to the encouragement of groups that were prepared to go through the picket lines and work normally.

■ The work of Belbin and Margerison and McCann provides managers with the techniques to design teams through selection and training.

■ It provides the opportunity to improve the probability of success as defined by management.

■ It is also likely that such groups produce a more satisfying experience for members.

■ This could be described as a form of insidious control.

■ Training is an attempt by managers to shape the behaviour and attitudes of employees.

■ The institutionalization of group working provides a means by which corporate norms can be reinforced.

■ In order to achieve the objectives of the organization, two main conditions are necessary:
 – There must exist appropriate sub-groupings.

– Within individual groups there needs to be appropriate mechanisms to meet the purposes set for them.

■ Also the informal groups within the organization should not be hostile if success is to be achieved.

Group dynamics and effectiveness: a management perspective

■ In the previous chapter it was suggested that groups are in an almost constant state of flux.

■ This affects the way that groups operate and the processes through which they go.

■ Because of the significance of groups managers need to develop the ability to make effective use of them.

■ The influences arising create a situation where uncertainty and risk are high.

■ Circumstances change and the range of influences acting upon the situation may well create a change in collective attitude.

■ Because of the risk and uncertainty involved it is tempting to suggest that surplus capability is required within a group.

■ Groups make different provision for the need to deal with uncertainty and risk, depending upon the possible consequences.

■ Management is a political process as well as a decision-making one.

■ If groups are a key aspect of organizational life then management has a duty to ensure that they perform well.

■ Organizations obtain an operational advantage from teamwork.

■ The difficulty facing managers is how to realize that potential.

■ Within the complex web of organizational activity it is all too easy to create a situation where forces are acting in opposition to each other.

■ One common example is the encouragement of teamwork in operational activity, but reward being determined by individual effort.

Conclusions

■ In this chapter, we have considered how it is that groups set about structuring themselves; how they function and take decisions.

■ It is in making effective use of the ideas contained within this chapter that management can attempt to ensure that internal effectiveness is enhanced and external threats from even more effective groups minimized.

■ Groups, both formal and informal, are an important part of organizational life.

■ As the pressure on managers to produce ever higher rates of return from ever fewer resources increases, the significance of achieving forms of self and team management becomes apparent.

■ In this chapter we have introduced some of the main issues surrounding the ways that groups operate and achieve success.

Discussion questions: outline answers for selected questions.

3. Explain in your own words the team roles described by Belbin.

This question would require students to undertake some research into the Belbin team roles from the works of Belbin himself. They should then be in a position to describe them in their own words, reflecting to the marker a general understanding. The stronger students might also be able to include examples of such roles from their own experience of working in groups at college or in a job.

5. Define in your own words the team management role preferences described by Margerison and McCann.

This question is very similar to Question 3 above. The answer for all practical purposes would also be the same, other than might be expected as a consequence of the differing models.

7. It has been suggested that experiments like those carried out by Milgram are unethical and should not have been carried out. Make a case for and against the Milgram experiments.

This question seeks to draw out from the student an understanding of the ethics and practicalities of experimenting. At one level it could be simply argued that unless physical, psychological or other 'real' harm is being performed or threatened then any experiment that contributes knowledge should be valid. However, this reflects a very simplistic perspective and other aspects should be expected to be brought into the discussion, depending upon the background, level and course of study for the students. Issues such as the creativity of researchers and the limitations of experiments carried out on largely university students should however feature in most answers.

11. Figure 7.7 describes a hierarchy of group inter-relationships. Describe such a hierarchy for a tutorial group to which you belong.

This question sets out to draw out from students some analysis of the richness involved within and between the groups that they become involved at college or university. The analysis at its most restricted level might only reflect the tutorial group as a sub-set of a larger class or course. However it should be expected to incorporate some reflection of the boundary spanning links with family, friendship, potential employer, retail and other supplier groups.

Case study

The inclusion of a case study in this chapter is intended to provide lecturers with the opportunity to use this method of teaching which requires students to analyse a situation and form a judgement about their preferred solution. Groups of student could be encouraged to challenge each other on their solutions in order to deepen their understanding of the material and of the need to fully justify courses of action. This process should also provide lecturers with the opportunity to demonstrate that very rarely is only one solution available and that alternative routes might be equally (or more) valuable depending upon the forces acting upon the situation and subsequent events.

This activity is based around Management in Action 7.6.

Management in Action 7.6: dispelling the macho myth

In that panel the subject of outdoor training is raised. Consider the nature of outdoor training and find out as much as you can about it from a range of the providers of such programmes. Identify the programme contents and the objectives set for the delegates. Equally, consider these in relation to teamwork. Attempt to identify how the outdoor training that you have found out about seeks to develop team working skills among the people attending the programme. Specifically consider the work of Belbin and Margerison and McCann in this respect. How does outdoor training relate to the concept of team roles and the idea that individuals have work preferences that predispose them to function in particular ways in a team context.

Student tasks

In groups review all of the information that you have been able to find in relation to outdoor training and the work of Belbin and Margerison and McCann. Specifically, prepare a brief presentation (not more than 15 minutes) on:

1. The advantages of outdoor training for developing teamwork skills.
2. You know that your chief executive is a great believer in the use of the Belbin (or Margerison and McCann) approach to creating effective teams. Include specific advice for him on how outdoor training complements or is irrelevant to these approaches to teamwork.

Present your ideas to the rest of the class. Be prepared to answer questions from your classmates and also to defend your ideas.

CHAPTER 8

Communication, decision making and negotiation

Chapter outline

This chapter introduces the concepts of communication, decision making and negotiation. It begins with a review of the relationship between each of these concepts and organizations. The chapter then moves on to consider each concept in detail. The discussion examines the nature of each concept, its theoretical basis and its significance within an organizational setting. This is followed by a critical assessment of the implications of each and the management perspectives on them.

Learning objectives

After studying this chapter and working through the associated Management in Action panels, discussion questions and research activities, students should be able to:

- Outline the concepts of communication, decision making and negotiation.
- Describe communications, illustrating the process involved and the media options available.
- Explain how decision making takes place, differentiating between programmed and non-programmed decisions.
- Understand how communications, decision making and negotiation are linked together.
- Appreciate the organizational significance of communication, decision making and negotiation.
- Discuss how communication, decision making and negotiation link to other chapters in this book.
- Detail how principled negotiation is intended to achieve a satisfactory and consistent result for all parties.
- Assess the organizational significance of communications, decision making and negotiation.

Teaching notes and chapter summary

Introduction

- Communications is a process of providing information and influencing others.
- Decision making is a means of selecting a particular course of action from among the many options available.
- Negotiation is a process of difference reduction through agreement between individuals and groups.
- There are strong links between these three activities.
- Not all communication involves decision making or negotiation.
- Decision making requires a flow of information.
- Every negotiation requires communication and decision making.

Communications and organizations

- Communication implies a two-way process.
- Watching a news programme is information transmission because there is no direct interaction involved.
- The nature of communications within organizations is reflected in Figure 8.1.
- Managers engage in a considerable degree of communication with external groups.
- Complexity in communication is an exponential function of the number of people involved.
- The communication process needs to be managed carefully if total chaos is to be avoided.
- There are many ways in which this is achieved including:
  - Limitation.
  - Procedure.
  - Teamwork.
  - Automation.
  - Separation.

Decision making within organizations

■ There are many areas of decision making from short term to the long term.

■ Decisions are taken by all levels of employee.

■ The major distinction between types of decision are scale of the decision and the time frame for the impact.

■ At the lower levels decisions are focused on immediate events and the use of current resources to achieve the desired daily/weekly output.

■ The directors, however, may only review the financial results of the company every quarter.

■ At senior levels decision making can take considerable time.

■ Margaret Thatcher began to court Japanese business leaders in the mid-1970s, well before she became British Prime Minister.

■ It was approximately 10 years after this level of approach that Nissan became one of the early Japanese companies to invest in England (Garrahan and Stewart).

■ The foregoing discussion illustrates the third property associated with decision making: risk.

■ The three elements associated with decision making can be reflected in a diagram, see Figure 8.3.

Negotiating and organizations

■ Managers are involved in negotiations much of the time.

■ Negotiations can take place either formally or informally.

■ The annual negotiations between managers and trade unions over rates of pay are typical formal negotiations.

■ Informal negotiations take place every day between people at all levels.

■ For example, the sales director might seek to persuade the production director to change the priority on a particular order.

Communications

■ Figure 8.4 reflects the main interaction networks which form the basis of communication for managers.

■ Communication serves four functions within an organization:
  – Information processing.
  – Co-ordination.
  – Visioning.
  – Personal expression.

■ The methods of communication that occur within organizations include:
  – Written.
  – Oral.
  – Non-verbal.
  – Electronic.

The communication process

■ The process of communication is a social activity involving two or more people across time (Figure 8.6).

■ Taking each element described in the model:
  – Source/receiver.
  – Encoding.
  – Transmission channel.
  – Decoding.
  – Feedback.
  – Noise.

Interpersonal communication

■ Interpersonal communication involves two people in a dyadic interaction.

■ Non-verbal signals are the least obvious yet carry much information (Table 8.1).

■ Taking each category in turn:
  – Body language.
  – Paralanguage.
  – Proxemics.
  – Environment.
  – Temporal.

Electronic communications

■ In today's organization the use of computer-based technology to communicate is commonplace.

■ The facsimile (fax) machine is now a key piece of equipment for sending messages and documents between locations.

■ The use of copier and electronic mail allow information to be circulated widely and rapidly.

■ In manufacturing, the ability to design products on computer systems that produce parts lists and production schedules makes ordering and invoicing much easier.

■ The ability to call up a client file on computer allows transactions to be effectively tailored to client needs.

■ Computer systems allow designated individuals access to appropriate information.

■ Access to information can be restricted in various ways.

■ The potential of electronic communication needs to be balanced with the other forms in order to produce an effective process.

■ There is little to be gained from introducing teleconferencing between two locations only five miles apart when the usual communication between them is twice each year.

Communications and the law

■ Information is a source of power and that there is unequal access to it between managers and employees.

■ British employment legislation requires managers to communicate certain information to trade unions in specific circumstances.

- This includes areas of collective bargaining and proposals to declare redundancies.
- Limited liability organizations with more than 250 employees have to include some information in their annual reports.
- The introduction of works councils is now built into the European Union's employment legislation.

Approaches to decision making

- Decisions are about choice.
- If there were no choices then decisions would be unnecessary.
- The difficulty facing managers is that many options are in conflict.
- It is finding ways to balance the competing pressures that form the basis of decision making.
- Decision making takes time, is resource demanding and contains risk.
- In situations where the problem has not occurred before it is necessary to work out the options and relative benefits for each before deciding which to follow.
- The decision is taken before the result is known.
- The actual chain of events that will follow from any decision cannot be fully anticipated.
- The D-Day landings of the allied forces in France in June 1944 was the culmination of considerable planning and training.
- By chance a crack German armoured regiment was on exercise in the area of one of the landing zones and so was able to reinforce the defence of the area more effectively than anticipated.
- There was no opportunity for the military commanders to change the decision in the light of the new information.
- It simply had to be dealt with as the landings progressed.
- This leads to the notion of a stream of decisions rather than a single activity.
- Simon describes decisions as a continuum from programmed to non-programmed.
- Programmed refers to the existence of decision rules that lead from problem to solution.
- Non-programmed decisions are novel, new, cannot be anticipated, or do not have pre-existing methods of resolution.
- Comparing these two approaches to problem solving a number of conclusions should be apparent, including:
  - There is less risk of failure in a decision which is based on the programmed approach.
  - Reliance on non-programmed decision making incurs a higher cost.
  - Measured in units of output per person, the performance of an organization using a high proportion of programmed decisions will be greater.

  - Unique situations cannot be dealt with i grammed mode of operation, they must I nelled out and dealt with separately.
  - Where non-programmed decisions are the norm, the skill level of employees must be of a higher order than required for programmed decisions.
  - The structure of the organization will be effected by the approach to decision making.
- The approach described by Simon is based upon the need to apply differing levels of preplanning.
- Programmed decisions require thought and anticipation separated from the events themselves.
- Non-programmed decisions can be broken down into a network of sub-problems, many of them programmable.

Problem-solving preferences

- Another way to think about decision making is to consider the preferences that individuals have.
- The information gathering approach is defined in terms of either sensing (preference for facts) or intuition (preference for possibilities).
- The information evaluation approach is defined in terms of thinking (preference for logic) or feeling (preference for values) in analysing available information.
- This can be reflected in a diagram (Figure 8.8).
- Another approach to individual problem solving is that described by Thompson and Tuden:
  - Preferences for outcomes.
  - Beliefs about causation.
- This model provides an indication of the problem solving approaches that arise from these dimensions (Figure 8.9).

Decision-making models

- There are a number of models that attempt to describe how decisions are made:
  - Rational model.
  - Restricted rationality model.
  - Pragmatic model (Figure 8.10).
  - Political model. One form of this was described as a garbage can model by Cohen *et al*.
  - Conflict model (Figure 8.11).

Negotiation

- One of the key areas in which managers engage in communication and decision making is negotiation.
- Negotiation is frequently thought of as involving personnel managers and trade unions, but it is much more broadly based.
- For example, applicants for jobs invariably negotiate some aspect of their appointment with the prospective employer.

- Negotiation is often regarded as a formal process.
- However, it is often an informal process.
- Technically a superior is empowered to give 'instructions' to subordinates, who must then carry them out.
- In practice, any manager who relied on giving orders as the only way to lead would not achieve the best results.
- Negotiation is, therefore, best seen as an interactive process of making mutual agreeable bargains in situations where one party needs to influence the activities of another.

A negotiating framework

- Formal negotiation is a means through which differences can be resolved and agreement specified.
- Negotiation can be a reflection of the power balance.
- Figure 8.12 provides a framework for understanding the formal negotiation process within employee relations.

Negotiating tactics

- There are a number of approaches to dealing with conflict which are relevant to negotiations:
  - Avoidance (simply ignoring the problem).
  - Smoothing (seeking to 'patch up' a rift through calming actions).
  - Forcing (one's own point of view on others).
  - Compromise (seeking an acceptable middle ground).
  - Confrontation (facing up to the differences and seeking accommodation) (Torrington and Hall).
- Other factors include:
  - the preferred style of the individuals involved.
  - the relative power balance between the parties.
  - the degree of change involved.
  - the willingness of the parties to accept change.
  - previous encounters.
  - environmental influences.
  - training and experience in negotiation.
  - the dynamics of the process.
- Many negotiations are undertaken from a win–loose perspective.
- This is based upon the notion that the issues can only be shared out like cutting a cake into pieces.
- A piece once cut and allocated is no longer available.
- Often a deep diving approach is used on each item to be covered until a win is recorded before moving on to the next issue.
- Similar tactics include (Scott):
  - Probing from the outset.
  - Seeking to gain something before conceding anything.
  - The use of voice tone and other body language signals to create emotion in the process.
  - Good guy/bad guy.
  - The ability to manage body language and verbal cues allows some to cloak their feelings and intentions.

- The person producing the minutes is in a strong position to slant the official record.
- One side may understand the other's position without agreeing with it.
- Going over the head of the negotiating team to the boss is a threat that can be used to effect.
- There are various forms of force that can be used.
- There are various ways in which these tactics can be dealt with, but essentially it comes down to remaining in control of temper, emotions, content and process.
- There are few occasions where the power balance is completely one sided.
- Fisher and Ury describe principled negotiations.
- This requires negotiators to concentrate on four aspects:
  - Separate the people from the problem.
  - Focus on interests, not positions.
  - Invent options for mutual gain.
  - Insist on objective criteria.
- The authors include in their work a number of tactics for dealing with fighting situations, including knowing the alternatives to agreement.
- It may be in the best interests of one party to walk away from a particular negotiation, rather than reach an unacceptable agreement.

Communication, decision making and negotiation: a management perspective

- There are many applications of communications, decision making and negotiating in the field of management.
- Appropriate policies and practices are needed with regard to these issues.
- The challenge is how to achieve operational effectiveness without the unethical and inappropriate use of communication, decision making or negotiation.
- Most communication within an organizational context takes place between individuals and groups.
- Word of mouth should not be underestimated as a source of information and influence.
- Employees and managers invariably talk to other people as part of their social life.
- Not everyone is a good communicator and not all channels offer equal effectiveness (Table 8.2).
- Many of the situations relating to communication also involve decision making and negotiation.
- It is a management responsibility to establish who can negotiate what with whom.
- Poor communications (along with judgement and decision making) can also impact an organization in ways that were not intended.
- The chief executive of a large chain of discount jewellery shops found that sales dropped to nil overnight after a careless comment in an after-dinner speech in which he cast doubts on the quality of his company's products.

- Most of the shops closed down and he lost his job along with many of the staff.
- The political nature of decision making was described by Pettigrew.
- In decision-making terms the groupthink phenomenon is of particular importance.
- It is assumed that a group will take a better decision than an individual.
- In decision making there are number of creative approaches to the process of which those developed by Edward De Bono are perhaps the best known.
- In taking decisions managers have access to a variety of sources of information (Table 8.3).
- Limited rationality in the context of decision making leads to a notion of satisficing behaviour.
- Lindblom describes this as the science of muddling through.
- Decision making can be career limiting if the decision turns out to be wrong.
- There are many ways that individuals attempt to deal with this including the holding of meetings.
- Decisions can be categorized into one of three types: operational, tactical and strategic.
- The hierarchical structure of organizations can allow experience skills to be gained by individuals in a structured and relatively risk free environment.
- Junior staff are allowed to take comparatively small decisions and are usually monitored by more senior managers.
- Promotion brings with it the opportunity to become experienced in dealing with ever larger issues.
- One of the consequences of delayering has been to reduce the amount of practice in graded decision making and negotiating, with a possible increase in the level of risk.
- Communication can take place isolated from the other two.
- Decision making cannot take place without communication, but can take place without negotiation.
- Negotiation can only take place in conjunction with the other two.

Conclusions

- Communications, decision making and negotiation are three of the most important aspects of managerial activity.
- They are interlinked in a way that makes them difficult to separate and consider in isolation.
- From a manager's point of view they are all about the process of influencing others in some way or other.

Discussion questions: outline answers for selected questions

3. Describe some of the tactics used in negotiation.

How would you counter some of the aggressive tactics described?

The tactics are clearly identified within the text and students would be expected to be able to reproduce them without difficulty. The testing part of the question in terms of understanding and an ability to relate to the material comes from how the student is able to put together counters to the tactics indicated. Clearly some of these are also identified within the text and students should make use of them. However there is no shortage of opportunity to introduce a creative perspective to the counter tactics indicated. For example aspects of decision making and communication can be worked into a strategy that can improve the general climate and to reduce the likelihood of aggressive tactics being used. It is the creative aspects of the answer that would generate high marks.

4. Describe how communications can be thought of as a perceptual process?

This question seeks to encourage students to think beyond the chapter that they have been studying. Given that there are few mechanical links in the human communication process, signals received are subject to interpretation and many of the perceptual processes described in Chapter 2. From that perspective the issue of how much accuracy can be placed on what the receiver thinks is the 'message' arises and should be discussed.

5. Is rationality the only basis on which decisions are taken? Illustrate your answer from your own experience.

Again the basics for this answer are provided in the text. The key to a successful answer are in the ability of the student to demonstrate understanding through an effective description of illustrations which actually make the points about how non-rational factors play a part. Equally, students might be expected to question the notion of rationality. Who determines what defines rationality in any particular context is the basis of much of the critical literature on management and this should be reflected in the stronger answers.

9. Would it be possible for managers to operate in such a way that negotiation with trade unions could be avoided?

There is a point of view that suggests that if only every party to a negotiation understood the needs and wants of the others before the process began, then it could be avoided. For example, if the trade unions knew before a negotiation that management could be relied upon to state its true position and make sensible offers on wages then the trade unions would be able to accept that offer and negotiation would become unnecessary. However when this was tried it very quickly became unworkable because negotiation is not just about the reconciliation of difference, it is also about the ability to influence and an expression of freedom of choice. So one rationality suggests that it can be avoided, but there are many other forces at work. Trust, influence, freedom to express independence being just some of them. Students should be expected to go beyond the basics and explore some of these issues.

Case study

The inclusion of a case study in this chapter is intended to provide lecturers with the opportunity to use this method of teaching which requires students to analyse a situation and form a judgement about their preferred solution. Groups of students could be encouraged to challenge each other on their solutions in order to deepen their understanding of the material and of the need to fully justify courses of action. This process should also provide lecturers with the opportunity to demonstrate that very rarely is only one solution available and that alternative routes might be equally (or more) valuable depending upon the forces acting upon the situation and subsequent events.

Management in Action 8.3: The power of time

Student tasks

In groups of six people review the case study above in relation to the material in Chapter 8 on communications, decision making and negotiation. Split your group into

three. One team approach the issues within the case from the perspective of the managing director. Another team approach the case study from the perspective of the trade union. The final team approach the task from the perspective of the industrial relations manager. In general terms what conclusions do you draw from the episode described about the behaviour, objectives, intentions, attitudes and perceptions of the parties involved? How was communications, decision making and negotiation being used by the three parties to their advantage and the disadvantage of others? What lessons do you learn from this case study about the material discussed in Chapter 8?

Specifically:

■ Stage A. Bring the analysis and ideas of the three teams within your group together into an analysis of the situation from a management and trade union perspective.
■ Stage B. Prepare a brief presentation (not more than 15 minutes) on:
  1. What your group consider to be the chief communications, decision making and negotiation issues to be addressed by this company.
  2. Describe how as the company industrial relations manager you would seek to move away from the confrontational relationships that are described in the case by introducing communications, decision making and negotiation strategies based upon the material presented in Chapter 8.

Present your ideas to the rest of the class. Be prepared to answer questions from your classmates and also to defend your ideas.

CHAPTER 9

Organizational frameworks

Chapter outline

This chapter begins with the consideration of the significance of an organization's structure and introduces some of the factors that determine the choices made. This is followed by the introduction of the major structural variations adopted by organizations and a brief review of the work of Mintzberg in describing the process. The organizational life cycle is also introduced as a factor in the decision-making approach to design. The chapter concludes with a consideration of the management perspectives on organizational design issues.

Learning objectives

After studying this chapter and working through the associated Management in Action panels, discussion questions and research activities, students should be able to:

■ Outline the main structural choices available to organizations.
■ Explain why organizations operating internationally have more variables to take into account when deciding structural arrangements.
■ Describe the differences in design and control implicit in the product, process and matrix structural forms.
■ Understand how Mintzberg approaches the topic of structure together with the differences and similarities with other perspectives.
■ Discuss the limitations inherent in any organizational design.
■ Appreciate how the work of Taylor, Fayol and Weber has informed the approaches described in this chapter.
■ Detail how the need to compartmentalize the work of an organization is at variance with the need to integrate activities.
■ Assess the managerial significance of the structural choices made by organizations.

Teaching notes and chapter summary

Introduction

■ The need to arrange the resources of an organization has always existed.
■ Imagine the organization structure necessary to build the Great Pyramid of Cheops in Egypt.
■ It covers 13 acres and comprises 2.5 million blocks of stone, each weighing 2.5 tons.
■ Construction lasted some 20 years with a labour force of 100,000 men.

The significance of structure

■ Traditional approaches reinforced hierarchical control and segmented responsibility.
■ This is the essence of Weber's bureaucracy.
■ Fayol identified the operations necessary to run a company:
  – Technical.
  – Commercial.
  – Financial.
  – Security.
  – Accounting.
  – Managerial.
■ The managerial 'operation' or process he described in terms of:
  – Organizing.
  – Co-ordinating.
  – Commanding.
  – Controlling.
  – Forecasting.
  – Planning.
■ Fayol also identified a number of management principles which impact on structure.
■ They include:
  – division of work into compartments.
  – unity of command.
  – centralization and de-centralization.

- The size and complexity of operational activity creates the need for compartmentalization.
- Kanter describes differences in problem solving between bureaucracies and innovative companies.
- On the one hand structure creates differentiation (Figure 9.1).
- On the other hand there is a need for integration to complete the product or service.
- The significance of structure is its contribution to organizational objectives.
- Business process re-engineering is a modern approach to this.
- The structure of an organization will be a function of:
  - Objectives.
  - Technology.
  - Environment.
- Strategic decisions have a significant impact of organizational design (Figure 9.2).
- Structure is the means by which effort is co-ordinated and through which results are achieved.
- Porter argues:

  Each generic [competitive] strategy implies different skills and requirements for success, which commonly translate into differences in organizational structure and culture.

- Foucault considers many issues associated with the need for co-ordination and differentiation within an organization, including:
  - Enclosure.
  - Partitioning.
  - Ranking.
- The implication being that organization creates understanding as a precondition of the exercise of power and control.
- Organizations are a creation of management's imagination, designed to meet the requirements of the creator.
- Another view of organization suggests stage design as used in the theatre.
- Bolman and Deal claim that it is possible to interpret structure as:

  - An arrangement of space, lighting, props, and costumes to make the organizational drama vivid and credible to its audience.

- From this review of structure it is apparent that:
  - Management define the boundaries and content of organizations.
  - They construct the reality that other people must adapt to.
  - Structure provides management with benefits other than operational objectives.

Organizational structures

- The issues that can influence the organization design include:
  - Formalization.
  - Job design.
  - Height.
  - Orientation.
  - Centralization.
  - Co-ordination.

Entrepreneurial structures

- The entrepreneurial structure is typically found in small organizations where the owner plays an active role (Figure 9.3).
- Management activities are largely inseparable from the personalities and preferences of the owners.
- The relative lack of size and direct involvement of the owner require everyone to work together effectively.
- Individuals typically become involved with a wide range of tasks.
- It is not uncommon to find the owner rolling up their sleeves when necessary.
- Power and authority lie with the owner/manager.
- About 30% of new businesses go into liquidation within two years.
- Having survived early difficulties the entrepreneur is faced with the problems of success.
- Success brings with it the opportunity for growth and the need for change in the organization.
- At some point in time additional staff, new premises and equipment will be required.
- It is not unusual to find entrepreneurs limiting growth to retain personal involvement and control.
- The difficulties and choices facing the entrepreneurial manager were described by Greiner (Figure 9.4).

Product-based structures

- The product or service becomes the focus for the efforts of the people and resources.
- Typically, each product group would be the responsibility of the chief executive of a business unit.
- The key features of this type of structure are:
  - Product focus.
  - Single head.
  - Limited autonomy.
- Product-based structures are advantageous when:
  - There is a need to get close to customers.
  - The company offers products serving specific markets.
  - When the organization is required to be proactive across a broad front.
- An example is included as Figure 9.5.
- The main advantages of a product structure include:
  - Risk.
  - Evaluation.
  - Motivation and development.
  - Support.
  - Acquisition and divestment.
  - Change.

The disadvantages of a product-based structure include:
- Responsibility.
- Conflict.
- Short-term perspective.
- Relative size.
- Customer confusion.

Process-based structures

- Process-based structures split the organization according to function.
- The typical process-based structure of a manufacturing company would group together the resources under production activities, personnel, marketing, finance and engineering (Figure 9.6).
- The advantages of the process based structure are:
  - Specialization.
  - Stability.
  - Centralization.
  - Clarity.
- The disadvantages of the process-based structure are:
  - Co-ordination.
  - Budget orientation.
  - Succession.
  - Growth.
  - Political.

International organizations

- The most commonly found forms of international activity include:
  - Exporting.
  - Agents.
  - Licensing.
  - Franchising.
  - Management contracts.
  - Turnkey operations.
  - Contract arrangements.
  - Direct investment.
  - Portfolio investment.
  - Multinational enterprise.
- The main options for dealing with international activities include:
  - International division (Figure 9.7).
  - Product-based business units (Figure 9.8).
  - Geographic business units (Figure 9.9).
  - Functional orientation (Figure 9.10).
  - Matrix organization.
  - Holding company.

Matrix structures

- The matrix attempts to integrate both functional and product responsibilities.
- Matrix ideas attempt to enhance the integration through effective design, manufacturing and marketing of products and services (Figure 9.11).

- The level of success has been limited as a consequence of the existence of split responsibilities.
- Dual reporting relationships introduce additional complexity into the organization of work.

Horizontal structures

- Horizontal frameworks attempt to overcome the complexity of the matrix organization.
- This is achieved by removing the vertical reporting relationships.
- The purpose of horizontal links are to integrate effort across functions.
- This is organized around a number of key features, including:
  - Flat hierarchy.
  - Process organization.
  - Team activity.
- Activities would be organized around the customer experience of the company.

The holding company

- The holding company is a company in its own right which owns (fully or partly) a number of separate businesses (Figure 9.12).
- Within each subsidiary the structure could be any of the frameworks described above.
- In a pure form the holding company acts as a banker for the group.
- It brings together and divests organizations to create synergy within the group.
- The existence of separate companies provides the potential to manage according to profit or contribution.
- This should result in group company's displaying the following characteristics:
  - Objectives.
  - Market.
  - Motivation.
  - Funding.
- In practice, this approach is one step beyond the divisional structure.
- It attempts to provide greater benefits through federalism.
- Some of the problems with the holding company approach are:
  - Support.
  - Risk.
  - Part owned.
  - Cohesion.
  - Restrictions.

Design frameworks

- Structure is only one part of the design process.
- Other important elements include systems, procedures, communication, consultative and reporting mechanisms.

- The purpose being to ensure that integration of effort takes place.
- Structure alone will not guarantee success or failure.
- The weaknesses of a particular structural configuration can be partly offset by the support mechanisms introduced.
- Naturally, the converse is also applicable.
- Mintzberg provided a simple view of the structural components in the design of an organization (Figure 9.13).
- Each of the components has a different set of functions to perform:
  - Senior management.
  - Middle management.
  - Technical support staff.
  - Administrative support staff.
  - Functional core employees.
- A slightly different view was described by Handy. He classified by the type of activity undertaken:
  - Policy.
  - Innovation.
  - Steady state.
  - Crisis.
- Handy stresses that 'activity types' are not the same as functional groupings.

Organizational life cycle

- Products go through a life cycle.
- The Greiner model of organizational growth (Figure 9.4) reflects one aspect of this perspective.
- But is growth always followed by death, or even contraction in size?
- Many companies change form, are taken over or absorbed into other organizations.
- Have such companies died or ceased to exist in any meaningful way?
- Companies that go into receivership only to reappear under new ownership could be said to have died or survived, depending upon the definition.
- Quinn and Cameron describe four organizational life cycles:
  - Entrepreneurial phase.
  - Collectivity phase.
  - Formalization phase.
  - Elaboration phase.
- To the above stages a fifth phase can be added:
  - Organizational decline.
- Whetten identified four response options to decline:
  - Generating.
  - Reacting.
  - Defending.
  - Preventing.
- The generating approach should be the most effective way to remain in an integrated relationship with the environment.

- Being adaptive implies being close to the numerous elements within the environment.

Organizational frameworks: a management perspective

- Managers make the decisions about organizations.
- That is not to suggest that there are no business reasons for the choices made.
- The impression is easily gained that organizations consider at frequent intervals the structure that is best suited to their circumstances.
- This process is reflected in the Greiner model (Figure 9.4).
- However, the process is less well defined and less certain than that.
- Organizations evolve and in moving the structure tends to adjust.
- It is frequently only when a major crisis occurs that a fundamental rethink of structure is undertaken.
- To radically change the way that work is undertaken requires:
  - Time.
  - Additional resources.
- It also implies a:
  - Risk of failure.
  - Lower performance until employees become accustomed to the new arrangements.
  - Disruption to the service as mistakes inevitably occur.
- It is hardly surprising that evolutionary change is preferred to revolutionary change.
- Evolution also carries a risk and lack of clarity during the gestation period.
- Technology is an influencing factor in structure.
- Technology can control activity, increase efficiency and reduce cost.
- It influences the design of jobs and the configuration of the organization.
- Design is the macro level arrangement of activities and responsibilities.
- It is also the basis of defining the jobs done.

Conclusions

- This chapter brings together the main options for configuration of activity within organizations.
- The structure of an organization shapes the behaviour of the individuals within it.
- It determines the jobs that people do and the nature of interaction within and outside of the organization.
- It also determines the nature of any reporting and control relationships.

Discussion questions: outline answers for selected questions.

3. Organizational design is the same as organizational structure. Discuss.

The answer to this question will depend upon the definitions of the key terms that are adopted by students. At one level they are the same if design and structure are seen as the same. However, the more able students may begin to explore the semantics involved and identify possible distinctions between them. For example design could be described as the process through which structure is formulated. Equally design could imply the intended or optimal structure identified by management, with structure reflecting the actual framework achieved in practice.

5. 'The ultimate demise of an organization is as inevitable as the demise of the people who work in it.' Discuss this statement.

This question draws on the notion of life cycle. The statement implies that there is a natural cycle of events which eventually results in the demise of any organization. The opposite perspective would suggest that it is people who join and leave an organization and therefore its 'life' is separate and distinct from the individual human life cycle. Because people come and go it should be possible for the institution of an organization to reformulate itself to secure existence in perpetuity. Clearly the motivation of people joining the organization over time should be to find ways of continuing its existence, if for no other reason than their own self-interest. The stronger students should be able to explore these and related issues.

7. Why might it be difficult to change the design of an organization that has been in existence for some years?

In some ways this question has similar connotations to the previous answer. Many organizations experience a lethargy in being able to engender change within themselves. This can be for many reasons including experience, capability, perception, politics and power. Students should be expected to explore these issues and find ways of supporting their views on the truth or otherwise implied by the question.

8. 'Organizations with fewer layers of management will face significant problems in the future as their managers will not have the opportunity to gain experience in major decision making before they have that responsibility.' Discuss this statement.

This question identifies the issues associated with delayering. It raises the potential to discuss two differing approaches to management expertise development. Firstly the argument runs that frequent but small promotions provides the opportunity for practice at higher levels of decision making in a relatively safe environment and with plenty of more senior people about to prevent disaster. Secondly the argument runs that managers are paid to do a job and with adequate training in appropriate techniques and decision-making problems will not arise. Equally the lack of levels in the organization does not always run to rational protection of the organization, it encourages political and related behaviour that can detract from effective performance. Students should debate these conflicting perspectives and reach a conclusion.

Case study

The inclusion of a case study in this chapter is intended to provide lecturers with the opportunity to use this method of teaching which requires students to analyse a situation and form a judgement about their preferred solution. Groups of students could be encouraged to challenge each other on their solutions in order to deepen their understanding of the material and of the need to fully justify courses of action. This process should also provide lecturers with the opportunity to demonstrate that very rarely is only one solution available and that alternative routes might be equally (or more) valuable depending upon the forces acting upon the situation and subsequent events.

Management in Action 9.2: Business process re-engineering and Management in Action 9.5: What a way to run a company!

In this chapter the task is to compare two of the case studies and to reflect on the consequences for organizational structure. Management in Action 9.2 discusses the issue of business process re-engineering (BPR). Management in Action 9.5 discusses the issue of horizontal organizational frameworks.

Orticon (Management in Action 9.5) has re-organized its head office activities around the concepts of customer focus and horizontal organization. The impression given is one of a lack of formal organization or structure, with considerable freedom for individuals in work activities. Individuals have a high degree of personal responsibility to undertake work on behalf of the company. They are not closely supervised in these tasks and are put on trust to respond appropriately.

BPR as described in Management in Action 9.2 gives a strong impression that scientific management principles should be used to guide the elimination of all unnecessary activity. It is about the systematic and ruthless identification of the core elements of the business and the essential processes through which to achieve results. The distinct impression is that it offers an approach completely unlike that adopted by Orticon.

Under BPR employees would have their jobs and targets of performance closely specified.

Student tasks

In groups of six people review both of the Management in Action panels indicated. You should also search through the literature and other resources available to you for material associated with both BPR and horizontal organizational frameworks.

Imagine that you are the personnel manager of a medium-sized manufacturing company making and selling kitchen furniture. Your chief executive has been at a presentation on BPR and is keen to achieve the impressive results that have been claimed to be possible as a result of implementing it. Equally your marketing director is keen to implement the concept of a horizontal organizational framework as she feels that by doing so customers (trade and DIY) will be better served, complaints will reduce, order response times improve and their influence within the company increase.

You have been asked to prepare a brief presentation for the Board of Directors (not more than 15 minutes) on:

1. What your group consider to be the basis and implications of both BPR and horizontal organizational frameworks.
2. Compare and contrast the two approaches and identify what you would consider the main strengths and weaknesses of both approaches.
3. Describe how the company might go about introducing either of the two approaches, including the potential problems and difficulties involved.
4. Conclude on which (if either) approach you would recommend for implementation by the company, indicating why and what further work would need to be done before a final decision could be made.

Present your ideas to the rest of the class. Be prepared to answer questions from your classmates and also to defend your ideas.

CHAPTER 10

Contingency theory and beyond

Chapter outline

This chapter introduces the contingency approach to organizational design. It begins by introducing the background to contingency theory, followed by a review of a number of the perspectives on how organizations have operationalized these ideas over recent years. A number of alternative organizational forms are also introduced. The chapter concludes with a review of the management perspective on the topic.

Learning objectives

After studying this chapter and working through the associated Management in Action panels, discussion questions and research activities, students should be able to:

■ Describe the origins of the contingency approach to organizational design.
■ Explain the limitations of the standard organization chart in explaining activity within an organization.
■ Understand the concept of determinism and how it relates to organization structure.
■ Outline the socio-technical perspective on the structuring of organizations.
■ Appreciate how matrix structures and the flexible firm reflect some of the attributes of the contingency model.
■ Assess the contribution to organization design by the viable systems model.
■ Discuss the contingency model and its relationship to structure and environment.
■ Detail a number of alternative organizational forms and assess the degree to which they reflect a contingency approach.

Teaching notes and chapter summary

Introduction

The search for more effective ways of organizing exists in order to meet new competitive circumstances.

The contingency approach

■ The contingency approach arose out of a realization that the earlier perspectives were inherently limited.
■ Scientific management emphasized the tasks to be done.
■ The human relations movement emphasized the significance of people within organizations.
■ Human beings have free will and an ability to think.
■ Concentration on the people issues omits the commercial imperatives.
■ It was proposed that a broad range of factors influenced effectiveness, including structural arrangement.
■ There are two ways that the relationship between people, task and structure can be explained:
  – Separated.
  – Integrated.
■ Using the second approach, the design of an organization is said to be contingent upon the forces acting upon the situation.

Organizational metaphors

■ The way that an organization finds expression in the world is limitless.
■ The variation covers differences in:
  – Size.
  – Location.
  – Product or service orientation.
  – Culture.
  – Management style.
  – Level of profit.
  – Public or private sector.
  – Number of locations etc.
■ The umbrella term organization conjures up a generalized picture.
■ This is a simple expression of a metaphor.
■ Morgan identifies a number of organizational metaphors (Table 10.1).

- Metaphor provides a means to understand organizations and how they function.
- That understanding can include structure.

Limitations of the organization chart

- The organization chart describes structure and reporting relationships.
- It can also be an effective means of tracking:
  - Formal lines of communication.
  - Levels of responsibility.
  - Audit trails.
- Figure 10.1 is an example of the organization chart for a hypothetical medium-sized company in the fast food industry.
- Not included are:
  - Cross-functional relationships.
  - Decision-making processes.
  - Levels of responsibility held by the individuals.
- There have been attempts to reflect the relative seniority by scaling the vertical dimension (Figure 10.2).
- There are other ways of reflecting how an organization functions.
- A rich picture allows a dynamic situation to be reflected (Figure 10.3).
- Another means of reflecting activity is an influence diagram (Figure 10.4).
- Organizations are continually subject to change.
- Consequently organization charts need to be frequently updated.
- Townsend suggests that charts demoralize people as they reflect how far from the top most people are and the number of bosses that exist.
- The validity of an organization chart is a function of a number of factors, including:
  - Age.
  - Detail.
  - Purpose.
  - Need.

Two perspectives on determinism

- There are two approaches to determinism.
- The deterministic approach holds that structure is a function of technology, or other situational factors.
- The other perspective holds that structure is a function of managerial choice.
- From the determinism point of view there are two main schools of thought:
  - Technological determinism. This holds that the production technology of an organization determines the structural frameworks that are adopted (Woodward, Perrow).
  - Environmental determinism. This view holds that it is forces in the environment that determine how an organization structures itself (Burns and Stalker).

- Environmental determinism views an organization as an interactive part of its own environment (Figure 10.5).
- Lawrence and Lorsch reported that the most successful organizations integrated the way that they organized their activities relative to the environment.
- But that each of the industries required different forms of internal segmentation.
- Managerial choice is the other view of determinism.
- It is possible to reconcile these approaches.
- Even in the deterministic approach managers can be seen to be exercising decision making.
- Perhaps, managerial choice is an intervening variable between environment and structure, the consequences being apparent in the level of success.

Socio-technical systems theory

- The notion of a system originated in the physical sciences as a means of reflecting how a number of elements or sub-systems interact within a cohesive whole.
- Figure 10.6 represents an open systems view of an organization.
- As an open system the organization is in an interactive relationship with its environment.
- Within an organization there are a number of sub-systems.
- The socio-technical approach recognizes that it is necessary to incorporate both the social and technical aspects of work if an effective system is to be created.
- The first work in socio-technical systems originated in studies of coal mining in the north-east of England in the late 1940s and early 1950s (Trist and Bamforth).
- This approach is the contingency model.

The contingency model

- The contingency model postulates that the design of the organization is contingent upon a number of forces acting upon the situation.
- Figure 10.7 differentiates the traditional and contingency approaches.
- Figure 10.8 illustrates the contingency model.
- The main elements in the model are:
  - External contingency factors.
  - Internal contingency factors.
  - Managerial perceptions and objectives.
  - Organizational capability, will and politics.
- The contingency model is useful for explaining the diversity in organizational design.
- The Aston Group developed a research approach which examined three elements (Pugh and Hickson):
  - Change and complexity.
  - Institutional arrangements.
  - Multiple perspectives (Figure 10.9).

■ The use of the contingency model does not imply that there is only one approach to explaining the links between organization and environment.

■ The contingency model has been the subject of a number of criticisms.

■ These include that it assumes a relationship between organization and performance.

■ The contingency model does not take account of the exercise of power or control in work and its relationships.

Matrix structures and the flexible firm

■ A matrix organization utilizes a twin reporting framework to provide a more complex application of resource.

■ Vertical reporting relationships are integrated with horizontal linkages based on project or product grouping.

■ It was Ashby who first suggested the law of requisite variety.

■ In order to ensure that the variability (variety) experienced by any system is effectively controlled, it is necessary for the controller to match its complexity.

■ The matrix structure is an attempt to improve the level of requisite variety by providing a higher level of internal complexity.

■ There are a number of difficulties inherent with the matrix structure, including:
  – Complexity of operation.
  – Split responsibilities.
  – Split accountabilities.
  – Increased political opportunity.
  – Lack of clear focus.
  – Requires specific skills.
  – Conversion.

■ The flexible firm idea is based around the premise that employees can be trusted to do what is necessary.

■ It postulates that the horizontal perspective of an organization experienced by a customer should determine structure.

■ Another approach to the notion of the flexible organization is that described by Atkinson:
  – Numerical flexibility.
  – Functional flexibility.
  – Financial flexibility.

The viable systems model

■ The viable systems model is based upon cybernetic and systems principles.

■ Cybernetics originated from the study of control and communications in system functioning.

■ The viable systems model begins with the organization being an open system made up of a number of sub-systems.

■ Beer (1979) identifies the following systems:
  – System 1.
  – System 2.
  – System 3.
  – System 3*.
  – System 4.
  – System 5.

■ The viable systems model can be represented as a diagram (Figure 10.10).

■ The diagram should not be seen in the same terms as an organization chart.

■ It is not hierarchical.

■ Each system has its own responsibilities and functions that need to be integrated into an effective whole if success is to be achieved.

■ It is important to avoid the assumption that system equates with function.

■ Beer refers to one common problem for organizations as autopiesis, a tendency to over-elaborate and for support systems to seek to become viable systems in their own right.

■ The channels of communication are shown as passing from one system to another.

■ The model recognizes the need for communication channels that can, in special circumstances circumvent the normal routes, an algedonic system.

■ The model as described so far relates to a single organization, the system in focus.

■ Recursion describes the idea that every system is made up of sub-systems and is part of a larger system (Figure 10.11).

Alternative organizations

The human service organization

■ These include schools, hospitals, social work/welfare departments and public assistance providers.

■ There are differences in these organizations that make them a useful starting point for consideration as non-standard organizations.

■ Hasenfeld suggests that it is the common experience of the recipients of these services that they evoke a mixture of 'hope and fear, caring and victimization, dignity and abuse'. Employees of these organizations suffer a conflict between a personal need to provide high standards of service and the constraints and restrictions imposed by managers. He identifies a number of reasons that could account for this:
  – People as 'raw material'.
  – Human services as moral work.
  – Human services as gendered work.

■ Hyde describes the functioning of a number of feminist health centres.

■ The analysis begins with a review of the way that ideology influences organizational activity (Figure 10.12).

The co-operative and the kibbutz

- The co-operative and the kibbutz are both examples of consensual organizations (Iannello).
- Rothschild and Whitt define them as, 'any enterprise in which control rests ultimately and overwhelmingly with the member–employees–owners, regardless of the particular legal framework through which this is achieved.'
- This work identifies the that the following aspects differentiate consensual organizations:
  - Authority.
  - Rules.
  - Social control.
  - Social relations.
  - Recruitment and advancement.
  - Incentive structures.
  - Social stratification.
  - Differentiation of labour.
- The constraints arising from the conventionally organized world around the consensual organization constrains structure.
- Iannello indicates that the primary goal of consensual organizations is the humanization of the workplace in an attempt to re-establish the relationship between workers and society.
- The work of Greenberg identifies the major consensual organizations as:
  - Kibbutz.
  - Those in the former Yugoslavia.
  - That in Mondragon in Spain.

The virtual organization

- The term virtual organization appeared towards the end of the 1980s.
- The term originates from the computer world.
- Virtual memory reflects the appearance of more memory within a computer than actually exists.
- In an organizational context, it is a metaphor for an organization that appears to be larger than its resources.
- Such organizations have been in existence in some industries for many years.
- Small consultancies have used associates to expand their ability to accept large contracts.
- The virtual organization is a temporary network of independent organizations for a specific purpose.
- It could include suppliers, customers, competitors.
- The purpose being to take advantage of the particular strengths of each member of the alliance in achieving a specific objective.
- There are potential dangers with this type of approach.
- In terms of the structure and design issues, the hierarchy would be a minimum as each member of the alliance concentrates on only part of the process.
- There is a need for the integration of activity across the member organizations.

- Byrne *et al.* quote a number of key lessons including:
  - Marry well.
  - Play fair.
  - Offer the best.
  - Define objectives.
  - Common infrastructure.

Contingency theory: a management perspective

- From a managers point of view contingency theory offers a richer vehicle for organization design.
- This normative perspective delivers high useability to managers but little by way of explanation of what it is that creates structure (Legge).
- Organizations are composed of a number of smaller groups and these can have very different perspectives and interactions with the environmental (Figure 10.13).
- The implication of Figure 10.13 being that an organization has many internal and external environments.
- The discussion so far has concentrated on organizational adaptation to environmental forces.
- Another way of considering how organizations evolve over time has been the population ecology approach.
- Using Darwinian approaches this approach emerged in the late 1970s, but it has not yet produced a significant alternative explanation.
- Structure is the means of organizing within the enterprise.
- It allows specialization to be introduced in order to reduce the skill and training required.
- It also provides the simplified and repetitive tasks that can create alienation and a lack of commitment.
- It is a double-edged sword, providing benefits and disadvantages.
- It is in an attempt to offset some of the disadvantages that alternative organizations are important.

Conclusions

- The design and structure of an organization is an area in which managers make choices.
- The form of the organization is not something that occurs by chance.
- It is appropriate to view an organization as something over which people have stewardship for a period of time.
- They are therefore constrained by a number of forces in moulding the organization.
- The notion of a direct cause and effect link between environmental forces and structure is overly simplistic.
- It ignores the interactive nature of external and internal forces and managerial responses.

■ The use of metaphor was introduced as a means of describing the understanding that managers have of what an organization is and how it should function.

■ Contingency and systems approaches offer a richer means of attempting to understand the processes involved and a basis for future research.

Discussion questions

2. Describe how the contingency approach to organizational design emerged.

   This question seeks to draw out from students the evolutionary nature of theory development. However when the student describes the emergence it should be apparent from the work that it reflects an attempt to take account of the deficiencies in the earlier and more simplistic perspectives of either task or people perspectives.

4. In what ways might a virtual organization differ from a conventional one? Would you like to work in a virtual organization, explain why or why not?

   This reflects another relatively factual question. the first part of the answer requires students to demonstrate that they have read the appropriate material and that they understand the main differences and similarities. The second part of the question is a personal opinion type of perspective. There is no right or wrong answer to this question it simply expects the student to be able to position themselves relative to this particular framework. In doing so the student should demonstrate their understanding of the notion of a virtual organization and the employment implications of it.

5. In what ways does the concept of a metaphor as described by Morgan (1986) contribute to an understanding of how organizations are structured?

   Metaphor reflects a way of thinking and of making sense of the world in which we live. Consequently it helps to simplify much of the complexity and eliminate some of the ambiguity from the world. In that sense it reflects a way of making sense of organizations. Students should be expected to be able to reflect on these ideas and will probably draw heavily on the work of Morgan in doing so.

10. What is a flexible firm and how does it reflect the contingency ideas described in this chapter?

    This question requires the student to describe the notion of flexibility and perhaps even to develop the major models of it. In doing so they should be able to effectively link together the principles of the contingency approach with that of flexibility in all its forms. Stronger students might also develop the

issues of flexibility and contingency being ideas that reflect a desirable benefit, but from whose point of view?

Case study

The inclusion of a case study in this chapter is intended to provide lecturers with the opportunity to use this method of teaching which requires students to analyse a situation and form a judgement about their preferred solution. Groups of students could be encouraged to challenge each other on their solutions in order to deepen their understanding of the material and of the need to fully justify courses of action. This process should also provide lecturers with the opportunity to demonstrate that very rarely is only one solution available and that alternative routes might be equally (or more) valuable depending upon the forces acting upon the situation and subsequent events.

In this chapter the task is to reflect on the consequences for organizational structure of Management in Action 10.2.

Management in Action 10.2: Steelmaker that re-invented itself

Student tasks

In groups of six people review the Management in Action panel indicated. You should also search through the literature and other resources available to you for material associated with organizational metaphors and also organizational frameworks.

Universities are continually claiming that they do not have enough money to undertake their full range of responsibilities as fully and effectively as they would like. Under these circumstances it is also difficult to effectively take advantage of the commercial possibilities that might arise. You should reflect on the example of redesign and organizational activity contained in Management in Action 10.2. In what ways might your college or university go about improving its financial health and undertake the wide diversity of activity possible.

You have been asked to prepare a brief presentation for the senior managers of your college or university (not more than 15 minutes) on:

1. What your group consider to be the areas of activity that the institution should be involved with.
2. Assess the possibilities for funding the activity. For example will each activity loose money, pay for itself or contribute a surplus to the institution and how should these issues be dealt with?
3. Consider the staffing and structure of the institution in relation to your ideas. For example, is the current structure appropriate, in what way and how might it

be changed? Are there enough people with the right skills employed within the institution? If not how might such people be attracted to become involved in your plans?

4. Describe how the institution might go about achieving these opportunities, including the potential problems and difficulties involved.

5. Having presented your plans reflect on the metaphors that you used in the process and how the underlying assumptions and beliefs influenced your decisions.

Present your ideas to the rest of the class. Be prepared to answer questions from your classmates and also to defend your ideas.

CHAPTER 11

Organizational culture

Chapter outline

This chapter considers the concept of organizational culture. The chapter begins with a review of what culture means within an organization and the forms that it can take. The determinants of culture are then explored, followed by a consideration of the notion of national culture and its links with organizational culture. The relationship between culture and organizational design are discussed. The chapter concludes with a management review of organizational culture.

Learning objectives

After studying this chapter and working through the associated Management in Action panels, discussion questions and research activities, students should be able to:

■ Explain why the concept of culture is problematic as applied to organizations.
■ Describe the different levels of analysis used in cultural analysis.
■ Outline the forms through which organizational culture finds expression.
■ Understand the links between culture and organizational design.
■ Appreciate the relationship between culture as used within an organization and as used to describe national difference.
■ Discuss the significance of sub- and counter-cultures to an organization.
■ Assess the impact of the various determinants of culture on an organizational context.
■ Detail the management significance of the culture of an organization.

Teaching notes and chapter summary

Introduction

■ Culture began to make an impact in the late 1970s and early 1980s.
■ Culture originates from anthropological studies.
■ There is no single dominant view of how culture should be conceptualized.
■ According to Allaire and Firsirotu there are eight separate schools of thought on what the term 'culture' means.
■ 'The way we do things around here' is frequently offered as an operational definition of culture (Deal and Kennedy).
■ This may be a useful approach to understanding the parameters of culture, but it has little analytical power.

Definition of organizational culture

■ Kilman *et al.* suggest that culture reflects the ideologies, shared philosophies, values, beliefs, assumptions, attitudes, expectations and norms of an organization.
■ Jaques suggests that culture is the:

    ... customary and traditional way of thinking and doing things, which is shared to a greater or lesser degree by all members, and which the new members must learn and at least partially accept, in order to be accepted into the services of the firm.

■ Deal and Kennedy suggest a range of elements within culture, including symbolism and leadership as a means of achieving employee commitment.
■ The Kilman *et al.* view considers content and the Jaques definition process.
■ This assumes that individuals will either possess the same culture as the organization before joining it or that they will subsequently acquire it.
■ Particular cultures will be more supportive of management's objectives than others.

■ The Japanese achieved this through what Thompson and McHugh call compulsory sociability.

Levels of analysis

■ It is possible to identify three levels of cultural analysis (Figure 11.1).
■ Taking each level in turn:
  – Perceived culture.
  – Common values, etc.
  – Underlying assumptions.

The dimensions of culture

■ Schien identified six dimensions that reflected the composition of culture:
  – Behavioural regularities.
  – Dominant values.
  – Norms.
  – Rules.
  – Philosophy.
  – Climate.
■ The circularity between culture and organizations is reflected in Figure 11.2.
■ Culture produces behaviour and belief patterns, which influences what happens within the organization.
■ Actual events are then measured against management objectives and the consequences feed back into culture.
■ The implication being that if management perceive that a particular culture achieves the objectives being pursued it will be reinforced.
■ If not then management will attempt to change it.

Cultural forms

■ There are a number of different approaches to the question of how culture experienced in an organization:

Handy's four types

■ Based on the earlier work of Harrison, Handy describes four manifestations of culture:
  – Power culture (Figure 11.3).
  – Role culture (Figure 11.4).
  – Task culture (Figure 11.5).
  – Person culture.
■ There are obvious links between the concept of culture as described by Handy and structure.

Ouchi's type Z companies

■ Ouchi identified that Japanese firms operated from a different cultural base to that of Western organizations.
■ He considered that organizational culture originated from the societal culture.

■ He identified a number of key differences between Japanese and American organizations (Table 11.1).
■ Ouchi gave his idea the title theory Z because it extended McGregor's theory 'X' and 'Y'.
■ Ouchi's suggested that some American organizations contained some of the features described in Table 11.1.
■ A number of the claims made by Ouchi have been brought into question by later researchers.
■ For example, the notion of lifetime employment applies to only a small proportion of employees.
■ It is also suggested that the Japanese approach produces a more tightly controlled approach to work.

Peters and Waterman's excellence and culture

■ Peters and Waterman attempted to identify what it was that made some American organizations 'excellent'.
■ From this research the McKinsey 7-S Framework was developed (Table 11.2).
■ The seventh item in the list relates specifically to organizational culture.
■ A set of eight features emerged that Peters and Waterman suggest are commonly found among excellent organizations:
  – Bias for action.
  – Being close to the customer.
  – Autonomy and entrepreneurship.
  – Productivity through people.
  – Hands-on, value driven.
  – Stick to the knitting.
  – Simple form, lean staff.
  – Simultaneous loose-tight control.
■ The ideas developed by Peters and Waterman have been subjected to considerable criticism.
■ A number of the organizations ran into problems in the recessionary markets of the 1980s.

Deal and Kennedy's cultural profile

■ Deal and Kennedy developed two aspects of organizational culture.
■ Firstly, they describe the effects of risk and speed of feedback from the environment on culture:
  – Work and play hard culture.
  – Process culture.
  – Macho culture.
  – Bet your company culture.
■ The second perspective is that of the existence of strong and weak cultures.
■ A strong culture would be evident if most members supported it (Table 11.3).
■ A weak culture is one that is not strongly rooted in the activities or value systems of the group.
■ From Table 11.3 there are two items of interest:
  – The hero, a person who personifies the values and actions expected of the true believer.

– The use of ritual and ceremony as the basis of reinforcement of the desired culture.
■ Managers frequently seek to inculcate a strong culture.
■ However strong cultures become difficult to change as a result of there depth of commitment and unity.

Trice and Beyer's organization culture

■ Trice and Beyer describe culture as a device for providing common meaning for a particular group.
■ They describe 11 elements that make up an organizational culture, grouped together under four categories:
  1. Company communications. The means through which culture is described, communicated and continually reinforced:
     – stories
     – myths, sagas and legends.
     – folk tales
     – symbols.
  2. Company practice. The activities that demonstrate the culture in operation and reinforce its importance:
     – rites
     – ritual
     – ceremonial.
  3. Common language. A major part of the socialization of new members into a group involves them learning the common language. It serves to reinforce group cohesion in binding together the individuals through the common forms of expression.
  4. Physical culture. This reflects the tangible nature of culture:
     – artefacts
     – layout.

Sub- and counter-cultures

■ In the discussion so far culture has been used in a unifying or integrating context.
■ Culture can also be a differentiating feature of organizational life.
■ The existence of sub-units within the organization (both formal and informal) creates differences in culture.
■ Professional groups and departments for example.
■ It would not be surprising to find that the organizational culture was a blend of sub-group cultures.
■ Counter-cultures exist where one or more groups are disaffected and have objectives that run counter to those of the dominant group.
■ For example, when one company is taken over by another the integration process can create counter-cultures.
■ As the culture within society changes the dominant culture within an organization also comes under pressure to change.
■ This can be described as cultural diversity, or cultural fragmentation.

The determinants of culture

■ In the early days of an organization the culture is very much dependent upon the founders.
■ There are a number of parallels with the Tuckman and Jensen stages in group development.
■ Handy indicates a number of influences on the culture of an organization:
  – History and ownership
  – Size
  – Technology
  – Goals and objectives
  – Environment
  – People.

National culture

■ Organizations operate within a national setting.
■ They are subject to the same cultural forces that act upon every other aspect of life in that situation.
■ The convergence perspective suggests that within an organization the national culture is subservient.
■ This implies that organization are able to separate internal from external cultures.
■ Also that they are able to manage the internal culture as necessary to support business objectives.
■ The divergence view holds that national culture takes preference and that organizational culture will adapt to local cultural patterns (Lammers and Hickson).
■ It is not difficult to envisage that both views could be correct in appropriate circumstances.
■ Hofstede carried out an extensive series of studies over some 13 years.
■ He defines culture as mental programming, on the basis that it predisposes individuals to particular ways of thinking, perceiving and behaving.
■ This implies that there is a tendency to produce similar patterns of behaviour.
■ He developed four dimensions of culture from a factor analysis of his questionnaire based research data:
  – Individualism–collectivism.
  – Power distance.
  – Uncertainty avoidance.
  – Masculinity–femininity.
■ Table 11.4 provides an indication of those counties that exhibit high and low levels of each of the four dimensions identified by Hofstede.
■ Organizations from particular cultures may be more easily accommodated into locations with similar characteristics.
■ It is also possible that the Hofstede framework could be used to describe organizations.
■ Hofstede considered that power distance and uncertainty avoidance were the 'decisive dimensions' of culture.
■ The research can be criticized on the basis of its emphasis on description rather than analysis.

- Culture as defined by Hofstede reflects tendencies rather than absolutes.
- However, as presented the dimensions give no clue as to the degree of difference that could be expected in any context (Tyson and Jackson).
- Frans Trompenaars built up a database of the cultural characteristics of 15,000 managers and staff from 30 companies in 50 different countries.
- His views contrast sharply with those that suggest that the world is becoming a 'global village'.
- He argues that what works in one culture will seldom do so in another.
- Trompenaars identifies seven dimensions of culture.
- Five deal with the way people interact with each other.
- A sixth deals with people's perspective on time and the seventh concerns the approach to moulding the environment.
- These combine to create different corporate cultures including:
  - Family. Typically found in Japan, India, Belgium, Italy, Spain and among small French companies.
  - Eiffel Tower. Large French companies typify this culture.
  - Guided missile. Typical of American companies, and to a lesser extent found in the UK.
- Trompenaars advises companies to avoid a blanket approach to culture.
- He argues for a transnational approach in which the best elements from several cultures are brought together and applied differently in each country.
- Managers should also be trained in cross-cultural awareness and respect.

Changing organizational cultures

- Another view of culture holds that it is the glue or cement that holds the organization together.
- Turner criticizes the view that culture can be managed, suggesting that it cannot be manipulated because it is an integral part of the organization's fabric.
- In contrast Lundberg argues that it is possible to change culture through:
  - External. Identify external conditions that may encourage a change to the existing culture.
  - Internal. Identify internal circumstances and individuals that would support change.
  - Pressures. Identify those forces pressing for change in the culture.
  - Visioning. Identify key stakeholders and create in them a vision of the proposed changes, the need and benefits.
  - Strategy. Develop a strategy for achieving the implementation of the new culture.
  - Action. Develop and implement a range of action plans based on the strategy as a means of achieving movement to the desired culture.

- Each non-dominant culture in a specific context is likely to seek to increase its own significance.
- Consequently there are political, power and control perspectives to culture.
- Perhaps adaptation over time is a more realistic perspective on culture change.
- Equally to suggest that culture is static understates the experience of organizational life.
- Perhaps the 'problem' is not one of how to ensure that change happens, but of ensuring that it moves in the 'right' direction.
- Perhaps culture can be described as very difficult to change in the short term, but adaptable over time.
- It could also be amenable to rapid change in times of crisis.

The significance of culture for organizational design

- Culture influences how people interact in the course of their daily work.
- There are also connections between culture and structure.
- Choice is available to managers in how to compartmentalize activities in order to meet their objectives.
- A definition of 'how things get done' would imply that structure is at least partly a function of culture.
- Culture influences and shapes the understanding of how things should be organized in pursuing objectives (Figure 11.6).

Organizational culture: a management perspective

- From a management point of view culture occurs naturally.
- That does not imply that managers should not, and do not attempt to create specific cultures.
- The discussion has suggested that there is an active relationship between managers and culture.
- Figure 11.7, based on Payne emphasizes the managed nature of the process.
- The culture that emerges within an organization may not be appropriate for the achievement of the set objectives.
- For example, it could be that the dominant culture is hostile to management's intentions.
- This does assume that the goals being sought by managers are the 'right' ones and that they are the only ones worth pursuing.
- Culture provides managers with a number of opportunities.
- A culture supportive of management's objectives should make it easier and cheaper to manage the organization.
- This opportunity manifests itself in three main ways:
  - Control.
  - Norms.
  - Commitment.

- It is too simplistic to suggest that managers can decide, design, implement and maintain particular cultures.
- For example, the decision to move towards a more participative culture will fail if it is not supported by appropriate training, encouragement and tolerance of mistakes.
- The maintenance of a culture is also problematic.
- Maintaining a static culture does not arise, it will evolve over time naturally.
- The problem is one of how to retain control over momentum, direction and alignment with organizational objectives.
- Watson studied one company in depth at a time when it was undergoing considerable change to its culture.
- He describes a number of reactions to this process from people within the organization:
  - Resistance from all levels.
  - A lack of confidence in the commitment, understanding and ability of senior managers.
  - Confusion about what culture was.
  - A cynical view of culture change being just another initiative designed by senior managers to further their own careers.
- This reflects the political and situational reality within which culture exists and evolves.
- In the act of becoming a group, an out-group is formed.
- Out-groups are generally considered as different and in extreme cases regarded as the enemy.
- Strong cultures if they are supportive of managers are a positive benefit.
- There is unity of purpose and intent.
- On the other hand strong cultures are less amenable to change, they develop a life of their own.
- The ability to direct such cultures is also reduced.
- Attempts to develop strong cultures require that a figurehead is incorporated.
- In other words a protection device which allows control and influence through support for the leader.
- In terms of organizational structure, culture is one of the contingency factors that influence design (Figure 11.6).
- The cultural perspective on structure contains two main aspects:
  - Managing internationally.
  - Accommodating cultural diversity.

Conclusions

- Culture influences a wide range of behaviour both within society and within organizations.
- It is not a precisely defined concept and is capable of being misinterpreted and manipulated by managers.
- Culture is valuable in describing a range of activities and features associated with organizational life.

- It is not possible to manage every person all of the time that they are at work.
- Some internalization of responsibility and knowledge of requirements must be delegated if efficiency in management is to be achieved.
- Culture is able to deliver a way of accounting for these phenomena.
- The notion that strong cultures provide a way for managers to ensure harmony and the achievement of objectives is simplistic and does not reflect experience.

Discussion questions and outline answers for selected questions

2. Discuss the significance of 'culture' in the context of managing an organization.

   This question seeks to draw out from students the range of definitions of culture and the difficulty in offering precise prescriptions of its significance in the management of organizations. On the one hand organizational culture is commonly understood as an important feature of how thing are 'done' within the specific company. On the other hand every culture consists of sub-cultures and there are also counter-cultures that exist and which impact on the overall activity. From that perspective culture is a 'problem' to manage and students should make an attempt to reflect the competing complexities as well as the importance of managerially supportive culture for operational effectiveness.

4. 'The concept of culture is of little practical value to managers because it simply describes tendencies and ignores the variation between individuals.' Discuss this statement.

   To some extent this question is an extension of Question 2 above, except that it approaches the issues from a slightly different perspective. This question raises the imprecise nature of the notion of culture and that it can be argued to reflect tendencies rather than absolutes. Every person, professional group, department, etc. will have a slightly different culture and perspectives on the priorities within the operation and so the notion of a single or dominant culture begins to become problematic. For example a dominant culture could be so because it reflects the underlying beliefs to which everyone would subscribe, or it could be so as a result of coercion or manipulation. Clearly each of these situations could imply differing circumstances. Equally, emphasis on the collective significance of culture ignores the importance of the contribution made to organizational effectiveness of individuals.

5. It has been suggested that strong organizational cultures are essential to the achievement of success. It

has also been suggested that strong cultures could predispose an organization to failure. Can you find an argument that could reconcile these two positions?

This question raises another of the difficulties associated with culture, that of 'strength'. Clearly it should be easier to manage an organization and to achieve the objectives determined by management if there is a strong and supportive culture in existence. However the danger inherent in such desires is that managers might find themselves creating very strong counter-cultures that oppose the original intention. For example, creating a unified workforce in support of management could easily become a unified workforce opposed to management's intentions, if management are thought to have abused that trust. The heavy reliance on employee commitment and co-operation for initiatives such as just-in-time to work also makes the organization vulnerable to industrial action if employees become disenchanted. Equally, a strong culture could make it more difficult to flex or adapt the organization to the changing needs of the marketplace, particularly if the organization operates globally where the need for different culture might be expected to exist. The reconciliation of these two conflicting perspectives comes from the need to attempt to create appropriate cultures which encourage flexibility and adaptability, as well as avoiding highly centralized, prescriptive and rigid cultures.

Case study

The inclusion of a case study in this chapter is intended to provide lecturers with the opportunity to use this method of teaching which requires students to analyse a situation and form a judgement about their preferred solution. Groups of students could be encouraged to challenge each other on their solutions in order to deepen their understanding of the material and of the need to fully justify courses of action. This process should also provide lecturers with the opportunity to demonstrate that very rarely is only one solution available and that alternative routes might be equally (or more) valuable depending upon the forces acting upon the situation and subsequent events.

In this chapter the task is to reflect on the consequences for organizational activity of Management in Action 11.5.

Management in Action 11.5: Cultivate your culture

Student tasks

In groups of six people review the Management in Action panel indicated.

Identify a company that has recently undergone a major culture change programme. Arrange to interview members of the senior management team to find out what they sought to change from what they defined the new culture. Identify their business reasons for seeking the change and the processes that were used to identify the desired culture. Also identify how the culture change process was undertaken, over what period of time and with what success.

Attempt to identify any of the approaches described in Management in Action 11.5 as having been used by the company in seeking to bring about the new culture.

You have two tasks to achieve:

1. Prepare a briefing for your class on the findings from your research activity in this case study. This should not last more than 15 minutes and should cover what you discovered about the company and its culture change programme, also how what you found links with the approaches identified in the Management in Action panel.
2. Having found out a considerable amount of detail about the culture change programme, you should seek to discuss with the senior managers the options discussed in Management in Action 11.5. Draw out from the managers which of the approaches from that Management in Action might have been useful in their situation, and which would not have been. Also seek to find out why they hold those views. In your group review the outcome of this part of your task and identify the lessons to be learned from it in relation to culture change programmes.

CHAPTER 12

Job design

Chapter outline

This chapter introduces the approaches to the design of jobs within an organization. The range of tasks to be performed as part of the organizational activities must be combined into jobs in such a way as to minimize cost. At the same time they should ensure that the individuals employed have something meaningful to contribute and feel committed to the objectives defined by management. The forces impacting on the design of jobs will be reviewed as will the ways that working patterns and practices can contribute to the value of work for employees and managers.

Chapter objectives

After studying this chapter and working through the associated Management in Action panels, discussion questions and research activities, students should be able to:

■ Understand the nature of job design as it impacts on organizational structure and employee perception of the value of work.
■ Describe the main approaches to job design.
■ Explain how work study attempts to influence job design activities.
■ Outline the interrelationship between technology and job design.
■ Assess the contribution of the quality of working life movement and the use of quality circles as an influence on job design.
■ Appreciate how issues such as flexibility and the pattern of work can influence the design of jobs.
■ Detail what is defined by the concept of a job.
■ Discuss how the socio-technical approach to job design attempted to incorporate the need to balance technical, economic and human aspects of operational activity.

Teaching notes and chapter summary

Introduction

■ The structure of an organization determines the type of jobs that exist.
■ However that does not prescribe the nature of the jobs in any given context.
■ The design of jobs is frequently based on tradition.
■ Increasingly, the formal design of jobs is seen as a means of improving motivation, quality and commitment.

The nature of a job

■ It may seem obvious what a job is.
■ People hold jobs, careers are made up of jobs and jobs form the basis of many stories on television, film and in books.
■ It is widely understood what the job of a police officer or doctor is.
■ However, not all police officers or doctors do the same job.
■ Add to this the opportunity for individuals to adapt jobs to their own preferences and jobs can become unique.
■ Roy identified the use of informal breaks and playing 'games' as a means of coping with monotony.
■ The concept of work as we know it is a relatively new one, see Management in Action 12.1.
■ A job is a collection of tasks brought together as a practical chunk of activity.
■ A job is a social construction created and adapted by people.
■ The design of jobs serves particular interests.
■ There are examples where jobs have been designed for the benefit of the job holder.
■ Examples include the professions such as the law and medicine.
■ Jobs vary in two dimensions, vertical and horizontal (Figure 12.1).

- Taking each dimension in turn:
  - Vertical. This dimension reflects the responsibility incorporated into a job.
  - Horizontal. This dimension reflects the breadth of activity in a job.
- A job is not static or incapable of being manipulated.
- Jobs can be consciously designed providing managers with a means of control.
- Jobs provide employees with a basis for protecting a defined area of work.

Work study and job analysis

- Work study is commonly thought to have emerged through the work of FW Taylor and scientific management.
- There is evidence that medieval monks used job times to determine the duration of monastery and cathedral building.
- Currie identifies an extract from a contract in which an individual undertook to secretly time jobs in a factory and report the outcome to the owner:

  > I Thomas Mason, this 22nd day of December, 1792 solemnly pledge myself to use my utmost caution at all times to prevent the knowledge transpiring that I am employed to use a stop watch to make observation of work done in Mr. Duesbry's manufactory; and to take such observations with the utmost truth and accuracy in my power and to give the results thereof faithfully to Mr. Duesbry.

- Adam Smith is first credited with the notion of division of labour.
- Work study contains two distinct elements, method study and work measurement (Figure 12.2).
- Taking each aspect in turn:
  - Method study. A range of techniques that enable work methods to be described and analysed.
  - Work measurement. The use of timing techniques to identify how long particular tasks should take.
- Work study approaches to job design provide an opportunity to control the design of work and its delivery.
- Torrington and Hall identify this as the disciplinary aspect of management.
- Work study initiatives were frequently followed by job cuts and demands to work harder for less pay.
- Discipline is most effective if the underlying values are internalized.
- If employees adopt the same values, standards and norms as management then the job of management would become much easier.
- Employees would require less supervision and would naturally function in ways supportive of management's objectives.
- Torrington and Hall identify three levels of discipline reflecting this progressive internalization of discipline (Figure 12.3).

- Job analysis is a systematic approach to the identification of job content.
- It can be used to support a wide range of activities, including:
  - Resourcing.
  - Training.
  - Career development.
  - Payment.
  - Performance evaluation.
  - Equality.
- There are two main approaches to job analysis according to Ivancevich:
  - Functional job analysis. This approach requires consideration of four aspects of the work:
    - Employees activities relevant to data, people and other jobs.
    - The methods and techniques used by the worker.
    - The machines, tools and equipment used by the worker.
    - What outputs are produced by the worker.
  - Position analysis questionnaire. This approach requires consideration of six aspects of the work:
    - Sources of information necessary to the job.
    - Decision-making aspects associated with job activity.
    - Physical aspects associated with the job.
    - Interpersonal and communication necessary to the job.
    - Working conditions and there impact on the job.
    - Impact of work schedules, responsibility, etc.
- Job analysis identifies what a job should be.
- It is however only one part of the process.
- Work is a function of both organizational and individual factors (Figure 12.4).
- Two points are worth highlighting:
  - Management intentions are an influence on both job analysis and job design.
  - However a job is defined on paper employees perceive and interpret the work expected of them.

Technology and job design

- Technology influences job design through a number of routes.
- There is the technology used in the work itself.
- There are the administrative and procedural technologies that must be complied with.
- There are the social technologies that influence how people integrate with the other technologies.
- The three technologies combine to produce the form that jobs take:
  - Equipment. This category includes the machines, tools and work methods required by the process itself.
  - Administrative. Every organization needs procedures to identify and control the cost of operations.

- Social. There are opportunities for influencing the actual design of jobs through the ways that people are fitted-in around the other constraints.
- These relationship can be shown as a diagram (Figure 12.5).

Approaches to designing jobs

- The tasks to be undertaken in an organization need to be combined into specific jobs.
- Job design is usually about changing jobs that already exist.

Simplification and job engineering

- Historically jobs were based around whole activities and craft based skill.
- The division of labour was observed to reduce training times, increase skill through constant repetition and reduced waste.
- Fewer tool changes and machine set-ups were also required as a result of the batch nature of production.
- FW Taylor introduced the scientific management approach to job simplification.
- This approach is referred to as job specialization, job engineering or job simplification.
- Job specialization because that was the work study aim.
- Job engineering – engineering the one best way of maximizing output and minimizing labour input.
- Scientific management produced considerably simplified jobs – hence the third title.
- Job simplification represents a collection small tasks to make the most efficient contribution to the process.
- It is seen in many production jobs and assembly line processes.
- The aim of job simplification is to maximize output and minimize labour input.
- The difficulties with job simplification were recognized early.
- It can be argued that the human relations movement was a direct consequence of the de-humanizing effect of such work.
- As far back as 1952 Walker and Guest identified the dissatisfaction among car factory assembly workers, including:
  - Lack of control over the pace of the assembly line.
  - Repetitiveness (short cycles) of work.
  - Low skill levels required to undertake the jobs.
  - Limited social interaction with fellow workers.
  - No control over the tools used or the methods of work.
  - No involvement in a total product.
- This approach to job design can also be found in administrative jobs.

Job rotation

- Job rotation accepts that simplified jobs provide the most efficient methods of work.
- It also accepts the shortcomings.
- The simplest solution to this is to combine two (or more) simplified jobs into a pattern of work rotation.
- The rotation of jobs does not produce the expected benefits and can reduce the efficiency gained through job simplification.
- The argument follows thus:
  - Employees must learn a wider range of skills.
  - With the reduced practice opportunity employees do not build up the same level of skill, speed or proficiency.
  - Rotation round simplified jobs does not change the fact that the work is basically boring and monotonous.
- Job rotation can provide the ability of employees to take on a wider range of duties at short notice.

Job enlargement

- Enlargement seeks to build up a job by adding more tasks into it.
- It seeks to move a job along the horizontal axis in Figure 12.1.
- The potential advantage is increased perceived meaningfulness for the employee.
- Productivity may be higher as employees are likely to have more interest in their work.
- It can conflict with the purist approach of work study.
- Enlargement is frequently restricted to assembly line jobs, which even when enlarged remain relatively small.
- The benefits quickly dissipate and jobs becomes monotonous again.

Job enrichment

- Enrichment requires that activity and responsibility be added in a vertical direction.
- Herzberg identified six forms of enrichment that designers should seek to include in jobs:
  - Accountability.
  - Achievement.
  - Feedback.
  - Work pace.
  - Control over resources.
  - Personal growth and development.
- Another approach was developed by Hackman and Oldham.
- They suggest five core job dimensions which produce psychological responses and personal outcomes (Figure 12.6).
- Taking each of the core job dimensions in turn:
  - Skill variety.

- Task identity.
- Task significance.
- Autonomy.
- Feedback.

■ The first three core job dimensions are linked together because they lead to a feeling of relative meaningfulness.

■ Based on social information processing Salancik and Pfeffer argue that the assumptions behind the job characteristics approach were open to question.

■ They argue that evaluating the value of work for an individual is a complex process.

■ It is based upon the social reality for the individual.

Socio-technical job design and autonomous work groups

■ The Tavistock Institute brought together the Taylorist tradition and the human relations movement.

■ Trist and Bamforth studied the impact of mechanization in coal mining.

■ Traditionally cutting coal had been undertaken by small groups of skilled miners, supported by a number of labourers.

■ The introduction of machines and conveyor belts allowed much longer coal faces to be worked.

■ Small teams were combined into larger groups organized around the machinery.

■ As a consequence a number of non-work behaviours changed.

■ These included:
  - Poor communications between workers across shifts and jobs.
  - Blaming other shifts for problems.
  - Increased absenteeism.
  - Increased number of accidents.
  - Increased stress.
  - Deteriorating industrial relations.

■ Trist demonstrated that a particular technology could support different types of work structure.

■ Social and technical aspects of the work needed to be integrated in an interactive socio-technical system.

■ The Tavistock Institute has been involved in many similar studies using the open systems model.

■ Autonomous work groups are an extension of the socio-technical approach.

■ The job to be done is contracted to a work group who then decide how to undertake it.

■ They become responsible to management for the output and cost of operations.

■ It allows control of all aspects of work to remain within the group.

■ There have been a number of variations of the basic autonomous work group.

■ The most famous application of these ideas have been in the Kalmar plant of Volvo.

■ Socio-technical job design is also associated with concepts such as the quality of working life.

Flexibility, empowerment and patterns of work

■ The flexible firm has already been introduced in relation to organization structure.

■ An individual's perception of their job and its design are a function of many issues, for example:
  - Flexibility.
  - Empowerment.
  - Patterns of work.

■ The links between these aspects of work experience and job design are not direct.

■ For example, employees in a supportive environment are more likely to see a boring job in a positive light.

Job design, productivity and satisfaction

■ Job design and productivity are both organizational imperatives.

■ Productivity is a reflection of conversion efficiency and therefore cost.

■ The continued existence of an organization is largely a function of its relative productivity.

■ The search for productivity and control leads naturally to the job simplification approach to job design, based on the machine metaphor of organizational functioning.

■ A number of job design approaches attempt to incorporate satisfaction into work.

■ This is based on the assumption that workers contribute more if they are happy.

■ There are three possible links between performance and satisfaction (Petty *et al.*):
  - Satisfaction generates performance.
  - Performance generates satisfaction.
  - Satisfaction and performance link indirectly (Figure 12.7).

■ Vroom provides a clear indication that a satisfied worker is not necessarily a high performer.

■ The relationship is less direct and a function of forces from a variety of sources.

■ These include, the individual, the job, working environment, management and personal relationships.

Quality of working life and quality circles

■ The quality of working life (QWL) movement emerged from a belief in the need to improve the experience of work.

■ There is no single definition of QWL but one which captures the breadth of the approach is (Kopelman):

> A philosophy of management that enhances the dignity of all workers, introduces changes in an organization's culture, and improves the physical and emotional well-being of employees.

■ It attempts to integrate organizational needs and employee expectations in relation to work.

■ James describes QWL as being composed of:
  – A goal.
  – A process.
  – A philosophy.
■ QWL activity tends to be concentrated into eight areas (Walton):
  – Compensation.
  – Health and safety.
  – Job design.
  – Job security.
  – Social integration.
  – Protection of individual rights.
  – Respect for non-work activities.
  – Social relevance of work.
■ QWL initiatives have enjoyed mixed results, partly as a result of the complexity of the issues involved.
■ External forces also influence how employees react to company initiatives.
■ Job design is an important part of the overall experience of individuals at work.
■ The use of quality circles has been associated with continuous improvement.
■ Whilst not part of job design circles can play a significant part in shaping peoples experience of work.
■ A quality circle is described as the following by the Department of Trade and Industry:

> ... a group of four to twelve people coming from the same work area, performing similar work, who voluntarily meet on a regular basis to identify, investigate, analyse and solve their own work-related problems. The circle presents solutions to management and is usually involved in implementing and later monitoring them. The particular effectiveness of circles depends on these few key features which combine to give them a special character quite different from other proven forms of group working such as task forces. They are not always called circles but it is convenient to use this general term for descriptive purposes. The precise design too will vary from place to place but all circle-like groups follow an essentially standard pattern of approach to problems.

■ Quality circles originated in the USA but gained wide acceptance in Japan during the 1960s, since when they have been re-exported to the West.
■ For circles to be successful the members need to be trained in problem solving, communication and team working.
■ They also need to be taken seriously by managers.
■ There has been some hostility to the concept from trade unions, managers and employees for a number of reasons.

Job design: a management perspective

■ Not all jobs are in the gift of managers to design.
■ The more that an organization personalizes its jobs the more it is necessary to train employees.

■ Boring and mundane aspects of work cannot be completely eliminated.
■ What is boring and mundane to one person may not be to another.
■ No matter how much an individual enjoys their work there are times when it is undertaken less than willingly.
■ Managers also have multiple objectives to achieve which influences the design of the jobs for which they are responsible.
■ To persuade managers to divert time from productive activity through quality circles as an aid to subsequent improvement is not always easy.
■ The Taylorist notion that managers decide and workers labour is still evident in many operational situations.
■ There is an assumption that job design is about the work of people other than managers.
■ In deciding what combination of activities should define a job there are a number of factors to be taken into account:
  – Operations.
  – Philosophy.
  – Technology.
  – Market.
  – History.
  – Creativity.
  – Political.
  – Profitability.
  – Work patterns.
  – Preference.
  – Risk.
■ These influencing factors impact on the design of jobs in both direct and indirect ways (Figure 12.8).

Conclusions

■ Job design influences a considerable range of work aspects.
■ Job design can reflect a belief about the rights of employees to high-level involvement in the activities of the company, or it can reflect a basic view of workers being simply flexible (or necessary) alternatives to machines.
■ Job design can be used to draw out additional commitment to the objectives of management without any reward other than satisfaction.
■ A high level of trust is required if radical approaches to job design are adopted.
■ Trust is something that is hard to gain but easy to loose.

Discussion questions: outline answers for selected questions.

2. Why should managers be concerned with job design?

This question seeks to draw out from the student the various relationships between job design and organizational activity. For example organizational structuring, efficiency and control. However the more able students may also introduce aspects associated with social control, the organization of work within society as a whole, exclusion of non-'qualified' people and professionalization.

4. If job design is a function of the many factors identified in Figure 12.8 how can work study techniques offer any real value in identifying the most effective design?

This question should draw out from students the limitations of the 'one best way' approach advocated by scientific management. It should also draw out the limitations of the rational view of managing work activities and the ability for employees to find ways of 'beating' any management determined system of work organization. However it should also point out the benefits of a systematic approach to the identification of actual work activities and of the various pressures (legal, etc.) on management to prescribe what is expected from employees.

8. How does technology influence job design?

Technology impacts on job design in many ways. The technology used by an organization influences the work that people do as a result of the skills and activities needed to operate the equipment. In addition technology creates some jobs through the need to make and maintain it in a physical sense, as well as changing or destroying some jobs. But there are also other forms of technology than the equipment used by an organization. There are the administrative and social technologies that influence different aspects of organizational activity, including the work that people do.

10. Describe the main approaches to job design and justify circumstances in which each would be the most appropriate to adopt.

This is a comparatively straightforward question and seeks to draw out the common forms of job design such as simplification and provide examples that would illustrate situations where each would be appropriate. The more able students may also broaden the discussion to consider the potential to avoid the negative connotations of simplification approaches in any context.

Case study

The inclusion of a case study in this chapter is intended to provide lecturers with the opportunity to use this method of teaching which requires students to analyse a situation and form a judgement about their preferred solution. Groups of students could be encouraged to challenge each other on their solutions in order to deepen their understanding of the material and of the need to fully justify courses of action. This process should also provide lecturers with the opportunity to demonstrate that very rarely is only one solution available and that alternative routes might be equally (or more) valuable depending upon the forces acting upon the situation and subsequent events.

In this chapter the task is to reflect on the consequences for organizational activity of Management in Action 12.4.

Management in Action 12.4: Job simplification on a slicing line

Student tasks

In groups of six people review the Management in Action panel indicated. Your tasks are:

1. In your group consider the task of slicing bacon as described in Management in Action 12.4. You have been recruited by the company as an expert in management and organizational behaviour to redesign the operation described in Management in Action 12.4. This includes reorganizing the equipment and designing the jobs of the people involved in slicing bacon in the most effective way.

   If you have the opportunity try to find a bacon factory or butchers shop where they would undertake such work and find out as much as you can about the process and how it could be improved. In addition you should consider how you would persuade employees to accept your ideas.

2. Prepare a briefing for the company on the findings from your research activity. This should not last more than 15 minutes and should cover what you discovered about the process and jobs associated with cutting bacon. You should also recommend to the management how you would redesign the operation and jobs as well as how you would implement the new design. The briefing will be made to your classmates.

Be prepared to answer questions from your classmates on your presentation and also to defend your proposed actions.

CHAPTER 13

New technology and work

Chapter outline

This chapter is based on the notion that technology inevitably influences both the nature of work undertaken by people within organizations and also the purpose of that work. Technology is not static, it evolves and changes all the time as new applications are found for existing technologies and new technologies are created. It is the intention of this chapter to identify some of the current and future issues that surround the use of technology in an organizational setting. It is not the intention to introduce a technological perspective, rather the behavioural and sociological points of view will be explored.

Learning objectives

After studying this chapter and working through the associated Management in Action panels, discussion questions and research activities, students should be able to:

■ Understand what is meant by 'new technology' and how it influences the context and jobs that people undertake.

■ Describe how new technology influences the operational and support activities within organizations.

■ Explain the relationship between new technology and the managerial perspective of organizational functioning.

■ Outline the technological determinism debate.

■ Assess the links between new technology and change.

■ Appreciate the relationship between new technology and rationality in managerial decision making.

■ Discuss the notion of diversity and the potential conflict between uniformity through technology and differentiation.

■ Detail the relationship between new technology and control.

Teaching notes and chapter summary

Introduction

■ Technology is a broad term incorporating social, procedural and equipment aspects.

■ From a historical perspective technology reflects a process of solving real problems, experimenting with new ways of doing things or simply finding new knowledge.

■ Technology is not static.

■ There would appear to be four major implications that emerge from a historical perspective on technology:
  - Experience. All technology is new technology at some point in time.
  - Loss. Political, military, religious and social events can conspire to loose a particular technology.
  - Erratic. The development of technology does not follow a smooth or continuous pattern across time and location.
  - Human. Decisions relating to technology are taken by people and it can support their objectives.

■ This assumes that technology is not fundamentally distinguishable from new technology.

■ Usage today implies that new technology incorporates computer-based technology.

■ It is a term used in a specific sense reflecting the application of a particular technology.

■ Forester suggests that it is high (computer) technology that impact directly on work.

Information technology

■ Information technology argues Zuboff differs from the technology used in nineteenth-century in only one respect.

■ It combines the replacement of people with machines and it provides a higher level of transparency.

■ He uses the phrase 'informates as well as automates'.

- It is the control potential from the transparency that is the new dimension.
- Buchanan and Boddy suggest four aspects of information handling that differentiate computer systems:
  - Capture.
  - Storage.
  - Manipulation.
  - Distribution.
- It has been argued that the failure to obtain the full potential from information technology is because of the continued use of outdated paradigms of organizational functioning.
- The new paradigm sees organizations as bundles of decisions.
- Decisions being based on an appropriate allocation of bundles between humans and systems or a combination.
- Information technology is not restricted to computer applications.
- The portable telephone has made an impact on a number of job functions.
- Compact discs store vast quantities of data.
- Electronic-mail (E-mail) can eliminate the need for the traditional memo and provide immediate access to senior managers.
- The development of neural networks leads the way for the next generation of information processing.

New technology: applications

- Few organizations are purely manufacturing or service.
- Manufacturing is the production of goods for subsequent consumption.
- Service involves the creation of intangibles consumed at the time of provision, with the customer taking away the benefit.

Manufacturing

- Machines can demonstrate a relatively low level of thinking ability.
- This leads to more integration of activity as computers talk to each other.
- It was the continuous process industries that were the first to adopt automation.
- The complexity in line and batch manufacturing operations creates a totally different context.
- The first machine tool was introduced just before 1800 with the development of the screw-cutting lathe.
- The technology did not change much until the numerically controlled (NC) machine appeared in the 1950s.
- Machine centres were the next development.
- Computer numerically controlled (CNC) machines appeared in the 1960s when paper tape was replaced by a computer.

- The use of the computer allowed design and specification data to be held at the worksite.
- The operator needed for a different range of computer skills.
- Robots with the ability to pick up, move and position items began to appear in the 1960s.
- They were used for paint spraying, spot welding and stacking operations.
- Automatic trains could also follow a predetermined path around a factory.
- With the incorporation of vision and touch devices robots were used for a wider range of tasks.
- Advanced manufacturing technologies (AMT) and flexible manufacturing systems (FMS) have also incorporated the computer.
- The purpose being to link together machines so that items can be automatically transferred between them in successive stages of production.
- These systems attempt to replicate the economy of large-scale production with small quantities.
- Just-in-time originated in Japan as part of a philosophy of eliminating waste within operational systems.
- Stocks of raw materials and components are considered as a major source of waste.
- This reflects a pull approach to manufacturing.
- The design of manufactured items has also been subjected to computer technology.
- Computer-aided design (CAD) with computer-aided manufacture (CAM) allows technology to create and produce products.
- This can be integrated into computer integrated manufacture (CIM).
- This is a very difficult and has yet to be achieved on a significant scale with any degree of success.
- Forester reviews a number of texts and reports from Europe, the USA and Japan that reflect ambiguity in the success of technology:
  - Take-up. The adoption has not been as dramatic has might be expected. In the USA in 1983 only 4.7% of machine tools were numerically controlled.
  - Cost. Organizations that have opted for high levels of new technology have not enjoyed significant financial benefit over other organizations.
  - Reliability. Production systems become more vulnerable than if they consist of individual machines not linked together.
  - Japanization. Productivity gains of up to 50% were reported in US motor manufacturers during the early 1980s.
  - Government policy. Governments in the major industrialized nations adopted different policies towards new technology.
  - Employee impact. Yamazaki (a Japanese machine tool manufacturer) claim that 12-day workers plus a night watchman using FMS can produce as much as 215 workers and four times as many machines using traditional methods.

- Managerialism. Part of the lower take-up of high technology in the USA and Europe could be the result of low levels of technological expertise among managers.
- Social factors. The social factors associated with high technology influence general attitudes towards it.

Service

- Among the major elements include:
  - Fax.
  - CD-ROM.
  - ATMs.
  - Laptop/personal computers.
  - Medical equipment.
  - EPOS.
  - Multimedia.
- The effect of new technology on employment in services has been noticeably different to that in manufacturing.
- The service sector was just beginning to develop when computer technologies arrived.
- The growth of the service sector was enabled because of the release of labour from manufacturing as a result of technology.
- Jobs have not been obviously lost in the service sector.
- Reed argues that there is an unevenness in the effect of new technology on different categories and level of job in the service sector.
- For example, the medical profession have considerable influence in the application and job impact of new technology.

Administrative

- Prior to the computer developments were adaptations of the typewriter and telephone.
- By the early 1960s most large companies had a mainframe computer undertaking routine processing of accounting and payroll.
- The original aim of administrative automation was a paperless office.
- Systems bring together expertise in:
  - Computer hardware and software.
  - Centralized data processing.
  - Telecommunications management.
  - Management of network facilities.
  - Support to user departments.
- The development of new technology in the office has concentrated on three main areas:
  - Convergence. The multimedia workstation is rapidly making an entry as the major application of new technology.
  - Visibility. The use of networks and data analysis packages allows greater visibility of information among managers.
  - Integration. Integration is about creating an office system as a single set of processes not a separate set of tasks.
- The impact of new technology in the office has not been as rapid as originally envisaged.
- The computer industry could not reach agreement on technology standards which spawned many different incompatible systems.
- Many users have found that systems have not lived up to the initial expectations.
- Many users found themselves locked into a particular supplier or system.
- The effects of new technology on work in the office can be summarized under four headings (Forester):
  - Employment.
  - Job quality.
  - Health and safety.
  - Social relations.

New technology: impact

Structure

- The impact influences three areas of structural design:
  - Scale.
  - Function.
  - Integration.
- Where technology dominates operational activity Mintzberg describes the structure as an adhocracy, typified by:
  - Few levels of management.
  - Little formal control.
  - Decentralized decision making.
  - Few rules, policies and procedures.
  - Specialization of work function.
- This can be particularly useful when work does not fall into regular patterns and is complex.
- Typical examples might be a hospital casualty area, or a consultancy.
- Expert systems attempt to harness some of the decision rules and diagnostic skill in such situations.

Job design

- New jobs are created by technology.
- Some jobs have also disappeared.
- Punched card operators were essential with early computers.
- Other jobs have been changed as a result of the application of technology.
- For example, secretaries, '... as a group, have been affected by the introduction of word processing and their jobs look set to change further with the spread of computer systems offering electronic mail, diary management, graphics, spreadsheets and desk-top publishing' (Thompson).
- Job performance has been changed through the application of new technology to training.

Managerialism

■ Managerialism refers to the ability of that group to maintain control of the organization through the imposition of their perspective.

■ It is management that determines the technology used and how it will be utilized.

■ Some organizations pride themselves on being at the forefront of technological applications, others prefer to be followers.

■ Management also decides the degree of employee involvement in determining the human interface with new technology.

New technology: determinism, rationality and control

■ There are compelling arguments that technology is independent of any particular organizational context and universally applied.

■ Friedman and Cornford use the term autogenerative to suggest that computer innovations are as much a function of the user as they are the original designer.

■ This view could support the deterministic perspective in that the development of technology is part of a cyclical relationship with the designer and user both developing the technology for each others benefit.

■ However, it can also be used to support the opposing point of view.

■ If the user can influence the innovation process they are in a position of control.

■ Management objectives play a significant part in the way that the environment is interpreted.

■ Decision making is a political process.

■ For example, the director in charge of a computer department may seek to ensure that the company takes decisions that further the position of the department.

■ In that sense it is more effective to consider not a technological imperative as such, but to see things in terms of cause and effect (Figure 13.1).

■ This view is perhaps closer to that of McLoughlin and Clark who argue for a complex definition of determinism.

■ So far rationality has been assumed.

■ Rationally might be implied in many decisions, but rational from whose point of view?

■ The justification of new technology is frequently based upon improvements in control.

■ Clegg and Dunkerley describe this as a vicious cycle of control (Figure 13.2).

■ It is easier to fit people around the technology than adapt the technology to the people.

■ Conversely, even sophisticated new technology is comparatively stupid by human standards.

■ It has been argued that the 'office of the future' is being held back because of poor new building design.

■ People on the other hand are flexible, they can adapt to changes in circumstances and are capable of solving problems for which they have not been programmed.

■ Computers control possibilities through structuring the time, space and activities of the humans with whom they come into contact.

■ There is another form of control through the political use of events and activities that engage with people's lives.

■ Braverman refers to this when he began what became known as the labour process debate.

■ Essentially this debate turns on the use to which human labour is put in the transformation of raw material into commodities for capitalist markets, and the part played by managers in the organization of that work.

■ It is management that determines the nature of any technology in any given context.

■ It is a management agenda that determines the use of technology and how human labour will be accommodated around it.

■ Is control to reinforce management's position, or is it to further the commercial business objectives of the organization?

New technology and change

■ Does change exist irrespective of a technology, perhaps driven by the need to change the product or service?

■ If so then the development of technology is a function of change, rather than the other way round.

■ The relationship between technology and work is not just experienced at a work level for example:
  – Employment.
  – Careers.
  – Products and services.
  – Economic activity.
  – Risk.
  – Internationalism.
  – Fashion.
  – Transition A phased change-over takes place (Figure 13.3).
  – Limitations.

New technology: innovation and diversity

■ Innovation is about creating new things, or creating new ways of doing existing things.

■ New technology is by definition an innovation.

■ New technology can also help organizations to innovate.

■ Betz describes innovation as falling into one of three categories (Table 13.1):
  – Radical.
  – System.
  – Incremental.

- Organizations require conformity.
- Products and services must consistently conform to the appropriate specification.
- One of the benefits of technology is that it can produce conformity to a higher level than human beings.
- Herriot and Pemberton argue uniformity is a weakness and though diversity comes strength.
- They argue that uniformity leads to situations where inappropriate decisions are taken.
- The Bay of Pigs (Janis) is one of many decisions used to illustrate the point.
- By encouraging difference and establishing learning processes based on its incorporation higher levels of innovation are encouraged.

New technology: a management perspective

- New technology from a management perspective presents both problems and benefits.
- It is developing at such a rapid rate that no sooner has a technology been introduced than it has been superseded.
- The successful adoption of new technology comes from its effective integration with other work activities and existing technology.
- In progressing their careers managers progressively move away from the operational levels of activity.
- Increasingly technology becomes something that other people use regularly.
- Managers inevitably rise through a particular discipline, accounting, personnel or production for example.
- At some point in their careers, managers have to take responsibility for disciplines of which they have no direct experience.
- When this happens technology continues to develop beyond that with which they were familiar.
- It is easy to see technology as an end in itself rather than a means to an end.
- Technology is not capable of running a company without input and support from people.
- Buchanan and McCalman studied the effects of computerized information systems and concluded that they offered a number of advantages, which they describe as a visibility theory:
  - Sharing.
  - Confidence.
  - Pressure.
  - Visibility.
  - Co-operation.

Conclusions

- New technology was considered in terms of decision making, rationality and as part of a change process.
- It is inevitable that any new technology will quickly become dated as suppliers and innovators create new technologies.

- The risk associated with new technology is that it begins to take a predominant position in organizational thinking and diverts attention away from human capabilities and diversity as an important element in survival.

Discussion questions: outline answers for selected questions.

2. What is new technology and how does it differ from previous technologies?

Students will undoubtedly address this question in terms of computer-based technologies. However they should also provide some recognition that every technology is a 'new' technology at some point in time. Because it is not possible to look forward with any precision it is not possible to know what it is that will form the new technologies of the future. In effect this position is very similar to the dilemma that arises from use of the concepts of modernism and postmodernism, what term can be used to describe what follows the period that follows modernism? What students identify that distinguishes 'new' technology from previous technologies will to some extent depend upon their experience and understanding. However it should provide some recognition of the ability for limited independent choice and action built into the technology.

4. Describe the areas of impact of new technology on the manufacturing industries and make an assessment of its effect.

In this instance the impact on new technology has been in the opportunity of the technology to replace human activity and its creation of new manufacturing opportunities. It has eliminated, changed and supported the work of people within manufacturing industry. Remember that manufacturing industry contains administrative, sales, managerial and specialist support staff as well as factory operators. New jobs have been created through the development of new technology, particularly those associated with computers. New industries have also emerged. The effect has been difficult to establish as there are so many other influences to take into account. Whole economies have undergone transformation as a result of the new technologies and the desire of governments to take advantage of its opportunities.

9. Does new technology manage managers, or do managers manage new technology? Justify your answer.

This question seeks to draw out from students the ability to think through and argue for their particular point of view. Either perspective could be argued. For example, if technology manages the managers it is suggesting that managers are subject to forces that they are unable to control. In that sense a manager who does not take account of the existence of new technology will inevitably lag behind and potentially suffer adverse financial conditions as competitors reap the benefits. From that perspective managers are led by the technology. From the opposite perspective managers have a degree of freedom of choice available to them and can make more or less use of the technologies available to them. Some organizations have made a commercial success out of being 'traditional' and of doing things in the old fashioned way. In that sense it is management choice that determines the form and use of new technology.

10. What effect has new technology had on structure and job design within organizations?

This question seeks to draw out a discussion on the impact of new technology on job design and organizational structure. New job creation and the elimination of other jobs are among the more obvious aspects that would be expected to arise. Equally the changes to job content as a result of the incorporation of technology into work activities should be covered. In terms of structure the creation of new departments associated with computers and technical support should find expression in the answer.

Case study

The inclusion of a case study in this chapter is intended to provide lecturers with the opportunity to use this method of teaching which requires students to analyse a situation and form a judgement about their preferred solution. Groups of students could be encouraged to challenge each other on their solutions in order to deepen their understanding of the material and of the need to fully justify courses of action. This process should also provide lecturers with the opportunity to demonstrate that very rarely is only one solution available and that alternative routes might be equally (or more) valuable depending upon the forces acting upon the situation and subsequent events.

In this chapter the task is to reflect on the consequences for organizational activity of Management in Action 13.5.

Management in Action 13.5: Which way now for the multimedia revolution?

Student tasks

In groups of six people review the Management in Action panel indicated. Your tasks are:

1. In your group consider the implications for work and job design of the continuing development of computer technology as suggested in Management in Action 13.5.
2. Prepare a presentation to the rest of your class on how you see work and jobs changing over the course of your lifetime. Undertake whatever additional research that you feel necessary to undertake this activity.

Be prepared to answer questions from your classmates on your presentation and also to defend your proposed actions.

CHAPTER 14

Management and leadership

Chapter outline

This chapter sets out to introduce the nature of management and leadership. The main theoretical perspectives on the subject of leadership will be introduced. Trait, style and contingency perspectives will be discussed, followed by a brief review of a number of other views on the subject. International aspects of leadership will also be introduced as will consideration of the nature and impact of meetings and humour in leadership activities.

Learning objectives

After studying this chapter and working through the associated Management in Action panels, discussion questions and research activities, you should be able to:

■ Understand the distinction between leadership and management.
■ Describe what it is that managers actually do when carrying out their jobs.
■ Explain the roles that managers perform and the skills that they need.
■ Outline what leadership as a process involves.
■ Assess the significance of the trait, styles and contingency approaches to leadership.
■ Appreciate the significance of humour in leadership.
■ Discuss international aspects and the impact of meetings on management.
■ Detail the 'other' approaches to leadership identified.

Teaching notes and chapter summary

Introduction

■ Is a manager automatically a leader and do leaders always manage?
■ Rothman light-heartedly concludes that birthdays are a key variable in selecting future leaders.

■ Leadership and management generate a vast quantity of published material, training courses and seminars.
■ There is little hard evidence for the success of any particular formula.
■ The complexity of variables involved requires an equally complex set of responses (Figure 14.1).
■ The non-specific forces identified in Figure 14.1 include:
  – Random factors.
  – Time and repetitive influences.
  – Interactive forces.
■ There are groups that attempt to operate without a formal leader.
■ They redistribute among members the activities and functions of the formal leader.
■ The training and development of managers is often undervalued by organizations.

Leadership and management

■ The terms management and leadership are synonymous, but only up to point.
■ The following provides some indication of the areas of distinction:
  – Role.
  – Situation.
  – Context.
  – Purpose.
  – Scope.
■ The usual differentiation is between senior, middle and junior management. Stewart identified another basis for the classification of management jobs:
  – Hub.
  – Peer dependent.
  – Man management.
  – Solo.
■ Figure 14.2 links together the traditional and Stewart views of management work.

What managers do

- There is such a wide diversity of management work that it is not possible to specify what every manager will undertake.
- Fayol identified the main activities for any organization, including what today would be described as management.
- In this he included the following functions:
  - Forecast.
  - Plan.
  - Organize.
  - Command.
  - Co-ordinate.
  - Control.
- A sociological perspective on management is provided by Reed's four themes:
  - Technical perspective.
  - Political perspective.
  - Critical perspective.
  - Practice perspective.
- These explanations reflect very little of what it is that managers actually do.
- Most studies of management reflect a job not at all like that implied by Fayol.
- Handy summarizes a number of studies into the job of managers, including:
  - Guest found that supervisors averaged 583 separate events in every working day.
  - Stewart found that on average managers enjoyed only nine 30-minute periods without interruption over a four-week period.
  - Mintzberg described activities for chief executives fitting into 10-minute bursts of time.
  - Mintzberg reported differences in activity between chief executives of large and small organizations.
- Mackenzie categorizes the activity of managers as either managing or operating.
- Figure 14.3 illustrates the changing balance of activity at different levels.
- The specific nature, range and pattern of work undertaken by any manager will depend upon a wide range of factors including:
  - Industry.
  - Role.
  - Pattern of work.
  - Level.
  - Exposure.
  - Contacts.
  - Personal factors.
- Luthans describes four general types of management activity:
  - Traditional management.
  - Routine communication.
  - Networking.
  - Human resource management.
- Simply doing something does not by itself result in achieving objectives.

- Promotion can depend on socializing and politicking rather than task-related activities.

The leadership process

- John Adair describes what a leader has to do in terms of a three circle model (Figure 14.4).
- Hellriegal *et al.* describe the leadership process in terms of:
  - Relationships.
  - Skills.
  - Power. In leadership situations the sources of power include:
    - Legitimate.
    - Reward.
    - Coercive.
    - Referent.
    - Expert.
- To be effective the leader needs to take account of:
  - the preferences of the leader.
  - the preferences of the group being lead.
  - the task to be achieved.
  - the context.

Trait theories of leadership

- For much of history it was assumed that leadership was a set of qualities that someone was born with.
- The significance of this approach is that leaders cannot be trained.
- This originated from the aptly named great-man (as at that time they were mostly men) view of leadership.
- Those traits associated with successful leadership include:
  - Intelligence.
  - Initiative.
  - Self-assurance.
  - Overview.
  - Health.
  - Physique.
  - Social background.
- To find a leader with every characteristic would seem to be an impossible task.
- There are too many exceptions to imply that each is essential for success.
- The terms themselves are imprecise.
- Trait approaches to leadership are used in many assessment centres.
- They are based on the view that there are personal characteristics that impact on effectiveness.
- Traits now appear as skill-based characteristics such as conceptual and human skills.

Style theories of leadership

- The basis of this approach to leadership is that subordinates will respond better to some styles than others.

■ It is assumed that a positive subordinate response creates the success sought by the leader.

■ There are many studies of this approach, each capable of classification on an autocratic – democratic scale.

The University of Iowa studies

■ Carried out in boys' clubs during the late 1930s by Lippitt and White leadership style was varied as follows:
 – Authoritarian.
 – Democratic.
 – Laissez Faire.

■ The democratic leadership group contained the least levels of aggression and apathy.

■ It is unfortunate that the original studies did not report measures of success such as productivity or achievement.

■ The studies are criticized as not specifically organizational and experimentally weak.

The Ohio State University studies

■ The Ohio Sate University studies began in 1945 and used a questionnaire to examine leadership.

■ The results were subjected to factor analysis and two factors emerged:
 – Consideration.
 – Initiating structure.

■ These studies established the importance of the task and people dimensions of success.

■ It has been argued that these studies don't identify actual leader behaviour but the perceptions of those completing the form.

Likert's four systems of management

■ Likert developed the four systems (or styles) of leadership:
 – System 1. Exploitative autocratic.
 – System 2. Benevolent autocratic.
 – System 3. Participative.
 – System 4. Democratic.

■ The most successful departments were described in terms of systems 3 and 4.

■ However, Likert's work has not been without its critics.

■ Muczyk and Reimann argue that not every organization can support participation effectively.

The Tannenbaum and Schmidt continuum

■ Tannenbaum and Schmidt utilize concepts of boss-centred leadership and subordinate-centred leadership (Figure 14.5).

■ Four main differences are identified:
 – Tells.
 – Sells.
 – Consults.
 – Joins.

■ This model leans towards the contingency approach in recognizing that success depends upon a range of factors.

Blake and Mouton's grid

■ This approach is based upon the idea that leadership is a function of:
 – Concern for people.
 – Concern for production.

■ The work has been revised several times, most recently as The Leadership Grid® (Figure 14.6).

■ The five stereotypes in the model:
 – Impoverished management.
 – Authority–compliance management.
 – Country club management.
 – Middle of the road management.
 – Team management.

■ Managers tend to have one dominant style and many have a backup style.

■ They found that many managers could vary their dominant style to some degree.

■ The factors that influence the style are shown in Figure 14.6.

Hersey and Blanchard's situation approach

■ This approach is based on the existence of two different styles:
 – Task style.
 – Relationship style.

■ There are similarities with Blake and Mouton.

■ The Hersey and Blanchard approach incorporates additional variables, based on the work of Fiedler.

■ Four actual styles emerge when the situation variable of subordinate readiness is added (Figure 14.8).

■ The four actual styles of leadership are:
 – Telling.
 – Selling.
 – Participating.
 – Delegating.

■ There are also similarities with the Tannenbaum and Schmidt work described earlier.

■ There have been a number of criticisms of this model.

■ The theoretical underpinning was argued to be weak.

■ The questionnaire used was also heavily criticized.

■ Nicholls argues that it breaks the three principles of consistency, continuity and conformity.

■ Naturally Hersey and Blanchard do not agree with the Nicholls perspective and defended their work.

■ This particular model spans the borderline between style and contingency theories.

Contingency theories of leadership

■ Contingency theory attempts to incorporate a wider range of variables.

■ The most appropriate style of leadership is contingent upon a range of variables from the context.

Fiedler's contingency model

■ This model identifies situational aspects of leadership and incorporates effectiveness.
■ Style is an expression of the leaders preferences for either a task or relationship approach.
■ Three situational variables are:
  – Leader–member relationships.
  – Task structure.
  – Position power.
■ The two levels of these constructs produces eight situational combinations.
■ These Fiedler combined into three levels of situational favourableness (Figure 14.9).
■ Fiedler developed a test which he called the Least Preferred Co-worker Scale (LPC).
■ Fiedler suggests that success is a function of the interaction between:
  – Relationships.
  – Task.
  – Power.
  – Preferred style of the leader.
■ Fiedler developed his work into a Cognitive Resource Theory.

House's path–goal leadership theory

■ The path–goal model of leadership links leader behaviour with subordinate motivation, performance and satisfaction.
■ House identified four styles of leader behaviour:
  – Directive leadership.
  – Supportive leadership.
  – Participative leadership.
  – Achievement-oriented leadership.
■ This is based upon the notion that individual leaders are capable of changing their style to match the needs of the situation.
■ The two situational factors are:
  – Subordinate characteristics.
  – Demands facing subordinates.
■ The model is reflected in Figure 14.10.
■ There have been some attempts to substantiate the model, with mixed results.

The Vroom, Yetton and Jago model of leadership

■ The model postulates that the degree of subordinate involvement in decision making is the major variable in leader behaviour.
■ There are four decision trees offered by the model, two for group problems and two for individual problems.
■ The decision tree offers a suggestion for a leader style that should generate the best decision in the circumstances.
■ For a leader to change style may create conflict, confusion or lower morale and productivity among subordinates.

■ Subordinates may also become accustomed to being involved in decision making.

Other approaches to leadership

The vertical dyad linkage model

■ It suggests that leaders behave differently with different subordinates.
■ Between the leader and each subordinate is an individual relationship, referred to as a vertical dyad.
■ The model postulates that leaders create an in-group and an out-group around themselves.
■ The in-group are a few special individuals, more trusted, given preferential treatment and special privileges (Figure 14.11).

Life-cycle model

■ Clarke and Pratt suggest that there are different requirements from a leader during the organization's life cycle.
■ They identify four different leadership patterns:
  – Champion.
  – Tank Commander.
  – Housekeeper.
  – Lemon Squeezer.
■ A variation on the this approach is that proposed by Rodrigues.
■ This is based on the experience for most organizations in functioning in a dynamic context.

Transactional and transformational model

■ Developed by Kuhnert and Lewis who suggested two types of management activity, each demanding different skills:
  – Transactional.
  – Transformational.
■ Bass identified the characteristics of both types of leader (Table 14.1).
■ Tepper found transformational leaders more frequently adopted legitimating tactics.
■ They were also able to achieve higher acceptance of objectives among subordinates.

Charismatic leadership

■ House characterized charismatic leaders as full of self-confidence, with a high level of confidence in subordinates and high expectations for results.
■ They also have a clear vision of the goal to be achieved, are able to communicate this effectively and lead by example.
■ Charismatic leaders can create problems for organizations.
■ Traits that may produce a charismatic approach include self-confidence, skills in impression management and social sensitivity.

■ Contextual variables that could encourage the emergence of a charismatic leader include crisis situations and high levels of subordinate dissatisfaction.

■ It is possible for charismatic individuals to abuse their capabilities to achieve an unquestioning following.

Attribution theory

■ The leader observers the behaviour of subordinates, imputes causes to it, and reacts on the basis of those interpretations.

■ The assumptions made by the leader may be wrong.

Leadership substitutes

■ Kerr and Jermier suggest three areas where substitution for leadership is possible:
  – Subordinate characteristics – professionally qualified, highly experienced or indifferent to the rewards that the leader can offer.
  – Task characteristics – highly routine containing immediate feedback on performance.
  – Organizational characteristics – highly routinized with little flexibility.

Leadership as symbolism

■ It is the symbolism associated with leadership that influences subordinate behaviour.

■ Individuals take a lead from the behaviour of their managers.

Leadership – roles and skills

■ In the theatre the actors perform roles written by the author and interpreted by the director.

■ There is a requirement that each actor will behave as expected for the whole performance to work.

■ Role provides individuals with an outline of what is expected of them in undertaking a particular function.

■ Zimbardo carried out an experiment in the role play of a prison.

■ Students were randomly allocated to the role of guard or prisoner.

■ Within six days the experiment had to be called off.

■ Both sets of players became so integrated into their roles that the well-being of prisoners was at risk.

■ Considering the notion of role there are a number of concepts that need to be examined:
  – Role set (Figure 18.6).
  – Role definition.
  – Role ambiguity.
  – Role incompatibility.
  – Role conflict.
  – Role stress and strain.

■ Mintzberg describes a number of roles undertaken by managers (Figure 14.12).

■ More recent studies have introduced including, visioning and motivator.

■ It has been suggested that this is a reflection of a 'pop-culture' in management.

International perspectives on leadership

■ There are tensions inherent in international leadership that do not arise in a single country context.

■ Early culture experience predisposes individuals to particular ways of relating to other people.

■ This in turn conditions particular ways of leading or being led.

■ Oh reviews the application of theory X and theory Y to management in China after the 1949 revolution.

■ It identified that managers allied with the communist ideology tended to adopt the theory Y perspectives.

■ Managers with less skill in the ideological areas tended to adopt theory X.

■ Leadership may be influenced by political, economic and culture.

■ Figure 14.4 reflects the interaction between these variables.

Meetings and humour in management

■ Meetings are an inevitable aspect of management.

■ Reasons for holding meetings include:
  – Decision making.
  – Collaboration.
  – Co-operation.
  – Conflict resolution.
  – Habit.
  – Political.
  – Courage.

■ Some meetings have a hidden agenda.

■ There are vast numbers of informal meetings in corridors and over coffee.

■ Mackenzie suggests that many middle manages spend up to 80% of their time in meetings and the approximately 50% of that time may be wasted.

■ Humour has been regarded as something incidental to management.

■ Levity could signal that business was not being taken seriously or that there was a lack of respect for senior managers.

■ However, that is not the only purpose of humour.

■ Barsoux considers that humour in the workplace:

   ... is rarely neutral, trivial or random. It is deployed for the achievement of quite specific purposes to do with self-preservation, getting things done or getting one's way.

■ Barsoux identifies the three main purposes of humour as:
  – Sword.
  – Shield.
  – Values.

■ Watson describes the role of humour in relation to communication and control.

Leadership: a management perspective

- It is hardly surprising that managers have for a long time been interested in leadership.
- Managers have an interest in the study of the subject to:
  - Protect their position.
  - Increase operational effectiveness.
  - Deal more effectively with other managers.
- The variables associated with the practice of management and leadership include:
  - The manager.
  - The managed.
  - The context.
  - The situation.
  - The task.
- Figure 14.15 reflects the linkages between these variables.
- It is the identification of the relationships between these variables that creates the difficulty in defining management and leadership.
- It is not possible to offer definitive models that ensure the best match between manager and situation.
- People can usually adapt behaviour to achieve a workable compromise between anarchy and perfection in specific contexts.

Conclusions

- The major theoretical approaches to the study of leadership have been introduced and critically evaluated.
- We have considered what it is that managers actually do and the roles that they adopt whilst performing their duties.
- International perspectives on leadership were also introduced.
- This chapter ended with a brief consideration of humour and meetings which account for much management time.

Discussion questions

3. Is an attempt to identify the most appropriate management style simply another attempt to identify a formula which is doomed to failure? Justify your answer.

   This question seeks to draw out from students the nature of research and its descriptive ability as opposed to the prescriptive possibilities. The implication being that there are some combinations of style and situation that are more useful/successful than others. It is tempting to go one stage further and to claim that if only the appropriate style could be identified then success could be guaranteed. This represents much too simplistic a set of relationships between the range of complex variables

involved in any situation. Students would be expected to discuss this aspect as well as the nature of leadership and management.

5. 'Come the hour, come the leader.' Discuss this statement in the light of the approaches to leadership discussed in this chapter.

   The statement argues for a situational basis for leadership. Students would be expected to explore both the view that in a crisis someone with appropriate style or the other necessary attributes will naturally emerge and that good management is about effective recruitment, training and development as well as having appropriate procedures and infrastructure in place.

7. Does humour have any part to play in management? Justify your answer.

   There are at least two perspectives on this question. The perspective that argues for a role suggests that it can help deal with stress, regulate behaviour, offset conflict and build teams among other benefits. The opposite perspective argues that it is an unnecessary diversion, detracting from the main business imperatives. Students should explore both perspectives and reach a conclusion that is supported by their discussion.

10. 'Charismatic leaders are not appropriate in the middle ranks of managerial jobs because they could provide a focus for an organization within an organization.' Discuss this statement.

    This question raises an issue that is often ignored in relation to charismatic leadership. Charisma is usually described in terms relevant to the main or senior leader positions, not the middle or lower ranks. But this perspective ignores the development of charisma in leadership at these levels. Issues that might be expected to find expression in this answer include the development or expression of charisma in people. Does it evolve or is it absent/present? Could an organization cope with charismatic leaders in the lower ranks under all circumstances, or just if the main leader is also charismatic? Would a charismatic junior manager be seen as a threat by others? These represent just some of the issues open for discussion in this question.

Case study

The inclusion of a case study in this chapter is intended to provide lecturers with the opportunity to use this method of teaching which requires students to analyse a situation and form a judgement about their preferred solution. Groups of students could be encouraged to challenge each other on their solutions in order to deepen their understanding of the material and of the need to fully justify courses of action. This process should also provide lecturers with the opportunity to demonstrate that very rarely is only one solution available and that alternative routes might be equally (or more) valuable depending upon the forces acting upon the situation and subsequent events.

In this chapter the task is to reflect on the consequences for organizational activity of Management in Action 14.7.

Management in Action 14.7: Who taught you to do what you do?

Student tasks

In groups of six people review the Management in Action panel indicated. Your tasks are:

1. In your group consider the implications for the training and development of managers of the material contained in Management in Action 14.7.
2. Prepare a presentation to the rest of your class on:
   - The extent to which management can be 'learned' in an environment separated from a work setting. For example, as a university course.
   - The extent to which management can be learned through any form of 'off-the-job' training.
   - The extent to which managers should be responsible for their own development, as compared to the organization having that responsibility.
   - The value of learning from other managers as individual careers progress. This could be part of a formal or informal mentoring process or it could simply be as a result of experience. Remember however that not all practising managers are 'good' examples and may provide poor role models.
   - Consider the special situation concerning directors (Management in Action 14.2). Should director training be classed as a form of management training, or is it different? Why or why not?

Prepare a brief presentation (not more than 15 minutes) for the rest of your class on the conclusions about the basis and form of effective management training. Be prepared to answer questions from your classmates on your presentation and also to defend your proposed actions.

CHAPTER 15

Ethics and employee involvement

Chapter outline

This chapter begins with the consideration of the links between ethics and moral philosophy before going on to discuss different approaches to the subject. This will be followed by a review of the major ethical dilemmas facing managers. The chapter will then review the links between participation and control before exploring the relationship between involvement and human resource management. The main forms of employee involvement will also be discussed.

Learning objectives

After studying this chapter and working through the associated Management in Action panels, discussion questions and research activities, you should be able to:

- Understand the basis of ethics and its links with moral philosophy.
- Describe the main forms of employee involvement.
- Explain the different classifications of ethical perspective.
- Outline the links between employee participation, power and control.
- Assess the ethical dilemmas facing managers.
- Appreciate the managerial activity that can be influenced by ethics.
- Discuss the approaches that managers take to resolving the ethical difficulties that they face.
- Detail the options for different forms of employee involvement.

Teaching notes and chapter summary

Introduction

- Ethics influences the process involved in making decisions and the criteria used to judge between options.

- It is not only managers that face ethical dilemmas.
- Employee involvement is also a difficult area for managers.
- Employees are unlike the other resource available to the organization.
- Humans decide which organizations to become associated with.
- They decide when to leave – usually.
- Whilst at work there are also many choices available to the human resource.
- Managers seek to find ways to manipulate the resource under their control.
- Manipulation is frequently regarded as having negative connotations.
- On the other hand a wood carver can create something of great beauty as a result of the manipulation of tools and pieces of wood.
- The managerial imperative to manipulate is intended to direct resources in pursuit of objectives.
- Unfortunately, life is not always so rational.

Philosophy and ethics

- Ethics is about doing the right thing.
- Philosophy is about, '... the critical evaluation of assumptions and argument' (Raphael).
- Moral philosophy takes as its sphere of interest a, '... philosophical inquiry about norms or values, about ideas of right and wrong, good or bad, what should and what should not be done' (Raphael).
- There are close associations between ethics and moral philosophy.
- Behaviour is judged by reference to the norms or values that are generally accepted within a particular context.
- There are four major approaches to the basis of moral decision making:
  – Naturalism.
  – Rationalism.

– Utilitarianism. Raphael identifies eight approaches to this approach (Table 15.1).
– Formalism. This provides a formalized approach to deciding between courses of action (Table 15.2).

■ Hosmer describes an approach to decision making that reflects this ethical perspective (Figure 15.1).

■ Figure 15.2 represents the impact of ethics on rational decision making.

Ethical perspectives in organizations

■ Ethical issues are about rightness, wrongness, good and bad.

■ Deciding the right thing to do can be difficult.

■ A subordinate who finds that their manager is falsifying expenses claims might:
– Do nothing.
– Report the manager to a more senior manager.
– Let the manager know that they have been found out.
– Send an anonymous letter to the chief executive.
– Report the manager to the subordinate's trade union.
– Write a letter to the press.
– Write a letter to the largest shareholder.
– Report the manager to their professional association (if they belong to one).

■ Each of the above options has a range of costs and benefits for the individuals involved in the situation.

■ In deciding a course of action the subordinate can adopt one of two approaches:
– They could decide on their judgement of the rightness or wrongness of the act that they have encountered.
– They could form a judgement based on the possible consequences for the principle stakeholders.

■ Cederblom and Dougherty refer to the two approaches as utilitarianism and contractarianism.

■ Within each model there are two versions.

Utilitarian approach

■ This approach is about utility or usefulness.

■ It requires an evaluation based on the future impact on those effected:
– **Act utilitarianism**. Every dilemma should be regarded on its own merits. For example, telling a lie could be justified if it created happiness for the people involved.
– **Rule utilitarianism**. The rule approach implies that it is necessary to create frameworks that serve as the basis for identifying appropriate courses of action.

Contract approach

■ This approach is grounded in the notion that agreements whether they be explicit or tacit should be honoured.

■ In contractual relationships individuals are required to apply the general test of fairness to their behaviour.

■ To create a fair set of rules individuals would be needed who had no vested interest.

■ A contract view looks backward at the obligations that have been entered into and assesses the implications of these for the future:
– **Restricted contractarianism**. This forces an individual to consider the rightness of any arrangement without knowing the impact on themselves.
– **Libertarian contractarianism**. This implies that once a contract is entered into, individuals have an obligation to abide by it and not to take precipitated action to terminate the contract.

■ Leys produced a diagram reflecting the conflicts between moral standards (Figure 15.3).

■ The model does not provide a basis for identifying a course of action to resolve the moral dilemma.

■ It simply identifies some of the conflicting areas.

Ethical issues in management

■ There are number of ethical dilemmas that face managers in their operational capacity:
– Work and society.
– Corporate and public interest.
– Obligations at work.

■ There are a number of areas of obligation that impact on employees (Figure 15.4).
– Privacy.
– Working at home.
– Pay, promotion and discrimination.
– Whistleblowing.
– Codes of practice.

Power, participation and control

■ Figure 15.5 reflects the interaction between these influences and the role of people within the organization.

■ People are not completely malleable at the will of others.

■ Lomax demonstrates how prisoners of war can maintain some measure of independence even in the most hostile of conditions.

■ The *Brave New World* by Huxley also provides insights into how some are able to resist the control of society.

■ From management's perspective the advantages of employing people must outweigh the disadvantages.

■ Finding ways of controlling the people resource is an important aspect of management activity.

■ From an employee perspective work includes the ever growing demands of industrialization.

■ This includes ever tighter control, reduced ability to adjust the pace of work and subservience to the needs of technology.

- Mills described the experience as a number of traps.
- Because managers seek controlled behaviour they do not automatically achieve it.
- Alienation was identified as an expression of independence.
- Compliance is not the same as commitment.
- Fordism was an early attempt to provide control and social engineering replaced it.
- One aspect of social engineering is to persuade employees to subscribe to the same values as managers.
- The more enlightened management approaches recognize that it is not possible to force or restrict the human qualities that employees possess.
- Among the strategies designed to address these issues are those intended to increase employee involvement.
- Not every employee would wish to become involved with the running of their organization.
- Forcing people to become involved introduces another form of direct control.

Employee involvement and human resource management

- The function with a particular interest in employee involvement is the human resource department.
- Marchington *et al.* suggest that there are four types of involvement:
  - Downward communication.
  - Upwards problem solving.
  - Financial participation.
  - Representative participation.
- There are a number of consequences that arise from the involvement of employees including:
  - Degree of involvement.
  - Role of management.
  - Role of trade unions.
  - Management's right to manage.
  - Rights of involved employees.
  - Responsibilities of involved employees.
- If involvement were to be beneficial then employees would absorb much of the need for management activity.
- Involvement could influence the design and structure of an organization.

Forms of employee involvement

- At the most simple level employees are involved with the organization as a result of the work that they do.
- There are many informal processes that exist for employee involvement, for example the grapevine.
- Gossip and rumour have a high credibility because they are not subject to editing and filtering by managers.

Downward communication

- Downwards communication is intended to inform, to lead opinion and form attitudes that would be considered favourable.
- Employees may interpret the content as an attempt to manipulate and adopt a totally different set of attitudes.
- Among the main forms of downward communication include:
  - Section or departmental meetings.
  - Team briefing.
  - In-house journal.
  - Roadshow.
  - Electronic.

Upwards problem solving

- This allows employees to utilize their skills and knowledge in the search for increased productivity, quality and commitment.
- This can include:
  - Suggestion schemes.
  - Quality circles.
  - Total quality management.
  - Group working.
  - Project teams.

Financial participation

- Financial participation provides involvement through a monetary stake in the activities of the organization.
- The main variations are:
  - Co-operatives.
  - Profit share.
  - Share options.

Representative participation

- This approach is a means of becoming involved through some form of representative arrangement.
- Forms of representative involvement include:
  - Collective bargaining.
  - Joint consultation.
- There are many different approaches and experiences associated with employee involvement around the world.

Ethics and employee involvement: a management perspective

- A considerable proportion of management activity is about taking decisions.
- Implicit in that is the notion that managers are faced with options and choices.
- In many situations there are dilemmas and conflicts between aspects of the decision.
- For example, offering a bribe to a potential customer may:
  - Be against company policy.

- May help to provide jobs in an area of high unemployment.
- May prevent the company from loosing money.
- And the product may be the best on the market.
■ Also, competitors may offer bribes.
■ Just because it is against one set of norms does not mean that it is against the principles and practices in every location.
■ This is just one form of ethical dilemma faced by managers.
■ It is not only managers that are faced with ethical dilemmas.
■ What should employees do when they find that an organization has been cheating its customers?
■ This chapter introduced some of the approaches based on moral philosophy that exist to guide decision making.
■ Each approach offers a view of what defines right and wrong in any particular context.
■ One dilemma for managers is the degree and form of involvement that employees should be allowed to have.
■ For at the heart of all capitalist systems is a contradiction, '... the need to achieve both control and consent of employees, in order to secure not just the extraction, but the realization of their surplus value' (Legge).
■ Involvement is done because managers see that it has advantages in helping them to achieve their objectives.
■ Scientific management has not been able to deliver the desired control and benefits.
■ Efforts begun under the human relations umbrella have now become more sophisticated.
■ At one extreme it could be argued that employees are a resource to be used and that they are paid to do management's bidding.
■ That view misses the potential to make use of the intellectual capabilities of employees.
■ Involved employees could make management easier, generate higher profits and generally improve operational effectiveness.
■ The difficulty facing managers is how to identify the most effective means of achieving that objective.
■ The difficulties with employee involvement in practice has been the commitment of managers to make it work.
■ From a manager's perspective any form of employee involvement might become a threat.
■ Equally not all employees would wish to become involved beyond their contractual obligations.
■ Consequently, dual levels of involvement have to be catered for.
■ Not all approaches to involvement offer equally effective results.
■ Poole identified that the intended purpose of involvement would determine which method would be most effective.

■ Deciding what the right thing to do is in this respect is an ethical problem as well as a managerial one.

Conclusions

■ Material included in this chapter provides a basis on which ethical dilemmas can be resolved.
■ A number of the more common areas of conflicting moral obligation were discussed.
■ Just as important in this light are the areas that have been omitted.
■ For example, giving to political parties and charity.
■ Employees are involved in their organizations as soon as they are recruited.
■ There is no perfect approach to employee involvement.
■ Power and control have a significant interaction with ethics and involvement in organizational activity.

Discussion questions: outline answers for selected questions

2. 'Ethics has no part to play in managerial activities.' Discuss this statement.

   This question gets to the heart of the problems for managers. It touches on the 'all's fair in love, war and making money' perspective to running an organization. Clearly there are two opposing perspectives on this issue and students should be expected to argue convincingly for whichever approach they adopt. Clearly it might be difficult to recognize the merits in an answer which argues for the 'anything goes' perspective, irrespective of how well it is argued. However even economics is beginning to incorporate a quantified element for the effects of ethics! Stronger answers might also incorporate issues associated with the commercial benefit to be gained from 'selling' and ethical dimension to products and services. The role of 'spin doctors' in putting the other point of view on behalf of managers might also be rewarded highly.

3. Discuss employee rights to privacy in the light of management's need to maintain good public and customer relations.

   In the light of commercial drives to provide (at least the illusion of) high levels of customer care, service organizations are placing ever higher demands on employees. This takes many forms and can make significant inroads into non-work time and activities. Split shifts, call-outs, unsocial hours, additional hours and taking work home being just some of the practices. Students would be expected to review these issues and the impact on people and organizations. The stronger answers might also touch on the contradiction between the consumers demanding higher levels of service being at the same time employees who are being subjected to the demands of employers to meet the perceived needs of other consumers. The issue of commitment might also feature in the answer in that it is often claimed that employees are keen to 'give' that extra service. Is that the case or is it compliance as a result of a lack of real alternatives as perceived by employees?

5. 'Profit share schemes are an attempt to turn employees into capitalists and so be sympathetic to management control.' Discuss this statement.

This question gets to the bribe or reward aspects of management. Are managers attempting to reward performance by employees through the improved company results improving pay, or they seeking to influence employee behaviour on a much wider scale. The notion of being an employee implies a contractual relationship to deliver a particular set of duties at the behest of the employer. It might be argued that if by becoming a participant in the profits the fundamental employment relationship can be changed to that of a stakeholder then all parties might benefit. This approach would encourage employees to understand management's perspective and adopt supportive patterns of behaviour. That should make organizations easier to manage. However the opposite could occur. As a stakeholder, employees might seek a more active involvement in the decision making of the company, almost upwards management. This might reduce management's ability to unilaterally control people and organizations. Students would be expected to discuss these issues.

10. How would you persuade a manager who thought that their job was at risk from an employee involvement initiative not to attempt to undermine the benefits from the programme?

This question attempts to draw out from students their understanding of involvement and how it might be perceived in both a positive and negative light. It also attempts to draw out from them how they might seek to change the negative perspectives, perhaps training, starting with 'soft' options and study trips might be mentioned. It could also be that some students will simply argue for a replacement policy for people who might resist, but this would need to be implemented sensitively and as a last resort.

Case study

The inclusion of a case study in this chapter is intended to provide lecturers with the opportunity to use this method of teaching which requires students to analyse a situation and form a judgement about their preferred solution. Groups of students could be encouraged to challenge each other on their solutions in order to deepen their understanding of the material and of the need to fully justify courses of action. This process should also provide lecturers with the opportunity to demonstrate that very rarely is only one solution available and that alternative routes might be equally (or more) valuable depending upon the forces acting upon the situation and subsequent events.

In this chapter the task is to reflect on the consequences for organizational activity of Management in Action 15.3.

Management in Action 15.3: Poverty pay of Barbie doll workers

Student tasks

In groups of six people review the Management in Action panel indicated. Your tasks are:

1. In your group consider the ethical implications of the material contained in Management in Action 15.3. For example is it 'right' for a company to make more profit because it can cut its cost of operations by using cheap labour? Is it any different in principle or practice paying low wages to humans, or cutting labour cost by the replacement of high wage human employees with automation?
2. What responsibility do consumers have in relation to paying 'fair' prices to companies for goods and services that reflect 'fair' wages that those companies pay to employees? How could such an arrangement be enforced?
3. Should companies be required to pay high wages in underdeveloped countries in order to 'pump-prime' economic activity in those areas, or should it be left to market forces?
4. If companies cannot 'take advantage' of cheap labour how could they be persuaded to relocate to areas that need opportunities?
5. Imagine that you are a manager working for Mattel, how would you deal with the situation described above and how would you advise your company to act in relation to the ethics of wages and company operations?

Prepare a brief presentation (not more than 15 minutes) for the rest of your class on the conclusions about the issues raised by the five questions above. Be prepared to answer questions from your classmates on your presentation and also to defend your proposed actions.

CHAPTER 16

Japanization and post-Fordism

Chapter outline

This chapter will introduce a number of perspectives on organizations that have emerged over recent years. It was the developments in manufacturing technology first introduced by Ford that allowed a fundamental change to be introduced in the way that work was practised. Since then many other views about the nature and practice of work have emerged and this chapter will review the approaches emerging from Japan, followed by the labour process theory and postmodernism. The intention of this chapter is to attempt to place the notion of work into a broader context than the functionalist perspective usually adopted by managers.

Learning objectives

After studying this chapter and working through the associated Management in Action panels, discussion questions and research activities, you should be able to:

- Understand the concept of Fordism as indicative of a particular way of working.
- Describe the main themes associated with the Japanization of work and management.
- Explain what is meant by the labour process approach to work.
- Outline the postmodernism view of work.
- Assess the contribution of labour process and post-modernism to the understanding work and management.
- Appreciate that there are conflicts and contradictions between approaches to the understanding of work.
- Discuss the distinction between real and pseudo participation as might be experienced in the Japanization movement.
- Detail the management perspectives on the ideas presented in this chapter.

Teaching notes and chapter summary

Introduction

- Over the centuries the control of work and workers has taken many different forms.
- Scientific management is frequently regarded as the beginning of modern management practice.
- It is also regarded as the basis of the deskilled, monotonous, repetitive, alienated work found in many organizations.
- Shortly after Taylor began to identify the benefits the weaknesses became apparent.
- Consequently other approaches to management and organization began to emerge.
- One of the major difficulties created by the market concept is that the relentless drive for cost reduction is unstoppable.
- Japanization reflects an assumed mixture of management approaches that was thought to be vastly different to that developed by Taylor and Ford.
- Labour process theory and postmodernism are different ways of thinking and theorizing about organizations.

Fordism and post-Fordism

- The factory system made available a greater variety and volume of goods.
- The systematic design and control of work provided the opportunity to reduce unit labour cost and increase output.
- Scientific management increased output from 'pig iron' loaders by more than 300% with only a small increase in pay.
- Post-Fordism has also been described as Neo-Fordism.

Fordism

- It was the fledgling motor car industry in which the ideas and principles which became known as Fordism were developed.

- At the turn of the century motor cars were traditionally made by teams of craftsmen.
- The process of manufacture could take up to 13 weeks to complete each vehicle.
- Partly assembled vehicles remained in one position whilst teams of workers moved around the factory.
- Early attempts to increase productivity included pushing vehicles between workstations.
- Early attempts required the workers to push each vehicle to the next workstation.
- This left control over the pace of work to the employee.
- It was Henry Ford who made a breakthrough by mechanically driving an assembly line at a speed determined by management.
- The breakthrough was of three forms:
  - Mechanically driving the assembly line.
  - Continuous line movement removed control of activity from workers.
  - The pace of the line became an integral part of job design.
- It is frequently associated with alienated workers performing boring tasks with no inkling or interest in the end product.
- An indication of the benefits of assembly line technology can be found in Table 16.1.
- It did not take long for the benefits of Fordism to become established across a wide range of industries and countries.
- Many employees were not able to tolerate the noise, pace of work and boredom, and so labour turnover was very high.
- The response of Ford was to raise wages, thereby allowing employees to become more avid consumers.
- Ford engaged a private police force to ensure that workers were committed and did not form or join trade unions.
- Employees were regarded as an extension of machines.
- The all pervading significance of Fordism is brilliantly captured in literature in the work of Huxley.
- The relentless pressure of an assembly line introduced an additional cause of stress.
- Supervisors were continually pressed for increases in line speed, jobs were deskilled and interaction eliminated.
- The human dimension of the organization was something that Ford actively discouraged, 'A big business is really too big to be human. It grows so large as to supplant the personality of the man' (Ford).
- Great emphasis was placed on the 'quality' of the working environment.
- Welfare provision included school, hospital, cut price shops and a newspaper.

- Industrial disputes began to emerge.
- In structuring production greater output and reduced cost had been achieved at the expense of vulnerability.
- This placed a considerable degree of power in the hands of employees.
- Goffee and Scase summarize a number of weaknesses associated with the Fordist model, including:
  - Alienation.
  - Product change.
  - Managing and doing distinction.
  - Inhibition of creativity.
  - Potential not fully realized.
- These difficulties soon became apparent and led initially to tighter control of the process.
- Considerable effort was put into method study and other approaches in seeking out solutions.

The post-Fordist model

- There are immense benefits to be gained from scientific management.
- However, there are forces that offset these benefits and they are one-off by definition.
- There are three areas in which Post-Fordism addressed the difficulties:
  - Market.
  - Methods.
  - Management.
- Figure 16.1 reflects the phasing process between Fordism and post-Fordism.
- As an ideal type the efficiencies available through Fordism retain their attraction.
- The difficulty is, it cannot be achieved in the long run.
- Humans are not machines and they react to being controlled by inflexible assembly lines.
- Pressures in the environment tend to encourage the retention of Fordism, including:
  - Risk.
  - Training.
  - Systems.
  - Preference.
- Goffee and Scase identify a number of features as paradigm shifts from Fordist to post-Fordist models (Table 16.2).
- Much of this can be attributed to the need to create new forms of flexibility.
- The need for a wider, diversified and more frequently changing product range, with shorter lead times and lower costs are frequently behind these moves.
- It is Japanese companies that have been both the trigger and model for many of these initiatives.

Japanization

- The quality and reliability of Japanese products decimated many long established producers.

■ Oliver and Wilkinson provide statistics which indicate the significance of the threat (Table 16.3).

■ The view was that a new way of managing provided such impressive results.

■ It was thought to be a reflection of:
– Japanese culture.
– Religion.
– An emphasis on the group rather than the individual.

■ Oliver and Wilkinson identify a number of features of Japanese methods that provide the scale of benefit, including:
– Quality.
– Just-in-Time.
– Continuous improvement.
– Work organization. Cellular manufacturing methods and U-shaped production lines allow for greater employee flexibility as well as improved control of the product and process. Figure 16.2 shows a U-shaped production line. Teams also provide an opportunity for people to work together.
– Structure and system.
– Personnel practice.
– Social, political and economic factors.

■ Western manufacturers found it necessary to respond or be eliminated.

■ One way of responding is to emulate.

■ Most of the major motor manufacturers have experienced years of frustration, negotiation and dispute in order to introduce some of the Japanese practices into UK factories.

■ In order to better serve export markets and to placate any suggestion of unfair competition, Japanese producers began to build factories in the West.

■ The introduction of Japanese companies provided an opportunity to observe Japanese management at first hand.

■ Of course many of the practices could not be translated directly but many of the others were.

■ There is the suggestion that transplanted operations are little more than screwdriver factories and that the transfer of manufacturing activity is far from the intention (Williams *et al.*).

■ Clearly Japanese organizations have found effective ways of organizing.

■ However, there are a number of questions that emerge:
– Is Japanization an approach to management fundamentally different to Fordism and scientific management?
– In whose benefit is effectiveness being pursued and why?
– What purpose does work serve?
– What is the effect of such approaches on employees?

Labour process theory

■ Labour process theory originated from the Marxist tradition and attempts to explain the nature of work.

■ It has been defined as:

> the means by which raw materials are transformed by human labour, acting on the objects with tools and machinery: first into products for use and, under capitalism, into commodities to be exchanged on the market (Thompson).

■ As an area of study it began with Braverman, who stimulated the rediscovery of the Marxist material on the nature of labour.

■ There are five core elements to a theory of labour process identified by Thompson:
– Labour as a unique commodity.
– Labour is a special focus of attention in capitalism.
– Capitalism forces minimization.
– Control is an imperative.
– Institutionalized conflict.

■ There are many who would argue with the views put forward by labour process theorists.

■ They include those who would see it as moving away from a traditional Marxist view of common ownership, and those who would prefer to see an emphasis on management as a social science.

■ It does however provide a way of considering the nature of labour in capitalist organizations and perhaps placing Fordism and Japanization into a broader context.

■ It is also inescapable that not all organizations are capitalist, even in a predominately capitalist society.

Postmodernism

■ Research approaches are given titles as an attempt to both differentiate them from other perspectives and to encapsulate some of the essence of the underlying thinking.

■ Carter and Jackson use the terms premodern, modern and postmodern to describe epochs of tendency (Table 16.4).

■ The trend evident in Table 16.4 is one of an increasing reluctance to accept the assumed natural order of things, towards one of uncertainty and an acceptance of a rule of thumb rather than formula management.

■ Research as well as organization is an integral part of the broader social milieu and is as much influenced as influencing within it.

■ Postmodernism is meaningful in terms of its juxtaposition with modernism and it is useful to begin by attempting to provide an indication of the modernist view.

■ Gergen identifies modernism as being characterized by:
– Reason and observation.
– Fundamentalism.
– Universal design.
– Machine metaphor.

■ For a number of writers the use of language to describe the observations from a modernist perspective became problematic.

■ Even if the things being observed and described formed the basis of the essentials of the universe the language used to articulate them did not.

■ So if there is a distinction between thing and symbol how accurate can the symbols be and how accurate can any inferences and conclusions be that are based upon them?

■ Reality and the language used to construct it are in effect separate entities.

■ Hassard brings together the work of a number of writers in order to identify the distinguishing features of postmodernism:
  – Representation.
  – Reflexivity.
  – Writing.
  – Difference.
  – De-centring the subject.

■ Postmodernism sets about questioning the place of reason and 'methodological unity' Hassard.

■ From its origins as a perspective on culture and art it has been used to provide interpretation on organizations as they exist in real time and space.

■ Postmodernism would suggest that it is only by facing up to the paradoxes that emerge that the otherwise hidden assumptions begin to emerge.

■ Not everyone would support the basic approach suggested by postmodern thinking.

■ It may be interesting to question rationality and to engage in deconstruction, but some experiences are very real no matter how they are described.

Japanization and post-Fordism: a management perspective

■ Managers engage in categorization, simplification and the application of procedure in order to carry out their duties.

■ This implies by that rationality pervades the management process.

■ Whilst this may be true part of the time there are also issues such as organizational politics, personal feelings and personality.

■ Scientific management appeared to provide an opportunity to apply rationality and science to the task of controlling work.

■ It proved to be an illusive but pervasive formula.

■ Problems with industrial relations, quality and commitment very quickly emerged.

■ The use of work study can be found in many factory and office sites in many countries.

■ The use of incentive schemes is also very common.

■ Ford was perhaps the earliest example of the adaptation of Taylorism with the introduction of the moving assembly line.

■ The concept of Japanization was at first associated with many apparently new and innovative practices.

■ This was achieved by more strongly unifying the interests of employees and management and by encouraging employees to be critical of organizational weaknesses.

■ However, it could also be argued that these practices are not as they appear at first glance.

■ For example, contribution to problem solving whilst voluntary on the surface is mandatory if the individual wishes to be regarded as an acceptable employee.

■ So perhaps the Japanization process is about being more Taylorist than Taylor, but in more subtle ways.

■ It is also necessary to remember that management practice has a strong cultural element to it and that what works in one place and at a particular point in time cannot be relied upon to have universal value.

■ It could be argued that labour process theory and postmodernism have little to offer practising managers.

■ However as attempts to throw light on the underlying processes they offer an insight into aspects of the management process.

■ This line of argument is based on the view that before being effective in managing others it is first necessary to understand oneself as both an individual and manager.

■ It also allows the behaviour of others to be placed into a context of their own assumptions and belief systems.

Conclusions

■ This chapter has attempted to provide an introduction to a number of the more recent perspectives on the work of Taylor and its impact on organizational activity and management.

■ It attempts to demonstrate how some of the ideas adopted post-Taylor have achieved the benefits of scientific management without creating the negative results.

Discussion questions: outline answers for selected questions

2. Why do you think that Japanese organizations would be happy to allow Western managers to study and understand their 'secrets of success'?

   This question sets a puzzle for students. It should allow them adequate scope to theorize (or fantasize) about the possibilities. Reasons that might be put forward include a spirit of co-operation and to demonstrate superiority. It could also encourage the more devious to suggest that perhaps Western managers are being subtly led astray by being encouraged to see certain practices as key elements when in fact it is others that form the basis of success. For example, Garrahan and Stewart demonstrate the 'other perspective' in describing empowerment or 'shopping' colleagues as one feature of Japanese practice.

3. Postmodernism is of no relevance to the study of modern organizations. Discuss.

There are different ways that this question could be tackled. It could be attempted from the perspective of the perceived value of postmodernism. Alternatively it could be addressed from the perspective of unfolding knowledge. From that point of view it might be argued that only after the event can any judgement be made about the value, relevance and effectiveness of any perspective and therefore it is not possible to judge relevance. In the unfolding of knowledge inevitably many 'blind alleys' will be pursued, but again these sometimes find new applications as knowledge grows. Whichever approach a student adopts it will be the quality of the argument that determines the mark rather than the perspective adopted.

6. Can a capitalist system ever hope to overcome alienation among workers? Justify your answer.

This question allows a good old fashioned Marxist discussion to be brought into the work of students. It will be interesting to observe how 'modern' generally managerial students tackle this question. I have not used this question myself, but my suspicion would be that answers would tend to be rather functional in approach. I would expect that students would approach the question by providing a rather sanitized review of the appropriate material, but with a managerial slant underpinning their perspectives.

8. Approaches such as just-in-time (JIT) place absolute power in the hands of the workers. Managers must therefore find new ways to offset this potential threat to production. Do you agree, and how might this be achieved?

The approach to this question will depend on the point of view adopted. It could be argued that as part of a process of greater empowerment and involvement JIT would encourage higher levels of commitment among employees. Consequently however levels of conflict are to be expected and so power is not an issue. On the other hand if power is seen as an inevitable part of employment life then the adoption of JIT will not change that. As a consequence a shift in the power balance could be expected and specific initiative necessary to limit the potential damage would be more likely. The stronger students may bring into this discussion the differences found in individual companies as a result of past experience, management attitudes, industry and location on the likely relationship between power and the use of JIT.

Case study

The inclusion of a case study in this chapter is intended to provide lecturers with the opportunity to use this method of teaching which requires students to analyse a situation and form a judgement about their preferred solution. Groups of students could be encouraged to challenge each other on their solutions in order to deepen their understanding of the material and of the need to fully justify courses of action. This process should also provide lecturers with the opportunity to demonstrate that very rarely is only one solution available and that alternative routes might be equally (or more) valuable depending upon the forces acting upon the situation and subsequent events.

In this chapter the task is to reflect on the consequences for organizational activity of Management in Action 16.6.

Management in Action 16.6: Trust: a new concept in the management of people?

Student tasks

In groups of six people review the Management in Action panel indicated. Your tasks are:

1. In your group consider the implications of the material contained in Management in Action 16.6.
2. Is trust essential for the effective running of an organization, is it desirable, or is it even possible? It could be argued that until employees become equal stakeholders with shareholders it will never be possible to generate trust with managers. Essentially it would be argued, managers are given the task to maximize the returns to shareholders and as such they have a fundamentally different agenda and set of priorities to employees. Conversely it would be argued that unless employees learn to trust managers organizations will never achieve their full potential.
3. Your task is to research and debate these issues within your group and reach a consensus.

Prepare a brief presentation (not more than 15 minutes) for the rest of your class on the conclusions reached. Be prepared to answer questions from your classmates on your presentation and also to defend your conclusions.

CHAPTER 17

Power and politics

Chapter outline

This chapter will begin by considering the related concepts of power, influence and authority and then go on to examine what generates power as used by individuals and groups within an organization. Power is frequently described as an influence on decision making and this forms the next focus. Political behaviour is examined in relation to attempts to influence the power balance already in existence. The chapter ends with consideration of how political behaviour can be managed.

Learning objectives

After studying this chapter and working through the associated Management in Action panels, discussion questions and research activities, you should be able to:

- Understand the nature of power as experienced within an organization.
- Describe the sources of power within an organization.
- Explain the relationship between power and decision making.
- Outline the concept of organizational politics.
- Assess the differences and similarities between the concepts of power, influence and authority.
- Appreciate how political behaviour is used by individuals within organizations.
- Discuss how political behaviour can be managed within an organization.
- Detail the value of power and politics to the running of an organization.

Teaching notes and chapter summary

Introduction

- The notion of power is endemic in organizational relationships.
- Industrial relations activity is directed towards a redistribution of the prevailing power balance.

- Politicking is frequently behaviour outside the accepted procedures and norms, intended to further the position of an individual or group.
- Both concepts of power and politics contain positive aspects.
- An effective power balance between capital and labour should allow both to function effectively without damage to the interests of either.
- If through the politicking of the marketing manager product changes are brought about which in turn provide commercial gains for the organization, then such behaviour was of benefit.

Power, influence and authority

- Power is a concept related to manipulation and influence.
- It is also something that is an accompaniment to authority.
- However this is relative as there are those with power irrespective of position.
- Power has been defined in many different ways.
- Pfeffer who brings together a number of views as:

  ... the potential ability to influence behaviour, to change the course of events, to overcome resistance, and to get people to do things that they would not otherwise do.

- Within an organization it is easy to envisage the linkage between power, influence and authority.
- There are also positions that do not have any formal authority yet the individuals are able to exercise considerable influence.
- Authority has been described as the legitimate expression of power (Handy).
- Employees generally accept the rights of managers to exercise authority over their behaviour.
- It was Chester Barnard who described authority in the following terms:

... the character of a communication (order) in a formal organization by virtue of which it is accepted by a contributor to or 'member' of the organization as governing the action he contributes; that is, as governing or determining what he does or is not to do so far as the organization is concerned.

■ Acceptance of the requirement to follow the order also acknowledges the authority of the giver of that order.

■ This is what Luthans describes as an acceptance theory of authority.

■ Handy introduces influence as both a noun and a verb to explain some of the confusion with power.

■ Influence is a broader and softer term compared to power.

■ Influence implies persuasion, co-operation and relationship based mechanisms.

■ Overt attempts to use power are likely to be met with resistance.

■ Consequently it is not uncommon to find more subtle mechanisms being used in order to obtain compliance.

■ By allowing employees to become shareholders managers might find it easier to achieve flexibility and lower pay expectations.

■ Forsyth identifies, in the context of whistleblowing, a number of influence strategies that they suggest are used in order to obtain compliance from employees (Table 17.1).

■ Where power is a feature of a relationship there is also dependency.

Sources of power

■ Power is invisible.

■ It is important to distinguish between power and the associated trappings which are detectable.

■ Stereotypic assumptions lead to implying that an individual holds power simply because they dress in expensive clothing or behave as if they were superior.

■ Power is something that only lives in the minds, attitudes, behaviours, expectations and perceptions of individuals.

■ There are situations where direct force (or the threat of it) is used to obtain results, but this represents the application of a particular form of power.

■ French and Raven identified a number of sources of power within a social context:
  – Coercive power.
  – Reward power.
  – Legitimate power.
  – Expert power.
  – Referent power.

■ There is also a sixth form of power (Handy):
  – Negative power.

Power and decision making

■ Decision making and politics are inextricably entwined.

■ Politics also influences the ability to implement a solution.

■ Former President of the United States of America Richard Nixon wrote:

> It is not enough for a leader to *know* the right thing. He must be able to *do* the right thing ... . The great leader needs ... the capacity to achieve.

■ Being able to ensure that a particular course of action is followed requires both power and political expertise.

■ Pfeffer identifies three aspects of decision making that provides for the concept of power to be incorporated into the processes:
  – Decisions change nothing.
  – Decision quality requires retrospective assessment.
  – Significance duration.

■ One of the consequences of this perspective on decision making is that it reflects a stream rather than discrete processes.

■ Within commercial organizations it is largely assumed that power is directly correlated with level in the hierarchy.

■ Trade union representatives in some organizations hold more power than line managers, at least to influence employees.

■ Managers must engage in co-operative behaviour in ensuring that their decisions are acted upon.

■ Competing priorities is frequently cited as the reason for one department or manager not being able to help another.

■ The danger in highly centralized structures in which power is restricted to a few people is that it can be abused.

■ Pfeffer identifies seven decision issues that should be considered as part of the process of decision making (Table 17.2).

■ The zone of indifference is the level of impact on an individual below the threshold at which they will respond negatively.

■ There have been attempts to create a contingency model of power (Figure 17.1).

■ In the contingency approach there is a relationship between the sources of power and the responses generated.

■ To be successful the power holder must have the ability to deliver reward as well as punishment.

■ Empowering and involving employees can be a way of encouraging them to adopt the underlying values of management.

■ This can be thought of substituting internalized forms of self-control for the less effective outward forms.

■ In effect relying on covert rather than overt forms of power application – power by socialization.

Politics within organizations

■ There are two different perspectives on organizational politics.

■ One views politics as a negative process that actively inhibits the effective running of an organization.

■ The other views it in a more positive light as an inevitable mechanism of conflict resolution and a process geared to reaching compromise.

■ One of the earliest works on the subject of politics was that of Machiavelli on the subject of serving princes and other rulers.

■ The negative view of politics imposes a definition that considers it to be outside normal practice, used to enhance existing power or to offset the power of another.

■ Politics increases the certainty that a preferred course of action (as defined by the person engaging in politics) will be followed (Mayes and Allen).

■ The more positive view of political behaviour regards it as an inevitable part of the need for individuals and groups to function in a collective context.

■ Most managers recognize the dual nature of politics within an organization.

■ Gandz and Murray carried out a survey in an attempt to identify how managers perceived politics in their working life (Table 17.3).

■ The positive view of organizational politics suggests that it will be rewarded if it is linked to success for the organization (Figure 17.2).

Using and managing political behaviour

■ The use of power within an organizational setting involves adopting one of three strategies:
  – Offensive.
  – Defensive.
  – Neutral.

■ Some of the tactics that are used politically are identified in Table 17.1 as influencing tactics.

■ Other researchers have identified categories that are framed slightly differently, for example Yukl and Falbe (Table 17.4).

■ Moorhead and Griffin bring together the work of a number of writers in order to identify the main techniques associated with political behaviour (Table 17.5).

■ Considering briefly each technique in turn:
  – Control of information.
  – Control of communication channels.
  – Use of outside specialists.
  – Control over work and meeting agendas.
  – Game playing.
  – Impression and image management.
  – Creating coalitions.
  – Control over decision-making criteria.

■ The degree to which it is possible to manage political behaviour in others is difficult to specify and depends upon:
  – The style of management.
  – The personality of individuals.
  – The skill level of individuals.
  – The networks of individuals.
  – The decision-making processes.
  – The level of resource availability.

■ To minimize the harmful effects of politics competition should be encouraged without allowing hidden agendas to flourish.

■ Specifying how decisions will be made and not allowing power to become a means of acquiring resource, for example.

■ Separating the evaluation of resource allocation from performance and promotion issues are other options.

Power and politics: a management perspective

■ Power and politics within an organization is very complex.

■ Managers without power are likely to have little influence.

■ The close relationship between power and influence provides a breeding ground for the political behaviour.

■ The use of political behaviour can enhance the level of power and influence held by an individual or group, thereby increasing their status and perhaps career prospects.

■ Etzoini provided a categorization for the basis of power as:
  – Normative (based on legitimacy of authority).
  – Utilitarian (based on the payment of inducements).
  – Coercive (based on the ability to apply sanction).

■ It is through the application of the latter two categories that the potential for the misuse of power and political behaviour is created.

■ However it is also important to recognize that there are three caveats to the use of power in an organization:
  – Balance. Only on very rare occasions is there a complete imbalance in the power held between the parties to a particular situation.
  – Domain. Few sources of power are likely to be valid across time and in every context.
  – Relativity. The application of power is only possible if the source is of value to the target person or group.

■ Kotter identified a number of characteristics shared by those managers who were able to use and manage power effectively:
  – Sensitivity.
  – Intuitive.

- Repertoire.
- Career.
- Investment.
- Maturity.

■ Politics can be seen as a means of sharing power among interested groups and individuals.

■ It can provide a mechanism for allowing the relative power of departments to rise and fall without adversely effecting performance of the overall organization.

■ However just as power can be misused so can politics.

■ Cliques are a form of group whose prime motivation is the defence of the members against the interests of other groups.

■ Cabals are a form of group that attempt to take the initiative to the advantage of its members.

■ Cabals represent a proactive approach to the acquisition and use of power through political means.

■ Political behaviour is encouraged in situations where formal roles and authority are unclear.

■ There are a number of issues that emerge about organizational informality or lack of clarity.

■ A number of new structural forms attempt to take out the formality and rigidity of bureaucracy.

■ The informality and lack of clear role definition could provide the basis on which political behaviour flourishes.

■ Delayering and downsizing impacts directly on the number of management jobs available.

■ No longer can managers expect to be protected from the harsh realities that have faced many other occupational groups.

■ Managers find it necessary to take a more active role in managing their own careers.

■ Political behaviour can be a means of influencing decisions about job security and career development.

■ There are links between the type of organization and the form that politics takes.

■ For example, in bureaucratic organizations it is the audit functions that enjoy a high degree of power and influence.

■ In organic organization it is the advisory functions that have most power.

■ In this latter situation organizational politics would tend to be aimed at holding or changing the power balance between line and staff functions.

Conclusions

■ Power and politics are important aspects of organizational behaviour.

■ They are inseparable from the needs of organization and the needs, aspirations and inclinations of the individuals that work within them.

■ There are individuals who introduce an element of game playing intended to enhance their power base and as a means of making work more interesting.

■ They can also introduce a source of much fun and enjoyment in observing the behaviour of others.

■ They are also the basis of much conflict within organizations.

Discussion questions: outline answers for selected questions

3. Is power and politics linked to organizational design? Justify your answer.

   Students could argue this answer from two different perspectives. They could argue that it is people who engage in power and politics and that they will do so irrespective of design. They could also argue that it certain design features encourage power and politics to be displayed. Of course it is possible to argue a combination of both perspectives. For example, successful power and political 'animals' have the opportunity to create designs that allow them to engage in their whims, which might be to encourage 'sport' among subordinates, or to limit the threat to their own position. Equally the points made in the text about how to limit the negative effect of power and politics would be expected to feature in the answer.

5. Describe the main sources of power and provide examples of each from an organization.

   These are described in the text and students would be expected to be able to recount them without difficulty. The examples used to illustrate them might be contrived or simplistic among students with little organizational experience, but a rich source of insight into real organizational politics, etc., from more experienced individuals and groups.

7. Identify the differences and similarities between the concepts of power and influence.

   This question should be capable of being answered directly form the text. Power as the ability to influence and the ability to influence without formal power should be aspects that feature heavily in the answer.

10. Management is ultimately about acquiring and using power successfully. The best leaders are successful politicians. Reconcile these two statements.

    The ability to reconcile these two statement depends upon the definitions of the key terms. For example if power is seen as the means through which to influence and politics is regarded as the achievement of the possible then they can be quite easily reconciled as related to achieving effective leadership and management. On the other hand if they are regarded in a negative light, or are regarded as necessary evils then it becomes more difficult to reconcile the statements. Whichever approach students adopt they should provide a sound justification for their answer.

Case study

The inclusion of a case study in this chapter is intended to provide lecturers with the opportunity to use this method of teaching which requires students to analyse a situation and form a judgement about their preferred solution. Groups of students could be encouraged to challenge each other on their solutions in order to deepen their understanding of the material and of the need to fully justify courses of action. This process should also provide lecturers with the opportunity to demonstrate that very rarely is only one solution available and that alternative routes might be equally (or more) valuable depending upon the forces acting upon the situation and subsequent events.

In this chapter the task is to reflect on the consequences for organizational activity of Management in Action 17.5.

Management in Action 17.5: Getting rid of a subordinate

Student tasks

In groups of six people review the Management in Action panel indicated. Your tasks are:

1. In your group consider the implications of the material contained in Management in Action 17.5.

2. Discuss what you would do if you were James. Would you have resigned after seeking another job or would you stay and fight? If you would stay and fight how would you do this and what do you think the consequences might be?

3. Discuss what you would do if you were the department manager. You were led to believe that you would be promoted in the near future and even allowed to recruit your replacement. However this is now unlikely to happen. James has an expectation that he will be promoted to your job and he has a much wider experience base than yourself. Could your director be considering replacing you with James? How would you deal with this situation?

4. Consider the company perspective. Is it possible for a company to prevent such situations arising, and if so how or why not? Is it possible for a company to find out if such situations have occurred, and if so how, or why not? Is it possible to identify ways of resolving such situations once they have arisen, why or why not? Does it matter that such situations arise and potentially good staff leave, as long as the company is profitable?

Prepare a brief presentation (not more than 15 minutes) for the rest of your class on the conclusions reached. Be prepared to answer questions from your classmates on your presentation and also to defend your conclusions.

CHAPTER 18

Conflict and control

Chapter outline

This chapter begins with an introduction to the concepts
of conflict and control. Conflict then becomes the focus
of attention in attempting to identify its sources, forms
and consequences. The forms and characteristics of
control are examined before the strategies for using it
are introduced. The chapter concludes with a consideration of the management perspectives on the topics
discussed.

Learning objectives

After studying this chapter and working through the
associated Management in Action panels, discussion
questions and research activities, you should be able to:

■ Understand the nature and impact of control within
organizations.
■ Describe the sources and forms that conflict can
take.
■ Explain the characteristic features of control
systems.
■ Outline the major conflict handling strategies.
■ Assess the relative strengths and weaknesses of the
various conflict handling strategies.
■ Appreciate that conflict is not automatically negative
in its impact.
■ Discuss the management perspectives on conflict
and control.
■ Detail the control strategies available to organizations.

Teaching notes and chapter summary

Introduction

■ The first definition of conflict in the *Oxford
Dictionary* is, 'trial of strength between opposed
parties or principles.'
■ Control can be used to refer to a range of actions,
including the control of machine processes.

■ It can also refer to the management of the
organization.
■ However it can also be used to reflect more sinister
processes.
■ It can be taken to reflect the manipulation of
employee behaviour.
■ There are examples of managers resorting to
bullying in order to force subordinates to comply
(Adams).

Conflict: sources and forms

■ Conflict can be considered as something that dis-
rupts the normal and desirable states of stability and
harmony.
■ Under this definition it is something to be avoided
and eliminated.
■ However it is also possible to consider conflict as
inevitable and if managed constructively offering
positive value.
■ Fox describes three major perspectives on organizations that each have a different perspective on the
nature of conflict:
  – Pluralism.
  – Unitarism.
  – Marxist.

Sources of conflict

■ There are six major areas within an organization that
can give rise to conflict (Figure 18.1).
■ Taking each of the sources of conflict in turn:
  – Intrapersonal. This represents the conflicts that
    arise within the individual.
  – Interpersonal. Whetten and Cameron identify four
    sources of interpersonal conflict:
  1. Personal difference.
  2. Role incompatibility.
  3. Information deficiency.
  4. Environmental stress.

– Intragroup. One particular context within which interpersonal conflict can be found occurs within a group (Figure 18.2).
– Intergroup. There are many different groups that exist within an organization and inevitably they will experience differences and conflict at some point in time.
– Intraorganizational. Individuals and groups play such a significant part in organizational activity that they inevitably account for much of the incidence of conflict. However, there are other features of organization that favour the emergence of conflict (Figure 18.3).
– Interorganizational. Markets provides a scenario in which organizations are inevitably in conflict with each other.

Forms of conflict

■ Conflict from a managerial perspective has the potential to create disruption within the organization.
■ Most organizations attempt to institutionalize the mechanisms for dealing with it.
■ Some of the forms that conflict can take are given below.

Individual

■ Some of the ways that conflict can find its way into observable behaviour include:
   – Sabotage.
   – Ethical dilemmas.
   – Interpersonal disputes.
   – Work manipulation.
   – Misuse of resources.
   – Choice.
   – Politicking and power.
   – Rumour and gossip.
   – Attitude.
   – Absence and leaving.

Group

■ Some of the forms of conflict identified under the individual classification can also find expression at the group level. The major forms of group conflict include:
   – Strikes and lock-outs.
   – Work-to-rule.
   – Work restriction.
   – Factionalism.

Conflict: the consequences

■ Everyone must work on the quality of relationships or conflict is likely to arise.
■ That is not to suggest that conflict can be eliminated completely.

■ There will always be individuals who do not get along at a personal level.
■ Minimizing conflict is something that requires positive action.
■ Conflict is a concept that can be argued to be either a negative or positive force.
■ Another viewpoint suggests that conflict can either be negative or positive depending upon the circumstances.
■ Too much or too little conflict is harmful, just the right amount of conflict can aid performance (Figure 18.4).
■ In this view conflict is defined as a pressurizing force.
■ Conflict is regarded as a force that can ensure that slackness is kept out of the organization.
■ If management cannot take for granted the loyalty and commitment of employees they will find it necessary to continually re-assess the working relationships.
■ With no conflict in existence a form of amnesia would result.
■ An organization would become slack.
■ At the other extreme excessive conflict would bring the organization to a standstill.
■ There are a number of consequences of conflict (Figure 18.5).
■ Most of the consequences identified in Figure 18.5 are self-explanatory, but some need further elaboration:
   – Training. Where conflict is a real possibility, training and other exposure activities can be effective means of exploring and resolving the difficulties.
   – Autocratic leadership. There is a view that conflict represents an unwillingness to compromise and a direct challenge to authority. Therefore one consequence could be to become autocratic in management style.
   – Low-quality staff. There are organizations who have a reputation for conflictual working relationships. Consequently potential employees tend to regard such employers as a last resort and only remain until something better comes along.
   – Less communication. When people are in conflict the level and quality of communication drops.
■ It should be possible to achieve medium levels of conflict through handling strategies such as negotiation and socialization.
■ Offsetting the negative consequences of conflict should improve performance.
■ The process of conflict resolution should provide greater levels of unity.
■ One potential weakness in Figure 18.4 is that organizations should encourage conflict up to a certain level.

Conflict handling strategies

■ There are a number of ways in which conflict can be managed within an organizational setting:

- Clarity and openness.
- Signals. The signals that managers and other individuals within the organization give also contribute to the likelihood of conflict breaking out.
- Training and socialization.
- Style and structure.
- Procedure. Among the more common procedural devices used are:

  A Operating policy and procedures. The purpose being to provide clarity of operational responsibility, prevent duplication of effort and to establish ground-rules for activity.

  B Communication and consultation procedures. Communication and consultation between the various groups that exist within an organization should facilitate an improved level of understanding and knowledge which in turn should reduce the prospect of conflict.

  C Decision-making practices. The processes adopted with regard to decision making can also be used to reduce the opportunity for conflict and assist with its resolution.

  D Negotiation. Negotiation provides a process by which individuals and groups can directly resolve their differences.

  E Discipline and grievance procedures The discipline and grievance procedures are the vehicles through which both parties have the opportunity to ensure satisfaction with the execution of the contract.

  F Industrial relations procedures. Armstrong indicates that, 'The primary aims of [industrial relations] policies and procedures are to improve co-operation, to minimize unnecessary conflict, to enable employees to play an appropriate part in decision making, and to keep them informed on matters that concern them.'

■ The above strategies provide an indication of the devices that are available but not how to respond.

■ Thomas identified five generic conflict handling styles based upon the balance between two dimensions (Figure 18.6).

■ The five conflict handling styles identified in Figure 18.6 are:
- Smoothing or accommodating.
- Avoidance.
- Collaboration and problem solving.
- Competitive or authoritarian.
- Compromise.

■ The style adopted in a particular conflict situation will be a reflection of a number of forces.

■ In an emergency situation it is more likely that a directive style would be adopted.

Control within organizations

■ There are many definitions of control.

■ One of the simplest is that provided by Dunford in which it is described as a process which:

> ... involves attempts to bring about desired outcomes.

■ Within an organization there are two distinct and opposite aspects to the existence of control:
- Firstly it provides the basis of order and predictability in operational activity.
- Secondly that control is restrictive, lacks flexibility, is manipulative and greedy with regard to the abolition of personal freedom.

■ It could be argued that many initiatives on employee involvement and participative management are covert attempts to find ways of retaining control within an illusion of freedom for the individual.

■ The net effect being the exercise of more subtle forms of control intended to minimize the risk of conflict and maximize contribution.

■ It has been suggested by Huczynski and Buchanan that control has three connotations:
- First, it is necessary as an economic activity, critical to the success of the organization.
- Second, it represents a psychological necessity in order to eliminate the ambiguity, unpredictability and disorder that would prevent individuals from operating effectively.
- Third, it represents a political process in which some individuals and groups are able to exercise control over less fortunate groups.

■ It possible to identify another purpose, physical.

■ Taking each briefly in turn:
- Physical. At the detailed control level jobs, processes and machines need to be organized and controlled effectively if they are to combine to produce the goods and services required.
- Economic. As an economic process control is geared towards achieving the financial objectives of the organization.
- Psychological. This process represents both the need among individuals to function within a predictable environment and the need that some individuals have to either control or be controlled.
- Political. Control provides the means by which existing structures and social conditions can be reinforced. Owners of capital insist on their pre-eminent right to ultimate determination of organizational existence. There are other political perspectives, for example, through the exercise of political skill a departmental manager may be able to increase their own significance and importance within an organization, thereby being able to exercise control over a greater range of resources.

Control: form and characteristics

■ Control and organization are inextricably linked.
■ Under the putting-out system owners could not directly control the activities of workers (Table 18.1).
■ The factory system was designed to change that.
■ A factory system provided owners with an opportunity to exercise in-process levels of control.
■ It became possible to break the manufacturing process down and to create jobs requiring low skill levels.
■ Lower skill levels are directly associated with cheaper labour.
■ The pace and method of work could be directly controlled in a factory, increasing the output per worker and reducing labour cost.
■ Very little control takes the form of force or pressure.
■ It is usually incorporated into the fabric of the organization and management practice.
■ If control is the ability to determine the behaviour of others it makes sense to exercise it in such a way that reduces the likelihood of conflict.
■ Creating an acceptance of the normality and necessity for control mechanisms is one way of achieving this.
■ The main forms of organizational control are:
  – Output control. This is based upon the premise that if the output achieved is as predicted, then the system is under control. It is a management-by-exception process.
  – Process control. This form of control relies on monitoring and controlling the means rather than the ends. It is premised on the view that it is necessary to control the process aspects of operational activity in order to ensure that the objectives are achieved.
  – Work design. The way that the tasks to be undertaken are clustered together into jobs is a reflection of the intentions of management in relation to how they view the business and the need to control activity in relation to the desired objectives.
  – Structure. It is the compartmentalization of activity that provides the opportunity to control through specialization. It also allows managers to be able to simplify complex activity into meaningful and understandable units.
  – Hierarchy and authority. The owners of the capital are held to be the people who have the ultimate right to determine what happens within an organization. In practice a power-sharing process must be entered into in order to define the relationships between the principle players. As a consequence of these processes a hierarchical arrangement of responsibility and control is introduced into the organization.
  – Skill. There are many other jobs in which skill or professional status provides an opportunity to exercise control in one form or another.
  – Technology. Machines can work at a predictable and stable pace until they breakdown or are switched off. People are not so programmable. It is frequently technology that determines (controls) the human participation in the production process.
  – Social control. There are many forms of social control, including those institutions provided by the state, the police, law and other government agencies. In addition, and of particular relevance to an organizational setting are institutions such as the education system which is intended to prepare children and young people for the world of work. Within an organization there are the induction; training; development; performance appraisal; pay; promotion and career development activities which all provide a basis for shaping behaviour patterns in one way or another.
■ Clegg and Dunkerley describe a vicious circle reinforcing the need for ever tighter means of control (Figure 18.7).

Conflict and control: a management perspective

■ It has been argued that the organizational history of the twentieth century can be described in terms of increasing management control and the potential for conflict and alienation that flows from it.
■ For managers control contains different connotations depending upon such factors as the seniority and job function.
■ For example, a chief executive should not be concerned with control over the purchase of pens.
■ They should assure themselves that someone is exercising control over the purchase and use of consumables.
■ A production supervisor would be expected to exercise detailed control over day-to-day production activities.
■ This could be taken to imply a rational and planned process (Figure 18.8).
■ Within such models there is limited recognition of the realities of organizational life.
■ The data essential for control purposes are not always available, accurate or available at the appropriate time.
■ The style of management and decision making are also variables that influence control.
■ Power and political processes influence not only the control processes but the interpretation of data.
■ Like all aspects of management the design of control systems are social processes.
■ There are different views about the impact of conflict within an organization.
■ The extended tea break, pace and diligence of work are some of the variables at the disposal of the

employee in demonstrating independence from total subjugation.

■ Recent managerial approaches can be categorized as attempts to delegate control in such a way as to provide the illusion of independence and encourage self-control (Figure 18.9).

Conclusions

■ This chapter has attempted to consider the related topics of conflict and control.

■ These subjects have strong links with negotiation, power and politics which were introduced in previous chapters.

■ Both conflict and control can be argued to be endemic to organizational life.

■ However, they can cause damage to individuals and the organization if they are not handled carefully and with respect.

Discussion questions: outline answers for selected questions

3. Can compliance as an employee response to employment ever form a basis for the creation of an effective organization? Justify your answer.

This question seeks to draw out from students the value of compliance in the sense of employees doing what they were employed to do and the use of intelligence and the other human qualities that are of value to any organization. Compliance in an unthinking and sheep-like manner is of little real value because it is not possible for managers to provide enough 'control' to ensure success. Students would be expected to discuss these issues and to form an appropriate judgement based on the quality of their argument.

4. 'Control does not exist in reality. Ultimately everyone is subject to some form of control by others. Consequently it is a device that provides an illusion of order and structure.' Discuss.

This question seeks to encourage a discussion of the 'direction' of control rather than the process. Control is frequently discussed in terms of 'how' a particular plan or set of criteria should be achieved. But what if the plan itself is faulty? The Charge of the Light Brigade is a perfect example of a well-executed and controlled process that could have easily been a disaster. So does control provide the illusion of order and effectiveness in the sense of 'doing the right or best thing as dictated by others' or does it actually provide a means of achieving results? Another feature that might be found in the better answers include social as compared to procedural control.

6. 'The trick in management is to find ways of control that are socially acceptable.' Discuss.

This question might draw out from students an analysis of the term 'trick' as related to management activity. This might imply slight of hand or some form of confidence trick as the basis of manipulating people in a work setting. The objective being to manipulate people to follow management's wishes. On the other hand it could be seen as a 'trick of the trade' in the sense of one of the approaches used by experienced practitioners to achieve better results. The student should then make some attempt to discuss the notion control in relation to power, politics and conflict. This should be followed by an attempt to relate the material to the achievement of business objectives and the need for employees to accept the forms of control being used.

8. 'Conflict management represents the biggest challenge for every manager.' To what extent and why do you agree with this statement?

This question almost assumes a negative connotation to conflict. The notion of genuine differences and the benefits to be gained by surfacing conflict and gaining commitment through difference resolution and compromise. Most students will probably answer this question in relation to industrial relations types of conflict. In that sense the answer will be oriented towards the need for consultative mechanisms and negotiation as avoidance and minimization processes. Recognition of the interpersonal and other forms of conflict should be rewarded as should an attempt to assess both their significance and opportunities for resolution.

Case study

The inclusion of a case study in this chapter is intended to provide lecturers with the opportunity to use this method of teaching which requires students to analyse a situation and form a judgement about their preferred solution. Groups of students could be encouraged to challenge each other on their solutions in order to deepen their understanding of the material and of the need to fully justify courses of action. This process should also provide lecturers with the opportunity to demonstrate that very rarely is only one solution available and that alternative routes might be equally (or more) valuable depending upon the forces acting upon the situation and subsequent events.

In this chapter the task is to reflect on the consequences for organizational activity of Management in Action 18.3.

Management in Action 18.3: Getting rid of the boss

Student tasks

In groups of six people review the Management in Action panel indicated. Your tasks are:

1. In your group consider the implications of the material contained in Management in Action 18.3.

2. You have just been recruited by the company to take over as department manager of the section described in Management in Action 18.3 (before the decision has been taken to close it down). The personnel director tells you that this is the last chance for the department and she wants to see a plan of action for redeeming the situation. You have to develop an appropriate plan that will address the needs of the situation, but will not cause problems elsewhere in the company. What would you do?

Prepare a brief presentation (not more than 15 minutes) for the rest of your class on the conclusions reached. Be prepared to answer questions from your classmates on your presentation and also to defend your conclusions.

CHAPTER 19

Managing change

Chapter outline

This chapter will consider the nature and impact of change on organizations and the people that are employed within them. The chapter will introduce some of the forms that resistance to change can take, as well as some of the reasons for it. This will be followed by a consideration of the major approaches to the management of change and the role of innovation as a coping and accommodating strategy. The chapter will conclude with a consideration of change from a management perspective.

Learning objectives

After studying this chapter and working through the associated Management in Action panels, discussion questions and research activities, you should be able to:

- Understand the range of forces that impact on an organization and which can require change to be made.
- Describe the organizational development approach to change management.
- Explain the difference between and significance of planned and unplanned change.
- Outline the association and implication between politics, power and change.
- Assess the value of managing innovation as part of a change strategy.
- Appreciate why people frequently resist change.
- Discuss the mechanisms through which managers attempt to control change.
- Detail the contingency and systems approaches to change management.

Teaching notes and chapter summary

Introduction

- The world has always changed and people, plants and animals have evolved and adapted to new circumstances.
- The rate of change is now much greater than ever before.
- Table 19.1 demonstrates some of the ways in which change can influence the working environment.
- Reluctance to adapt to change appears to be a normal reaction.
- Predictability appears to be a valued condition for many people.

Pressure for change

- For organizations there are particular events and experiences that instigate change.
- Some of these forces arise from outside the organization and some from inside it.
- Change can affect the individual, a group, or the entire organization.
- There are also changes that impact on society and which in turn influence organizations.
- Random or chance factors as well as natural disasters can also cause change.

internal external

Forces acting on organizations

- Table 19.2 represents some of the external sources of pressure for change.
- In addition to these sources of change, Hellriegel *et al.* identify the following:
  - Rapid product obsolescence.
  - Knowledge explosion.
  - Demographics.
- The internal forces for change include:
  - Efficiency.
  - Fashion.

- Control.
- Internal pressure.

■ Stewart identifies a number of changes that influence managerial careers, in addition to the points already made:
  - Business structure.
  - Business functioning.

■ There are four different ways in which change can be experienced by an organization (Figure 19.1).

■ Considering each of the cells in turn:
  - Surprise. This reflects situations that are both unplanned and relatively minor in nature.
  - Incremental. This could reflect situations which are anticipated yet relatively minor in nature.
  - Crisis. This represents both the unexpected and the serious.
  - Strategic. This represents major planned events that attempt to position the organization more effectively in relationship to its environment.

The scale of change impact axis of Figure 19.1

Adaptive change

Those changes categorized as adaptive are relatively small in scale and which as a consequence can be accommodated without major disruption and danger to the organization.

Fracturing change

This represents the major events that occur within the experience of all organizations. The scale of change represented by this category is very large and of a significance that could seriously damage or destroy the organization. It has the potential to fracture or break it.

The degree of planning that can be brought to bear axis of Figure 19.1

Planned change

Planned change represent those events that management intend to occur, or about which they can provide a predetermined response. It also represents the strategic moves made by organizations in order to position themselves to minimize the overall impact of declining markets and to capture the potential of expanding businesses. Planning for the many small changes that occur is part of normal managerial experience.

Unplanned change

This category represents the unexpected events that can never be completely eliminated. It is one of the primary responsibilities of management to anticipate events and to minimize the possibility of the unexpected arising. Also they have responsibility for the development of plans for dealing with such eventualities that cannot

be eliminated or totally harnessed. This contingency planning approach to change attempts to scan the internal and external environment and develop response scenarios for what might be expected to occur.

Resistance to change

■ Resistance to change implies that an individual or group have determined to frustrate the intentions of another to implement a particular course of action.

■ Kahn suggests that resistance behaviour during times of change is frequently indistinguishable from normal behaviour patterns.

■ The difference being a function of the perspective of the person classifying the behaviour rather than the behaviour itself.

Individual resistance to change

■ Individuals resist change for a number of reasons including those indicated in Figure 19.2.

■ Change can be a negative experience for many employees.

■ Experience soon indicates that managers do not always have the best interests of employees at heart.

■ Some of the reasons identified in Figure 19.2 need further explanation:
  - Symbolic meaning. Changes which impact on visible signs of position or status can be fiercely resisted even if they are incidental.
  - Change shock. The previous routine will have been familiar, individuals will have known instinctively what they were supposed to do. Change can destroy that level of familiarity and create situations in which less is predictable.
  - Selective attention and retention. Change can call into question established frames of reference and as a consequence be rejected. Individuals have a tendency to only pay attention and retain that information which supports their existing world views.
  - Dependence. Students are dependent upon lecturers for their intellectual development. However, taken to extreme, dependence can become a force which resists change as security is threatened. Dependence can also place significant power in the hands of those who are relied upon.
  - Security and regression. The need for security can lead to a search for the past when things appeared simpler and more familiar. This regression on the part of individuals is a clear force for resisting change.

Group and organizational resistance to change

■ Resistance to change at a group or organizational level comes in many forms (Figure 19.3).

■ Most of the categories of resistance identified in Figure 19.3 are self-explanatory, but a few could benefit from some explanation:

- Misinformation. Control over communication provides opportunities for a group to impart particular interpretations to information and so engineer resistance.
- Organization structure. The bureaucratic form of organization was designed to deliver consistency and predictability of operations. Consequently it is a structure that does not cope easily with change.
- Previous agreements. Arrangements entered into with another group or organization are designed to control events in the future. This restricts the ability to make changes over that period of such agreements.
- Fixed investments. The investments that an organization makes in buildings, land and equipment place considerable restriction on what can be done in the future. In practice they limit the ability to change because they represent assets that are not easy to liquidate in the short term.
- Overdetermination. The systems and procedures that organizations create to provide control can also restrict the ability to introduce change.
- Narrow focus of change. In considering change an organization very often takes the immediate zone of impact into account. It is possible for situations to arise in which groups not immediately affected by change resist involvement and so limit the benefits ultimately gained.

Managing organizational change

- Managers have a responsibility for both creating change and responding to it in pursuit of their objectives.
- One model of an organization attempts to reflect a basis for change management (Figure 19.4).
- Leavitt argues that change can influence any of the elements.
- Alternatively they can be changed individually in an attempt to influence other elements.
- A change agent is someone who plays a leading part in sponsoring the need for change or in its implementation.
- There have been a number of frameworks describing the forms of change agent activity.
- One of the more recent is that of Ottaway who produced a taxonomy linked to a particular model of change – that of Lewin.
- This model states that any situation exists as the result of a balance between the forces acting upon it.
- These forces occur in opposing directions, some driving for change whilst others are restraining that change by pressing in the opposite direction.
- It is known as the forcefield analysis model (Figure 19.5).
- The model is very simple to understand and can easily be applied to a wide range of situations.

- An analysis of absence levels might reveal the driving and restraining forces indicated in Table 19.3.
- If a change is desired then either the magnitude of the driving forces needs to be increased, and/or the magnitude of the restraining forces reduced.
- Lewin identified three stages of change associated with his forcefield analysis model:
  - Stage 1 – Unfreezing.
  - Stage 2 – Changing.
  - Stage 3 – Refreezing.
- Ottaway's taxonomy is based on this model of change.
- Three types of change agent are identified:
  - Change generators.
  - Change implementors.
  - Change adopters.
- Plant advocates Key Relationship Mapping in attempting to identify appropriate change strategies (Figure 19.6).
- Winners would not normally be expected to resist proposed changes, whereas losers would.
- Those who hold or have access to information have the potential to help or hinder change.
- In managing change it is necessary to utilize aspects from each of the models so far described.

Organizational development and change

- Organizational development (OD) can be defined as:

  a systematic application of behavioural science knowledge to the planned development and reinforcement of organizational strategies, structures, and processes for improving an organization's effectiveness (Cummings and Worley).

- The strands of theory and practice within OD include:
  - T-groups. Small unstructured groups meet and by exploring the interactive behaviour of the group learn about their own behaviour.
  - Survey feedback. The findings from attitude or similar surveys need to be communicated to the participants in a way that creates learning opportunities.
  - Action research. This reflects an active and iterative approach to research and change.
  - Quality of working life. The quality of working life (QWL) movement has been incorporated into the OD practice.
  - Strategic change. An attempt to integrate all organizational variables into a common purpose.
- OD assumes incrementalism as the best way to achieve change.
- Dunphy and Stace argue that not all situations allow for the slow process of evolutionary change.

■ OD as a process requires participation which, as Stephenson suggests, is not the panacea often claimed.

■ Individuals or groups intent on resisting change may not be persuaded by involvement and might slow down the process itself.

■ Involvement can expose, but not necessarily solve problems.

■ Compromise may not be the best option and changing opinions may not deliver as intended.

■ Figure 19.6 makes reference to power as part of the change process, this is lacking in the classic OD approach.

■ Recognizing this weakness Schein makes several suggestions for including a power and political perspective to OD, identifying with powerful stakeholders and attempting small projects first to gain credibility before tackling the more complex and risky projects, for example.

Power, politics and change

■ There are two major ways in which power and politics interact with change:
  - Process. Power and politics can be used to facilitate the process of change.
  - Purpose. Change can be used as the means to achieve another purpose. For example, the management of a company might 'engineer' the need for a redundancy in order to be able to dismiss particular employees.

■ Stephenson (1985) identifies the following tactics useful in the introduction of change:
  - Simple first.
  - Adaptation.
  - Incorporation.
  - Structure.
  - Ceremony.
  - Assurances.
  - Timescales.
  - Support.
  - Transition.
  - Unexpected.

■ In Nadler and Tushman's view there are three mechanisms required to manage the problems associated with the power, anxiety and transitional situations found in all change situations:
  - Mobilizing political support.
  - Encouraging supportive behaviour.
  - Managing the transitional process.

■ It could be argued that by acting in an overtly political way management could encourage others to act in a similar way.

■ Creating a deteriorating cycle of behaviour into a pit of intrigue and politics.

Contingency approaches to change

■ Contingency approaches to change incorporate a broader range of elements into the process.

■ They represent a directly managerial approach to the subject of change compared with OD.

■ One of the earlier approaches to the contingency view of change is reflected in the work of Kotter and Schlesinger (Table 19.4).

■ Taking each of the strategies for change in turn:
  - Education + communication.
  - Participation + involvement.
  - Facilitation + support.
  - Negotiation + agreement.
  - Manipulation + co-option.
  - Explicit + implicit coercion.

■ Dunphy and Stace introduce a two-dimensional matrix as a way of identifying strategies for the management of change (Figure 19.7).

■ The four change strategies are:
  - Participative evolution.
  - Forced evolution.
  - Charismatic transformation.
  - Dictatorial transformation.

■ The potential limitations in contingency models have been recognized by a number of writers.

■ Examples include the complexity of organization and environment relationships and the politics of managerial self-interest.

■ Managers have particular ways of relating to organizations, workers and the rights of stakeholder groups.

■ This leads to the creation of particular interpretative schemes, which play a determining role in strategy formulation.

Systems perspectives on change

■ Total systems intervention (TSI) is grounded in the philosophy of critical systems thinking.

■ This philosophy is based upon three principles: complementarism, social awareness, and human well-being/emancipation.

■ These principles reflect the view that techniques should be selected according to their appropriateness, that the social context plays a major part in determining the approach adopted and that the human dimension to work should contribute to the process of problem solving.

■ The TSI approach is a problem solving approach and has a wider application than the management of change.

■ TSI comprises three phases:
  - Creativity.
  - Choice.
  - Implementation.

■ The TSI methodology is intended to function as an iterative process.

- Within TSI there is the opportunity to utilize one or more systems methodologies.
- Each of the systems methodologies available are of benefit in particular contextual conditions.

Innovation as a change strategy

- Innovation and change are areas of activity that are strongly tied together.
- One dictionary definition of innovation is to bring in novelties and to make changes.
- Tom Peters for example has produced a stream of books all intended to drive the basic message 'innovate or die'.
- The degree of innovation demanded by such writers as Peters require nothing less than continuous revolution.
- Innovation carries with it a measure of risk because it involves doing things differently.
- There are some industries that are particularly prone to the risks associated with innovation.
- For example, restaurants and clothing are subjected to rapid and frequent changes in fashion and taste.
- Just as with change itself, innovation is an issue that finds resistance in many organizations for a number of reasons:
  - Inertia.
  - Control.
  - Operational effectiveness.
  - Predictability.
- Changing anything can create uncertainty, unfamiliarity and problems.
- Pascale points to a number of organizational features that restrict the ability to innovate and change (Table 19.5).
- There are different forms that innovation can take:
  - Radical.
  - Systems.
  - Incremental.
- The possible returns from the radical level of innovation are much higher than at the incremental level.
- Risk and return are strongly correlated, the higher the risk the higher the potential return.
- There is no aspect of an organization that is not amenable to innovative activity.
- Each of the elements in Figure 19.4 can sustain innovation in one form or another.
- Innovation is a process that is only dependent upon the ingenuity of the human resource within the organization.
- Another way of conceptualizing an organization is the Seven S Framework (Figure 19.8).
- Pascale revisits this model in the context of a discussion of stagnation and renewal as a cyclical process.

- Innovation and change represent dynamic processes in which change is followed by a period of stagnation as the benefits are harvested.
- This in turn produces a resistance to seek continuous change and so a disjointed process is generated.
- The Seven S Framework provides a basis for managers to consider each element on a regular basis and so limit the negative effects of stagnation.
- Schermerhorn identifies five elements of the innovation process:
  - Internal organizational sensitivity. Reflects the ability to be aware of the need for innovation and how to harness effort in support of it.
  - Idea creation. This involves generating new ideas and finding ways of adapting existing methods and procedures.
  - Initial experimentation. This reflects the development of prototypes and testing the ideas generated.
  - Feasibility determination. The determination of the practicality involves checking the financial viability, practicality and operational benefits.
  - Final application. This stage represents the commercialization of ideas and their adoption within the organization. In a perfect world it would lead to further innovation.

Change: a management perspective

- Management is a process of seeking a balance between change and stability.
- Stability is necessary in order to achieve the economies of scale.
- Change on the other hand is necessary because of the need to keep ahead of the competition and to ensure constantly reducing cost.
- The success of Japanese management methods is in being able to effectively harnessing these conflicting requirements.
- Too much change it can be argued is bad for operations, leads to confusion and reduces efficiency, quality and morale.
- Too little change results in stagnation.
- Many recent developments have been designed to allow greater levels of change to be adopted without loss of control.
- Just-in-time, teamwork, empowerment, quality circles and the other planning and control techniques all offer some ability to adapt operational activity to changes in product, technology or environment.
- Another way of looking at change is that is a natural part of life.
- The problems arise from stability, not from change.
- The changing seasons, weather, ageing, birth and death, sickness and health and family responsibilities represent just some of the ways in which change manifests itself in the life experience of human beings.

- Consider the changes in the range of skills and abilities of a human being between the ages of three and 12.
- Under these circumstances it is not stability that is the norm, it is change.
- Yet there is something that happens to human beings when they become adult and part of an organization that seeks to create security, stability and predictability.
- Perhaps it is the human experience of organizations that creates this 'change' in people?
- It is the responsibility of management to develop the structural, procedural and cultural arrangements that encourage the expression of human talents.
- For practising managers knowing what to change is frequently a difficult decision.
- How far change should go is another difficult area, resistance and cost inevitably increase with the degree of change.
- The process of change is another area with a number of dangers attached to it.
- The end result, once achieved may not meet the expectations predicted and fail to deliver the intended benefits.
- This exposes management to additional cost, loss of credibility as they seek to remedy the deficiency.
- So from a management perspective change is a dangerous practice that it is not possible to avoid and yet carries all manner of personal, professional and organizational risks.

Conclusions

- This chapter has analysed the nature of change and assessed the ways in which it impacts on organizations and management.
- The reasons for change were examined as were the forms of resistance to it.
- Change management approaches were evaluated as was innovation as part of the change process.
- Every aspect of an organization is subject to and involved with change in some way or other.
- From that perspective every other chapter in this book contains some aspect of change, its origins, impact and interacting variables.
- It is for that reason that change is a suitable conclusion for the book.

Discussion questions: outline answers for selected questions

2. Describe the McKinsey Seven S Framework and explain how it could be used to inform a change management programme.

   The first part of this question should present students with little difficulty. The second part should provide them with the creative opportunity to design a

change process of their own choice. Only in the light of the choice made by the student can an evaluation be made. The application of the model should reflect the integrated nature of the elements within it linked to one or more of the models discussed in the book.

5. Distinguish between planned and unplanned change, adaptive and fracturing change. What are the consequences of these distinctions?

   This question requires students to describe the model used in the early part of this chapter. They should also be able to draw conclusions from it in terms of the change strategies subsequently adopted.

8. Provide a brief explanation for each of the group and organizational reasons for resisting change identified in Figure 19.3.

   This is a straightforward question and requires students to reiterate material from the book with some degree of elaboration and their own understanding reflected in the descriptions used.

9. 'The true skill in management is to keep change happening so that everyone has to pay attention to what they are doing and they do not have any spare time to cause trouble for managers.' Discuss this statement.

   This question attempts to draw out from students the political perspectives on change. The statement might at first glance appear to be a way of offering managers the opportunity to keep employees busy and thereby avoid problems, but at what cost? The dangers and costs associated with change are such that for most managers the real or potential disruption would be worse than that caused by employees under all but the most extreme cases. Students would be expected to be able to recognize this aspect of the questions and respond accordingly.

Student exercise

On this occasion you are required to consider the notion of change as experienced in an organizational context as compared to that experienced by every human being as a child.

From birth every child undergoes a dramatic and continual change process that lasts for many years as development into adult human being takes place. Consider very young children and the rate of change that they experience as they learn to crawl, walk, as well as speak and communicate with their parents and other children. Very quickly they are able to influence events around them and frequently learn how to get their own way by a mixture of tears and smiles (punishment and rewards?). Every time a child learns a new skill they are desperate to practice it, show it off to other people and to learn a more advanced form or even new skills.

Consider by comparison adults working in an organization. Change is feared, resisted and regarded as a threat. It is not often regarded as welcome, a challenge, or the chance to enhance or develop new skills. Even with the techniques discussed in the text achieving change in an organization is a difficult, time-consuming and risky process. Not all change processes are successful, and many only partially so.

Consider these two different descriptions. Both involve human beings. Yet in the process of becoming an adult something changes the approach to change. Is it the education system that teaches people to expect predictability and certainty through the teaching methods used and subjects taught? Is it the experience of work and life which teaches people that humans outside of the family are not to be trusted and might do harm to the individual? Is it the way that managers treat the subject of change, using it as a lever through which to settle old scores or force people to do what managers want? What can managers learn about change and how to introduce it from thinking about human development and the ways that children learn in their early years?

Research and discuss these issues in groups of six. Prepare a short presentation for the rest of your class on your conclusions and your reasons. Be prepared to answer questions from your classmates and to defend your ideas.

OHP masters for the main figures

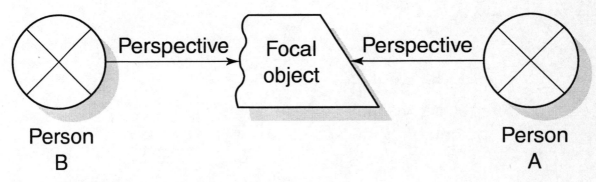

Figure 1.3 Different perceptions of the same focal object.

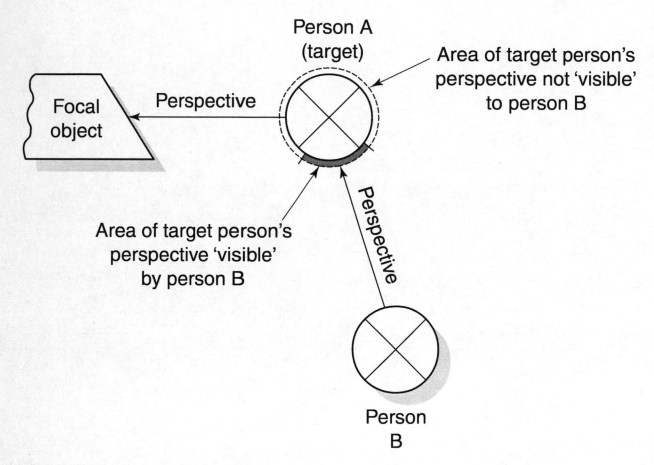

Figure 1.4 Understanding the perspectives of others.

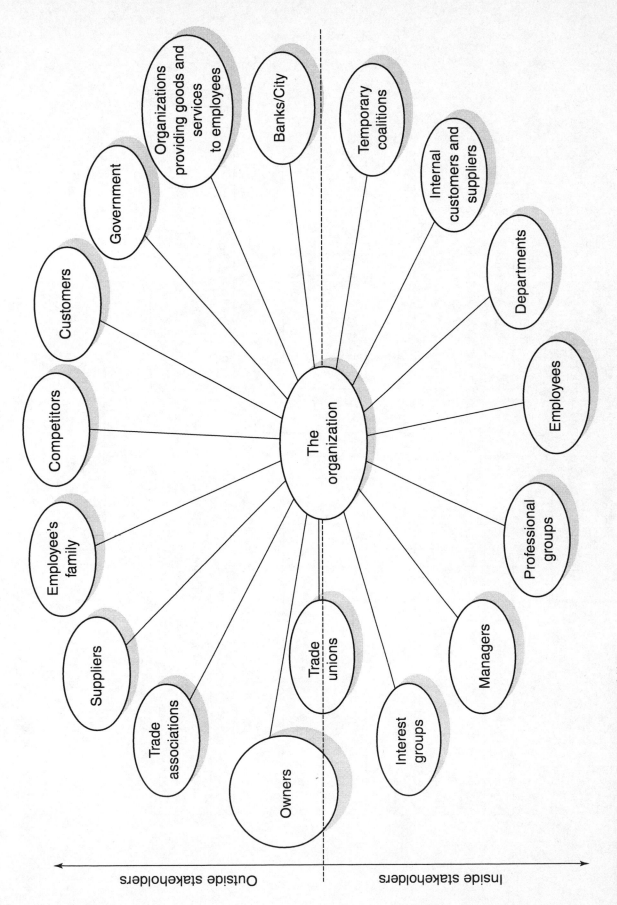

Figure 1.7 Major influences on management activities.

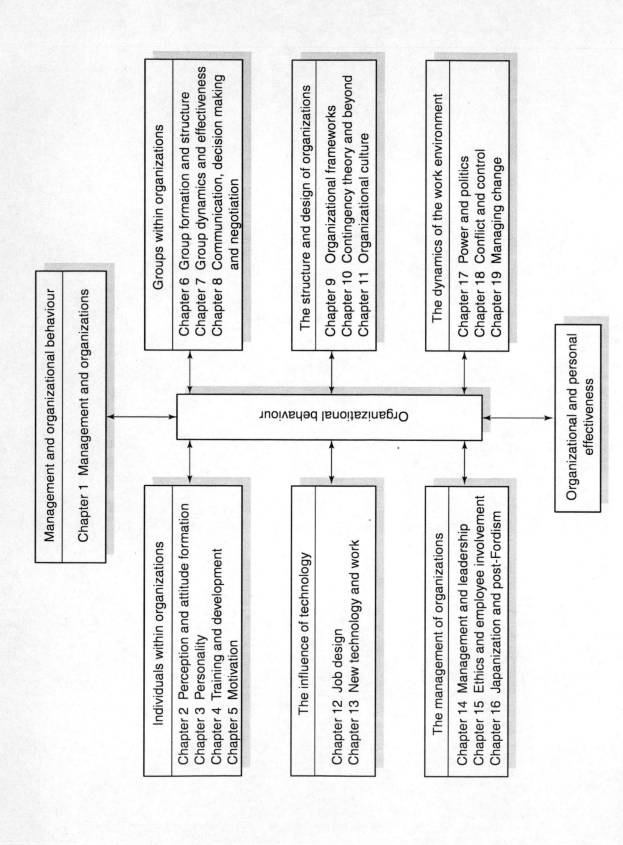

Management and organizational behaviour

Chapter 1 Management and organizations

Individuals within organizations

Chapter 2 Perception and attitude formation
Chapter 3 Personality
Chapter 4 Training and development
Chapter 5 Motivation

Groups within organizations

Chapter 6 Group formation and structure
Chapter 7 Group dynamics and effectiveness
Chapter 8 Communication, decision making and negotiation

The influence of technology

Chapter 12 Job design
Chapter 13 New technology and work

The structure and design of organizations

Chapter 9 Organizational frameworks
Chapter 10 Contingency theory and beyond
Chapter 11 Organizational culture

The management of organizations

Chapter 14 Management and leadership
Chapter 15 Ethics and employee involvement
Chapter 16 Japanization and post-Fordism

The dynamics of the work environment

Chapter 17 Power and politics
Chapter 18 Conflict and control
Chapter 19 Managing change

Organizational behaviour

Organizational and personal effectiveness

Figure 1.8 Organizational behaviour framework.

Figure 2.1   Ambiguous figure (originally published by Hill, WE (1915) *Punch*, 6 November).

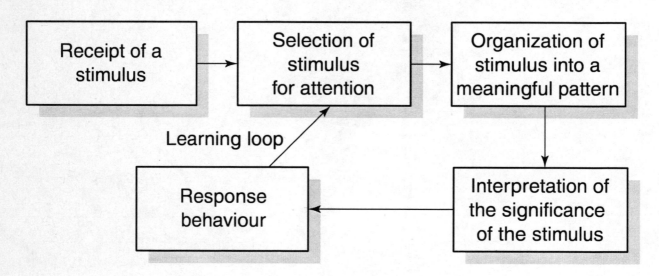

Figure 2.2 The perceptual process.

Figure 2.8 Reversible figures.

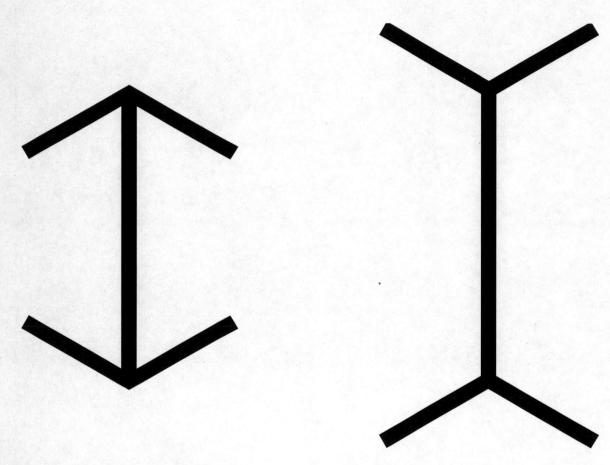

Figure 2.12 The Müller–Lyer illusion.

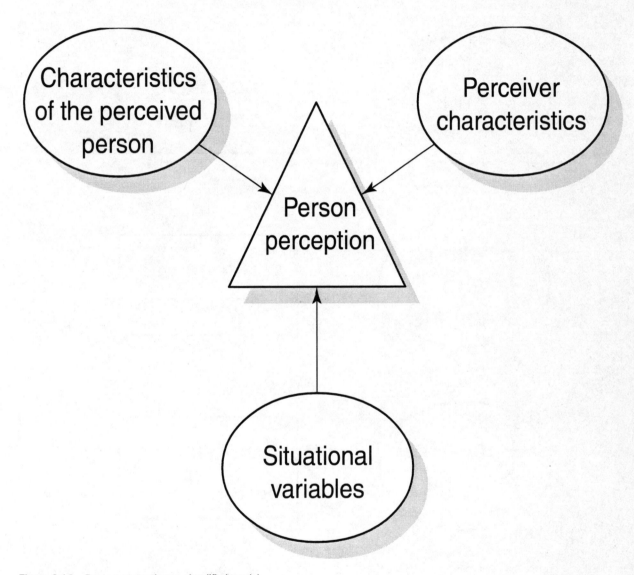

Figure 2.14   Person perception: a simplified model.

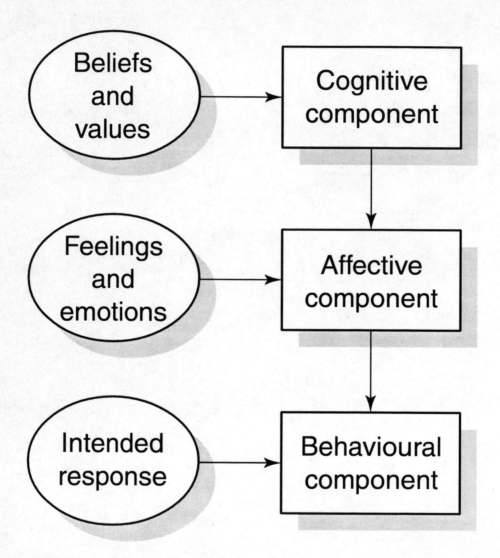

Figure 2.15 Construction of an attitude.

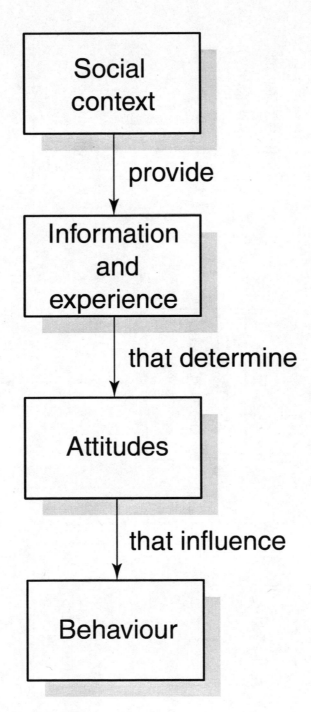

Figure 2.16 Situational construction of attitudes.

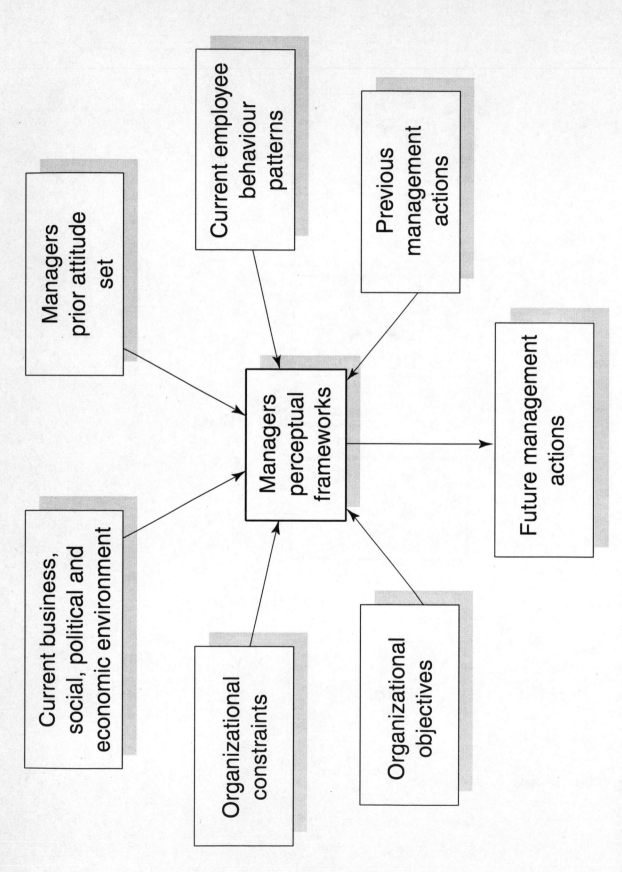

Figure 2.19 Managers perceptions and the impact on subsequent actions.

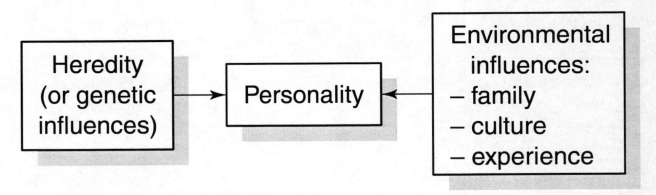

Figure 3.1 Relationship between the determinants of personality.

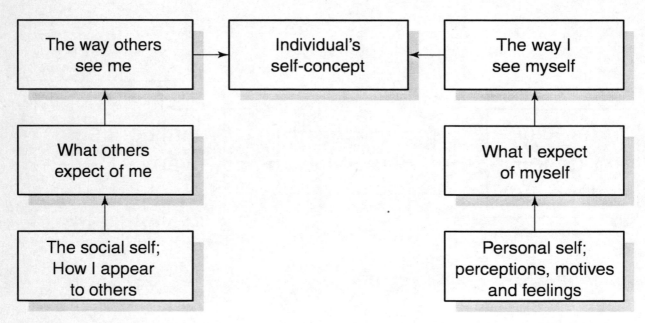

Figure 3.5 Rogers view of the 'I' and 'me'.

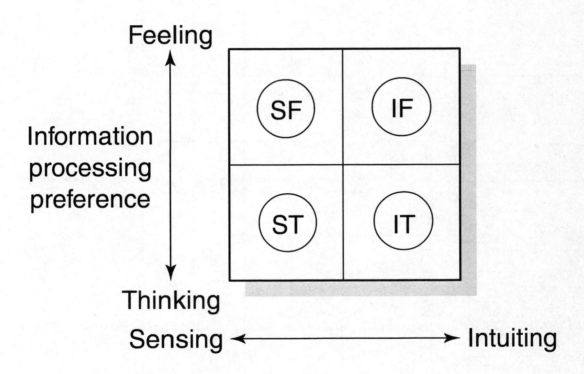

Figure 3.6 Jung's cognitive styles.

Significant people

Constructs	Self	Father	Mother	Brother	Friend A	Friend B	
Loving	1	1	1	0	0	1	Cold
Friendly	1	0	1	1	0	1	Unfriendly
Trustworthy	1	1	1	1	1	1	Untrustworthy
Helpful	1	0	1	0	1	0	Unhelpful
Like me	1	0	0	0	1	1	Not like me

Figure 3.9 Simplified repertory grid.

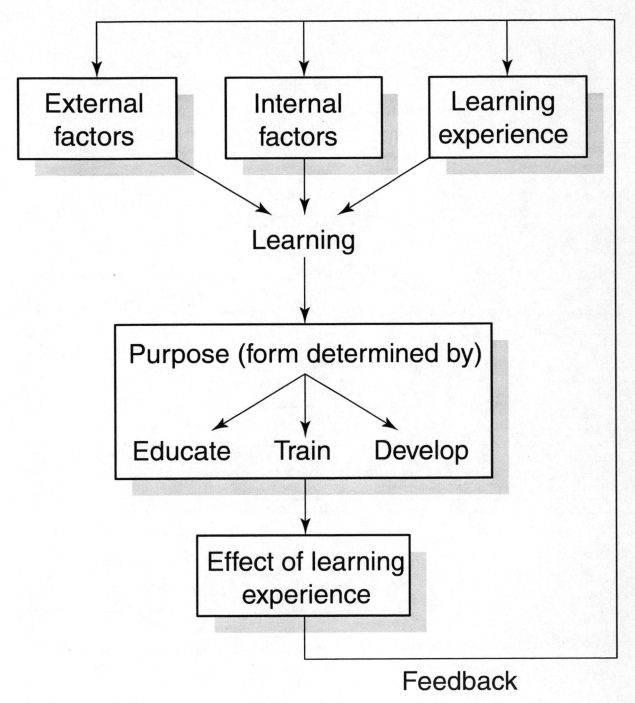

Figure 4.1 The learning process.

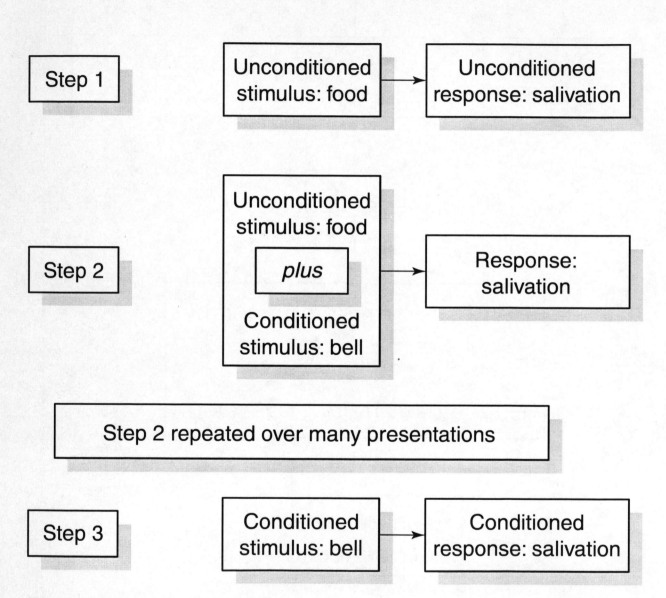

Figure 4.2 Pavlov's classical conditioning model.

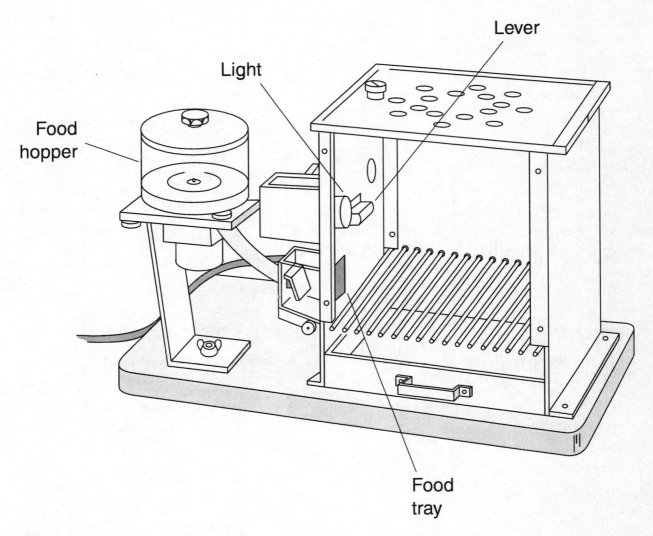

Figure 4.3 A Skinner box.

	Stimulus given	Stimulus taken away
Pleasant stimulus	Positive reinforcement	Omission
Unpleasant stimulus	Punishment	Negative reinforcement

Figure 4.4 Reinforcement framework.

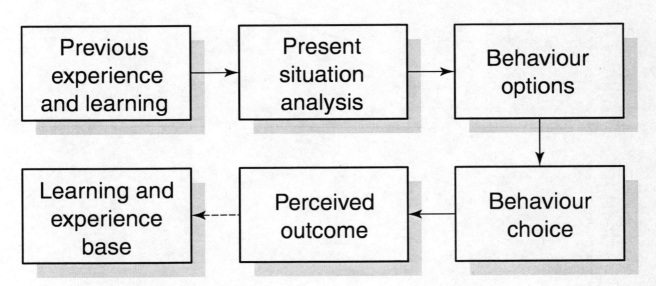

Figure 4.6 A cognitive model of learning.

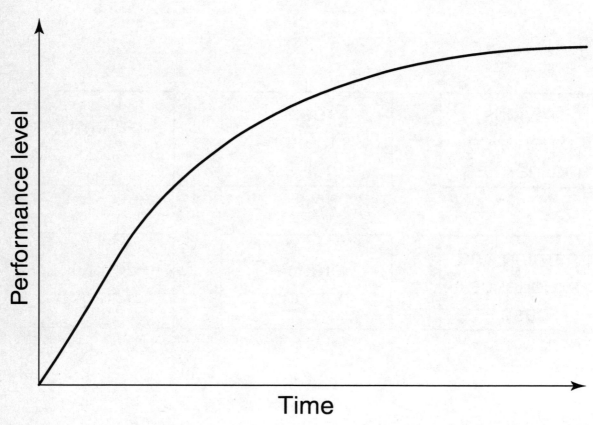

Figure 4.10 The learning curve.

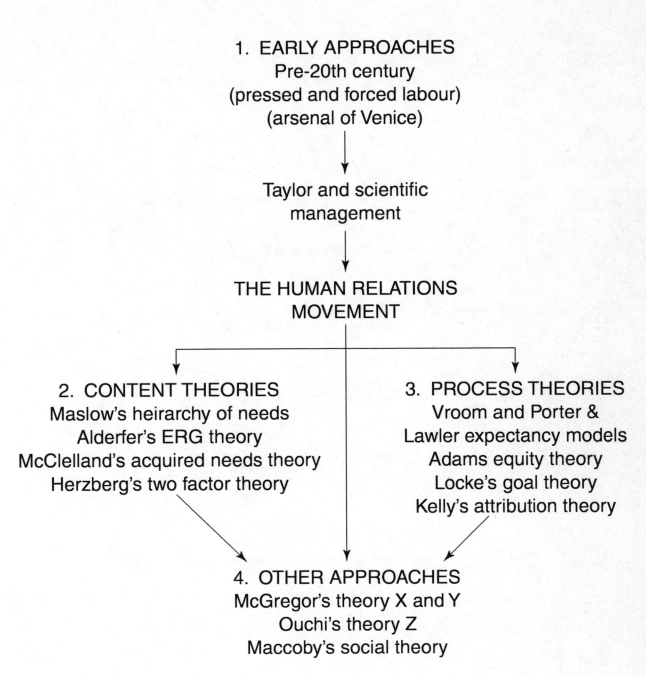

Figure 5.1 Evolution of motivation theory.

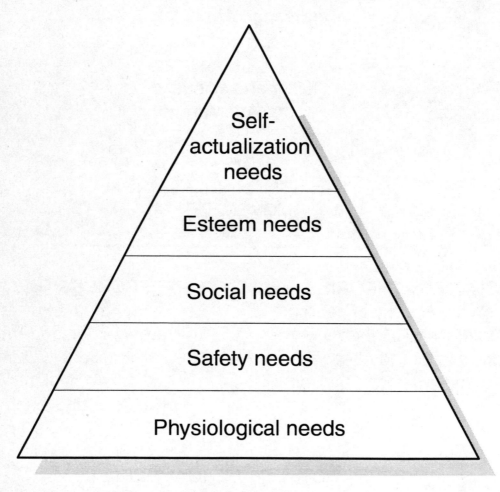

Figure 5.2 Maslow's hierarchy of needs.

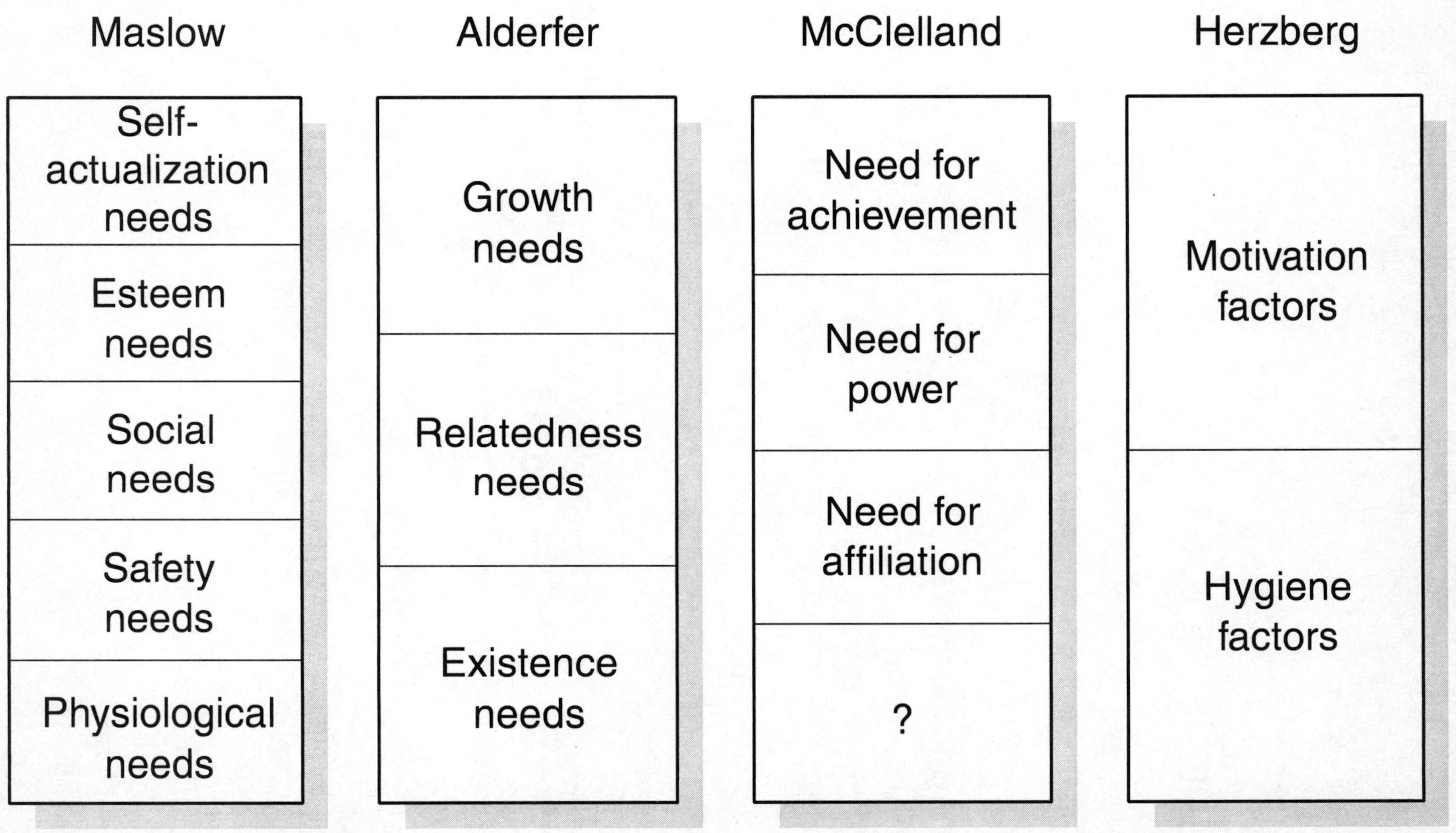

Maslow	Alderfer	McClelland	Herzberg
Self-actualization needs	Growth needs	Need for achievement	Motivation factors
Esteem needs		Need for power	
Social needs	Relatedness needs	Need for affiliation	Hygiene factors
Safety needs	Existence needs	?	
Physiological needs			

Figure 5.4 Comparison between the need theories.

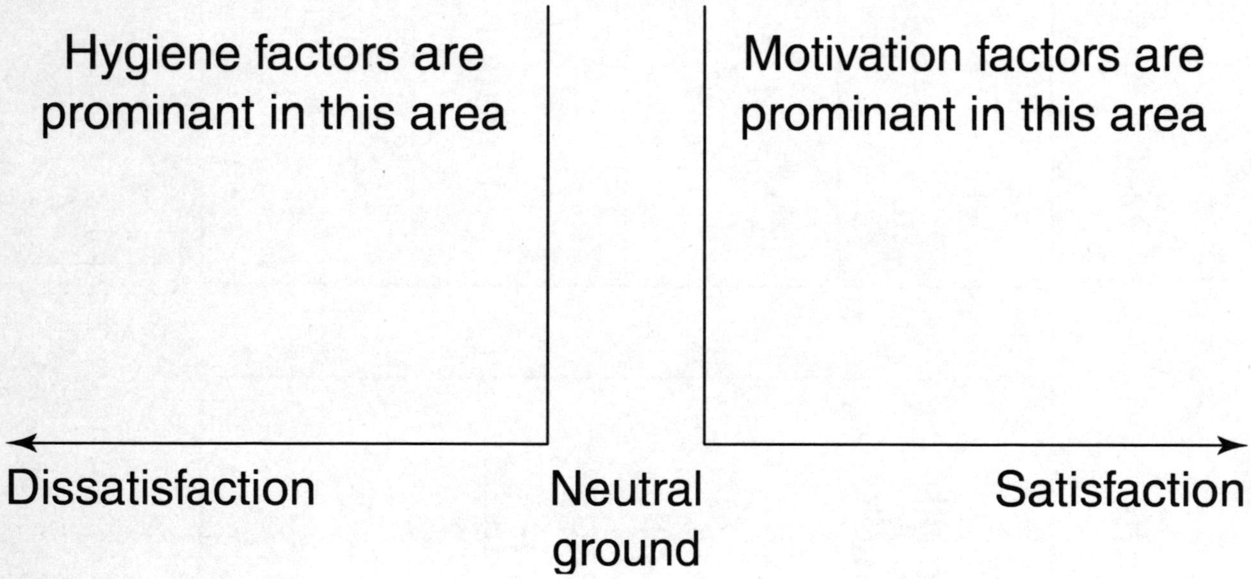

Hygiene factors are prominant in this area

Motivation factors are prominant in this area

← Dissatisfaction

Neutral ground

Satisfaction →

Figure 5.5 Satisfaction and Herzberg's two factors.

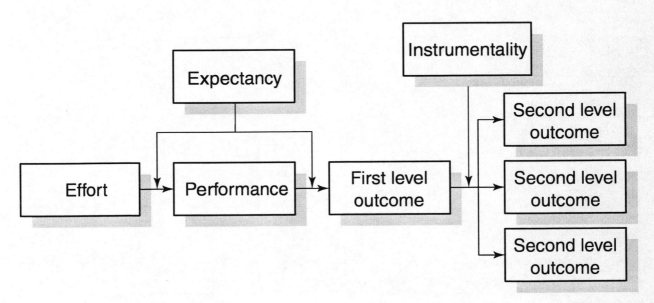

Figure 5.6 Vroom's expectancy model.

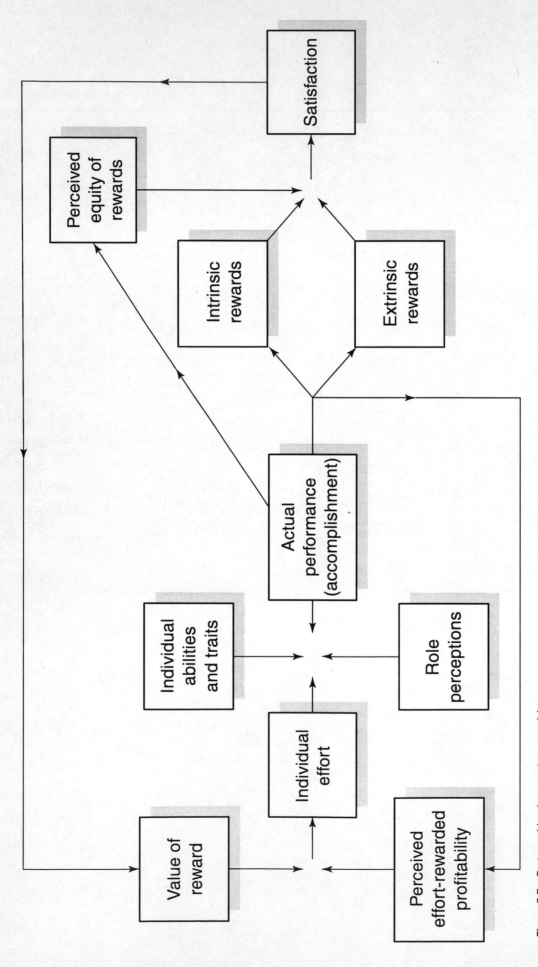

Figure 5.7 Porter and Lawler expectancy model.

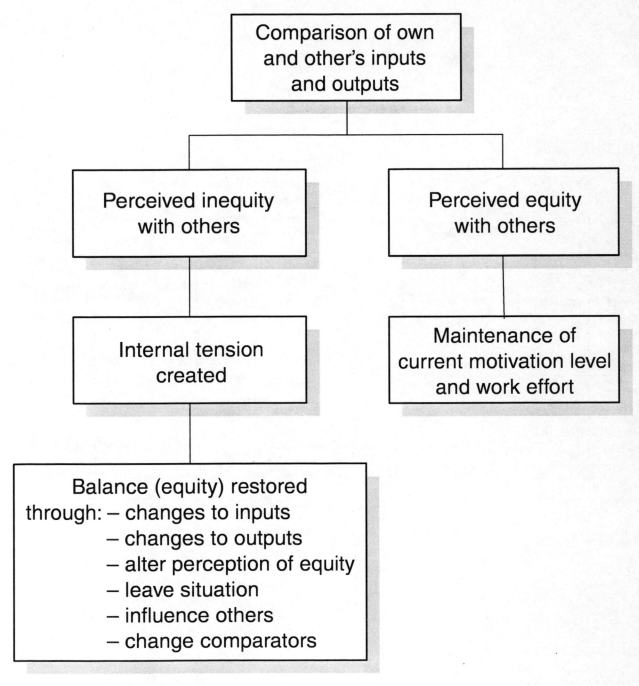

Figure 5.8 Adams' equity theory.

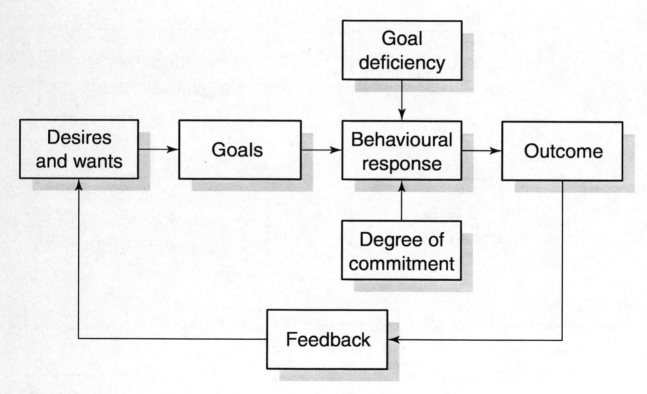

Figure 5.9 Goal theory.

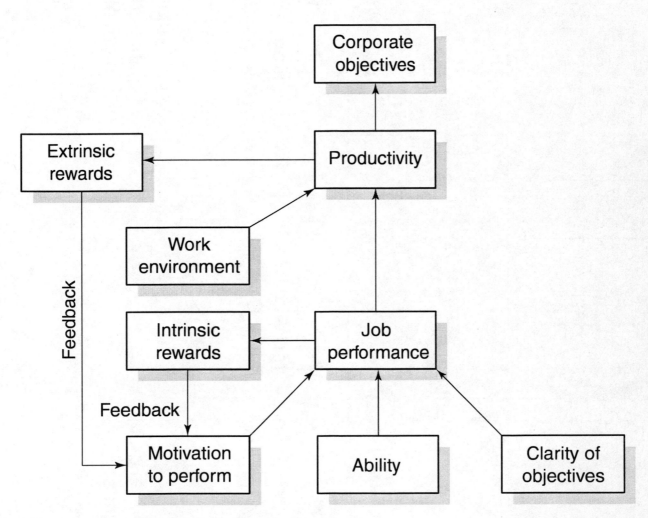

Figure 5.11 The links between motivation performing and rewards.

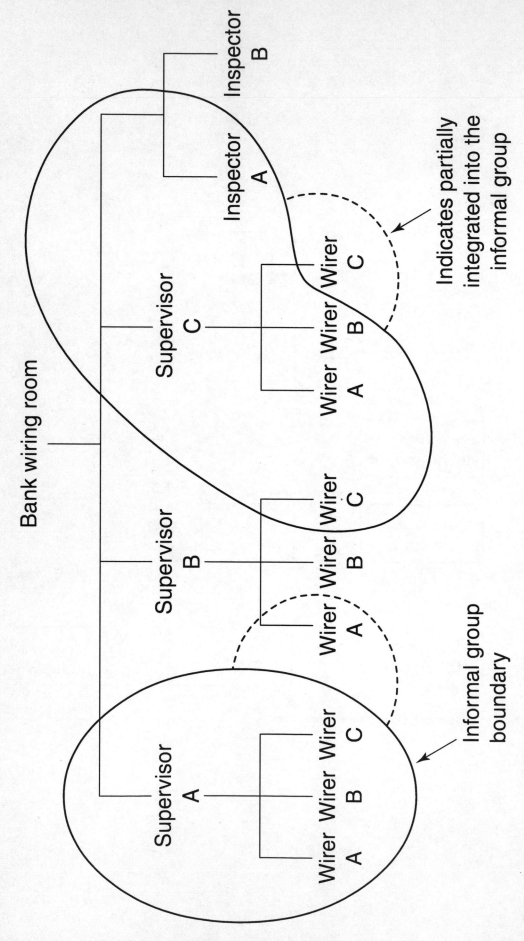

Figure 6.2 Formal structure and informal groups within the bank wiring observation room.

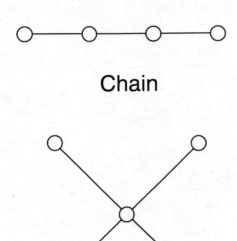

Chain

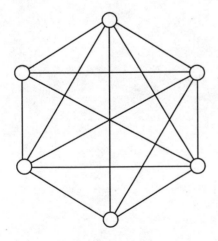

Wheel

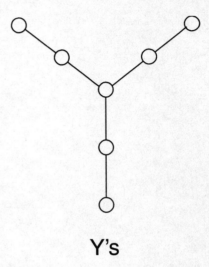

Y's

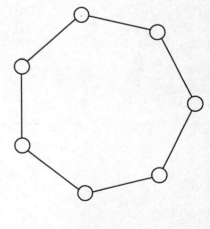

All channel

Circle

Figure 7.1 Communication patterns.

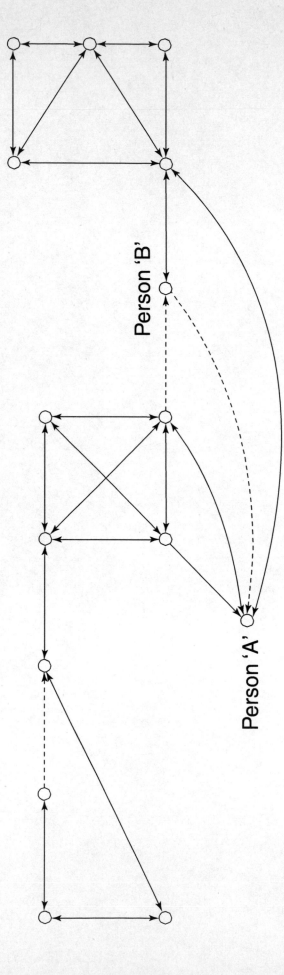

Figure 7.2 Example of a sociogram.

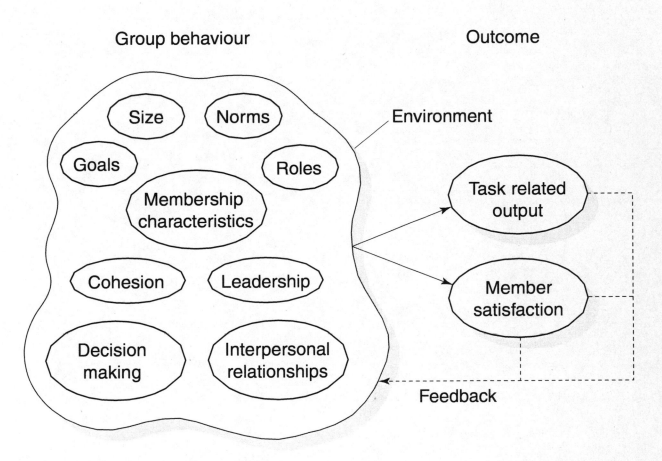

Figure 7.5 Determinants of dynamic activity within groups.

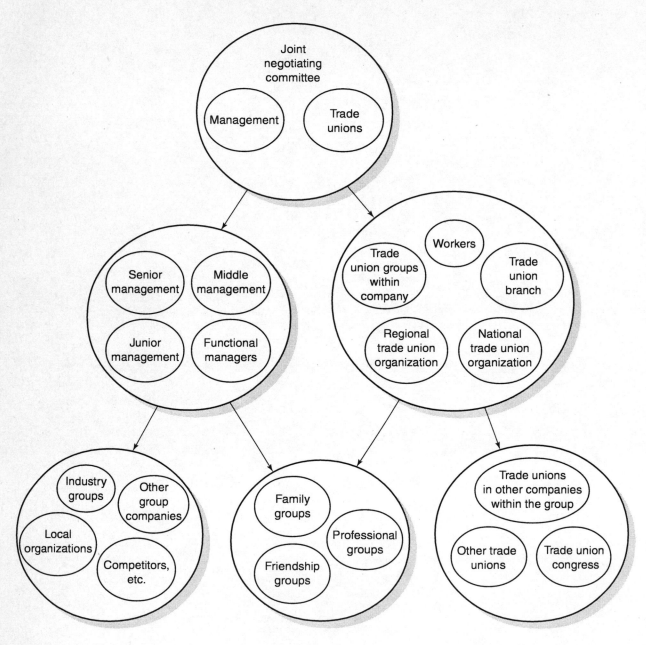

Figure 7.7 The group hierarchy.

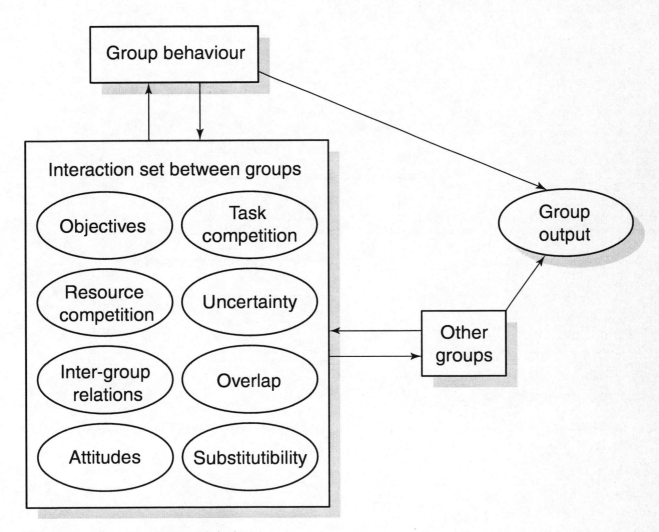

Figure 7.8 Influences on intergroup behaviour.

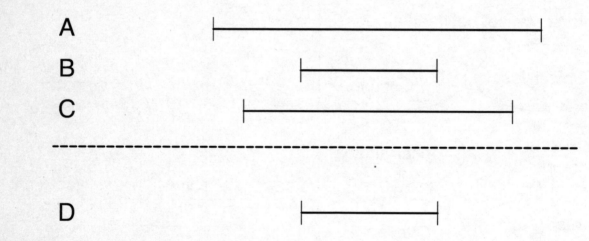

Figure 7.10 Diagram similar to that used by Asch.

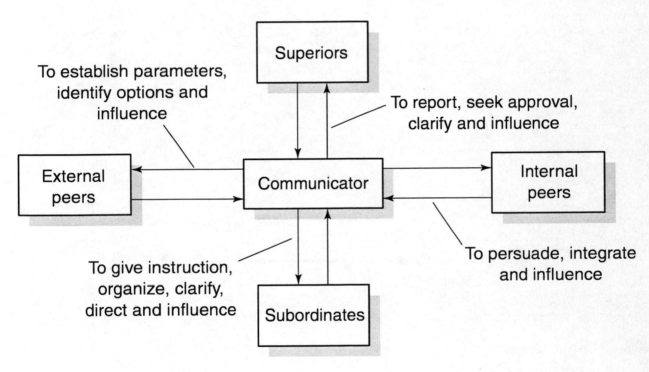

Figure 8.1 Organizational communications.

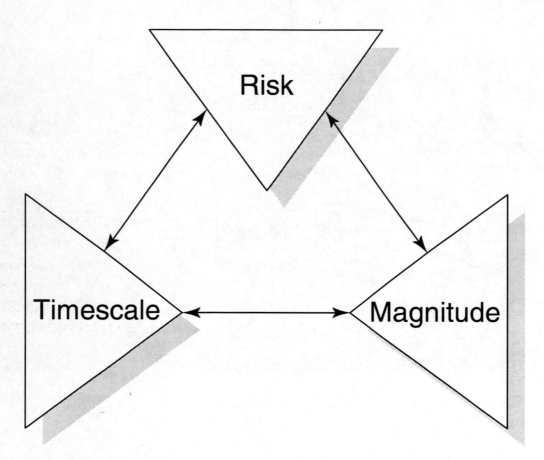

Figure 8.3 Dimensions of decision making.

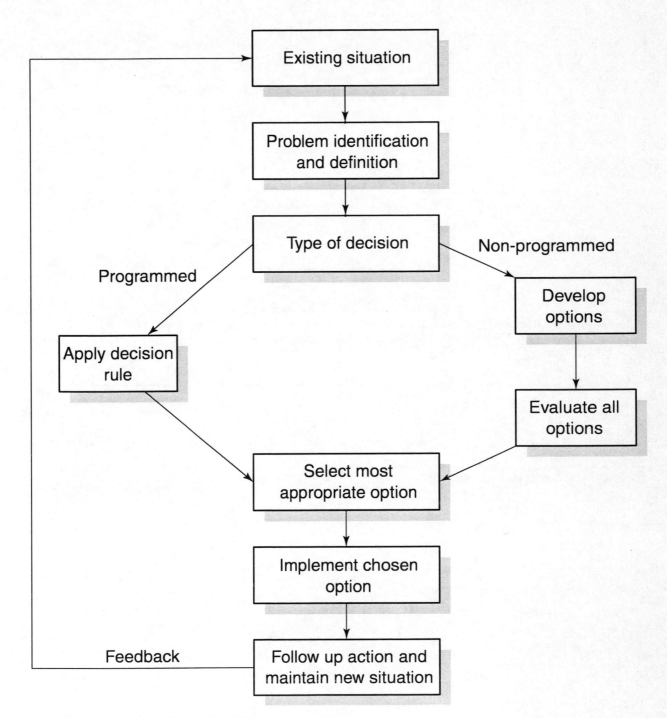

Figure 8.10 Pragmatic decision making model.

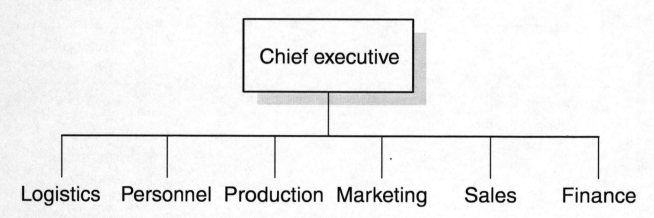

Figure 9.1   Functional organization structure.

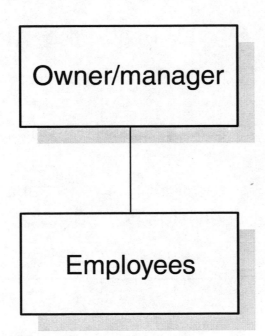

Figure 9.3 Entrepreneurial organization structure.

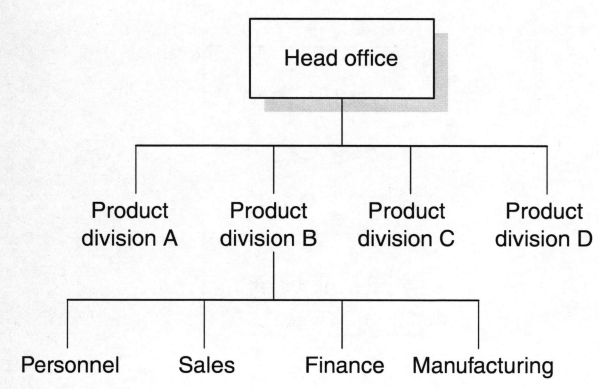

Figure 9.5 Product structure.

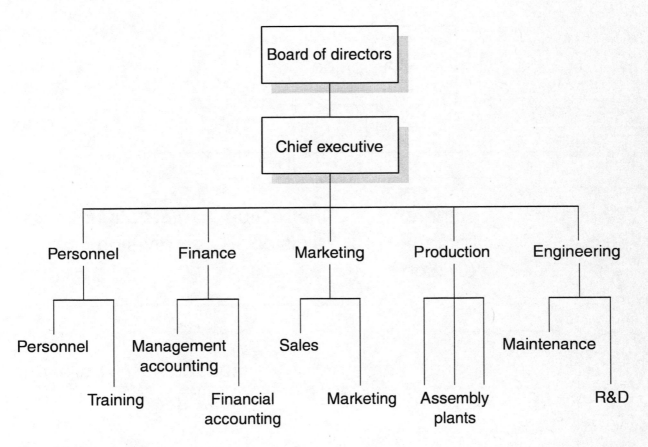

Figure 9.6 Process structure.

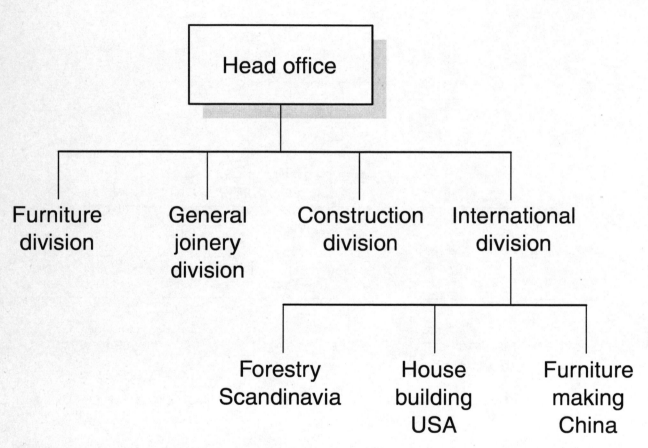

Figure 9.7 International operations as separate division.

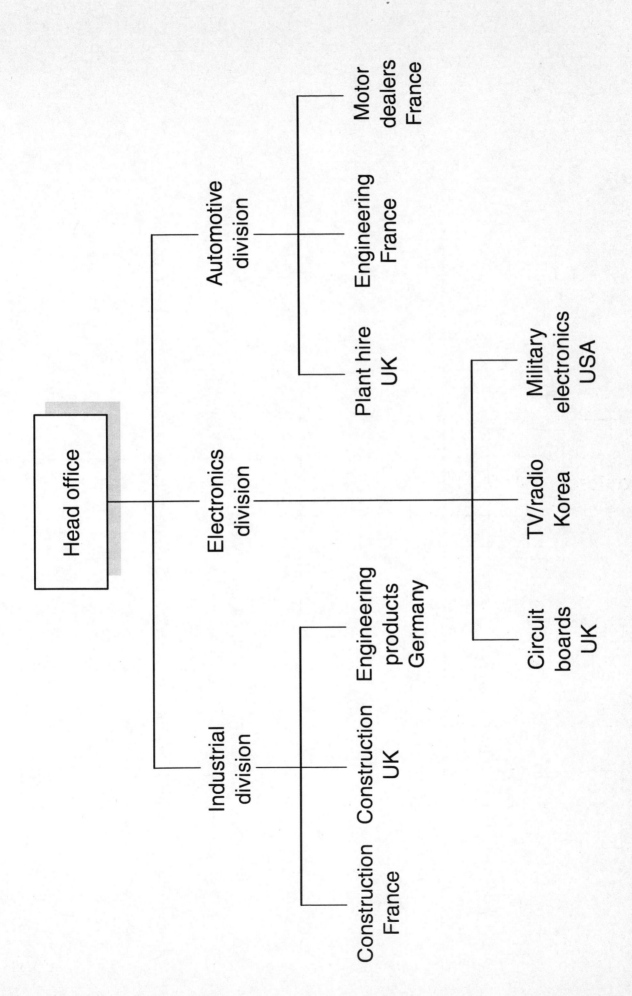

Figure 9.8 Product-based international operations.

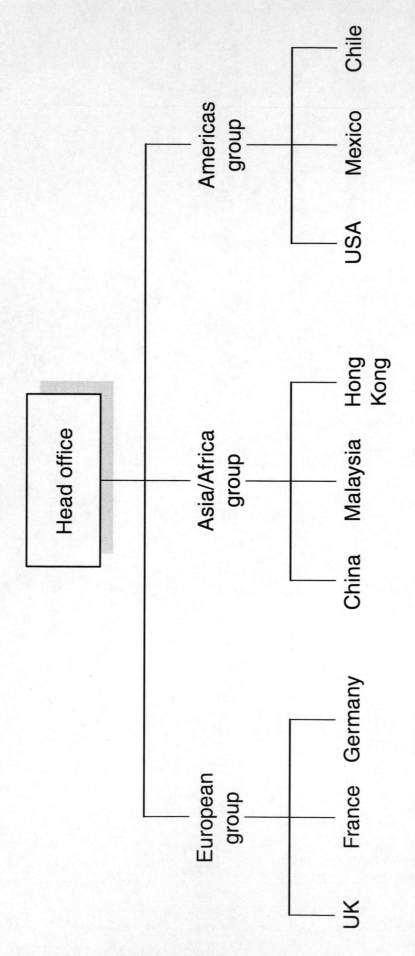

Note: There would be a differing range of business units within each country.

Figure 9.9 Geographic-based international operations.

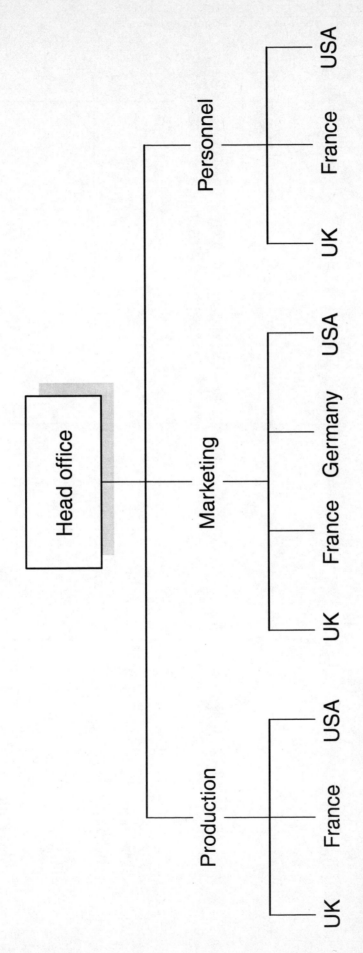

Figure 9.10 Functional basis for international operations.

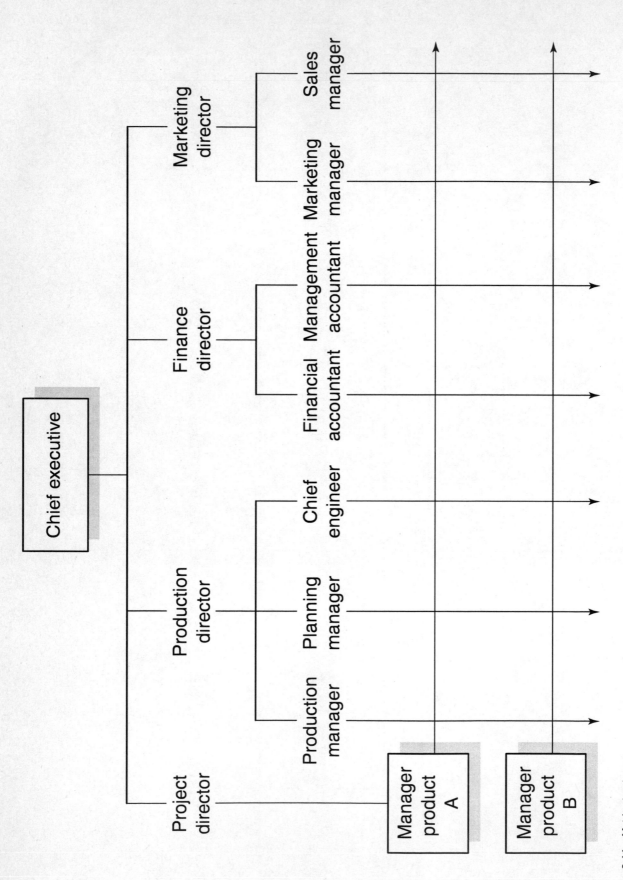

Figure 9.11 Matrix structure.

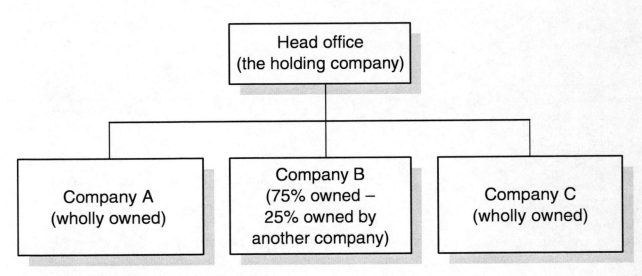

Figure 9.12   Holding company framework.

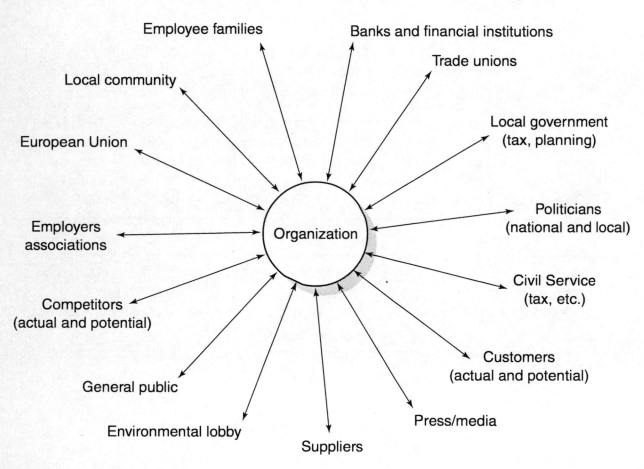

Figure 10.5 Organizational environments.

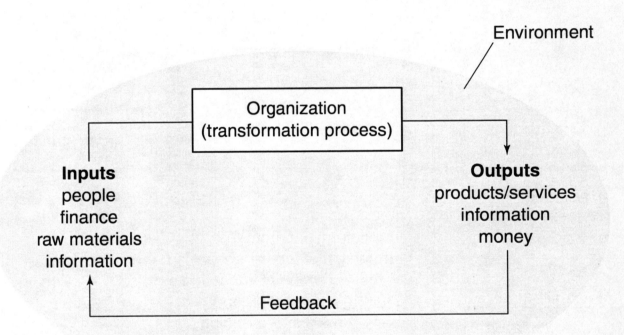

Figure 10.6 An open systems model of an organization.

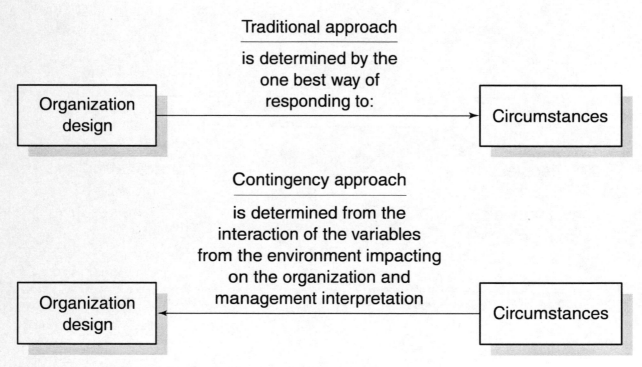

Figure 10.7 Traditional and contingency approaches to organizational design.

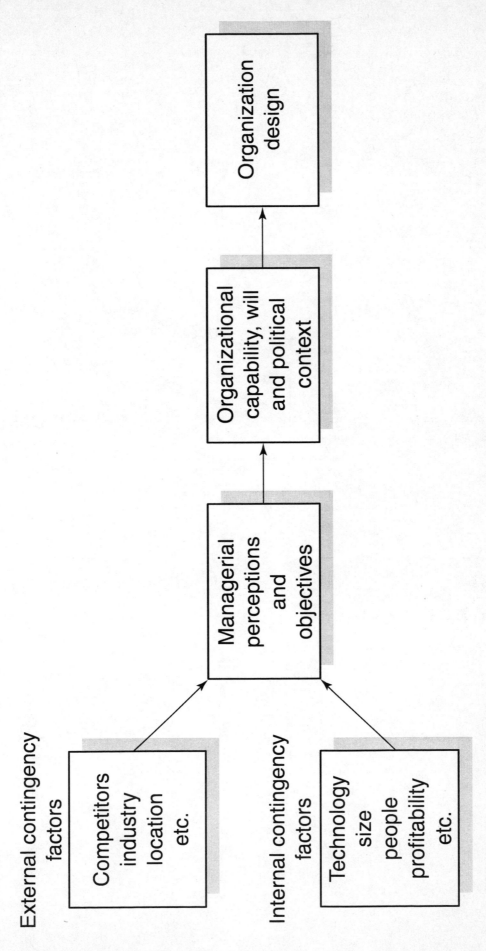

Figure 10.8 Contingency model of organization design.

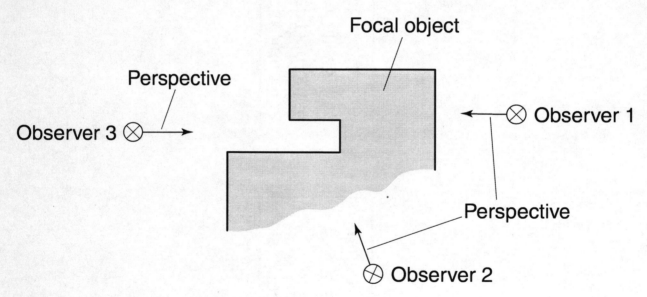

Figure 10.9 Multiple perspectives of an object.

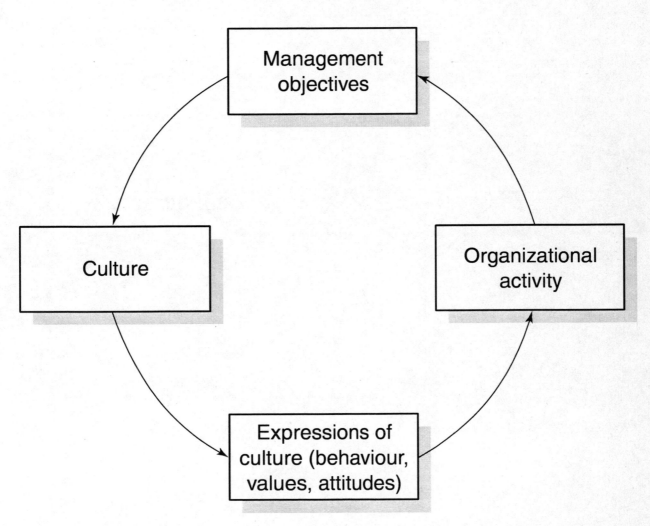

Figure 11.2 The cycle of culture.

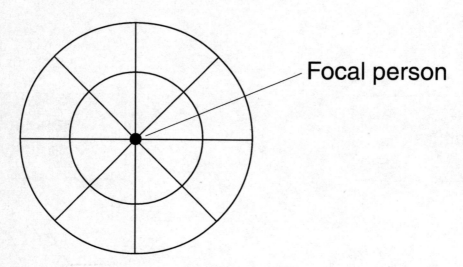

Figure 11.3　Power culture.

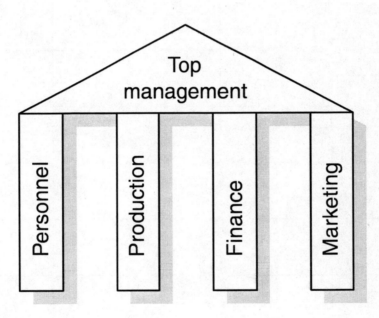

Figure 11.4 Role culture.

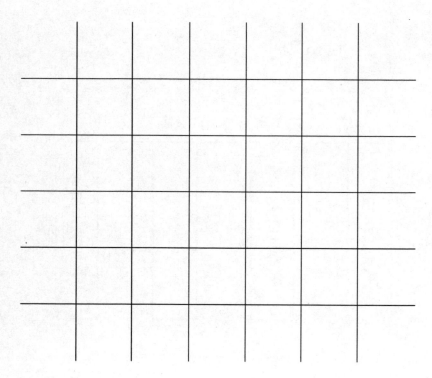

Figure 11.5 Task culture.

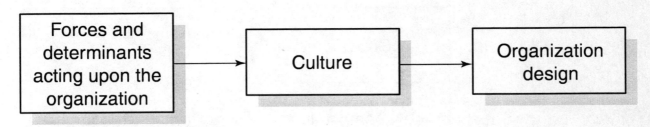

Figure 11.6 Culture as a design mediator.

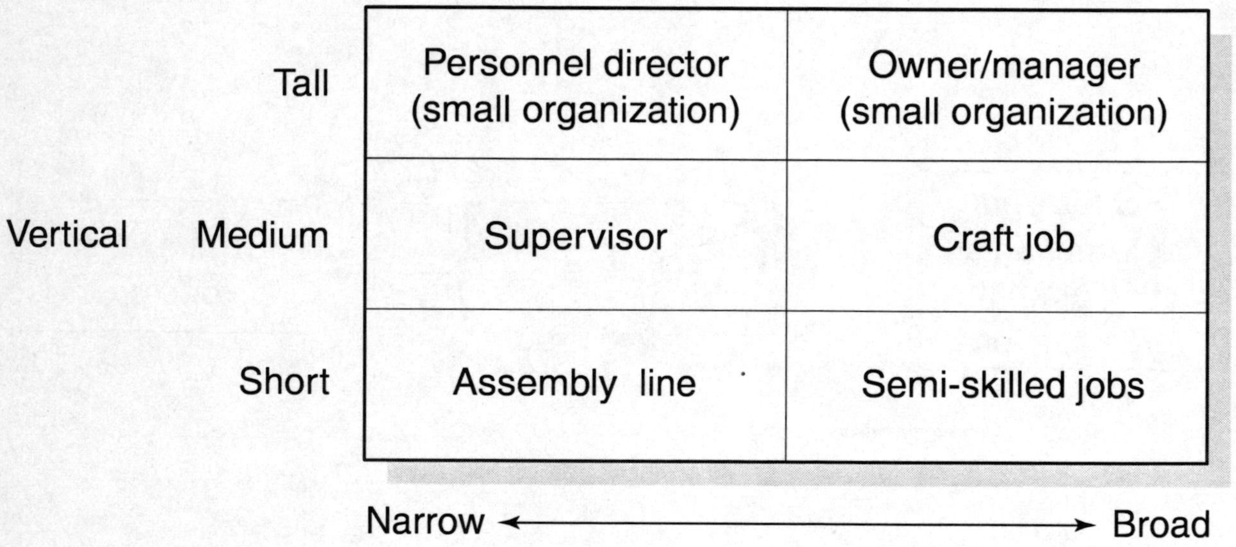

		Narrow ←	→ Broad
	Tall	Personnel director (small organization)	Owner/manager (small organization)
Vertical	Medium	Supervisor	Craft job
	Short	Assembly line	Semi-skilled jobs

Narrow ←——————————————→ Broad

Figure 12.1 Job dimensions.

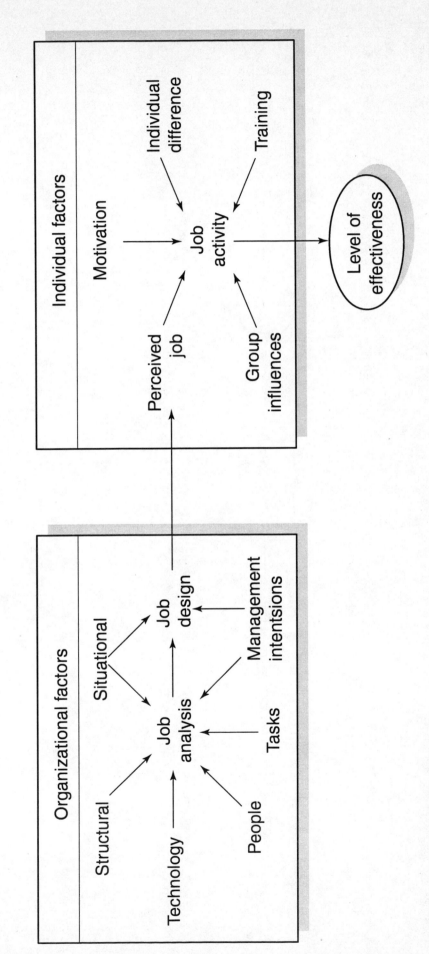

Figure 12.4 Job analysis and job effectiveness.

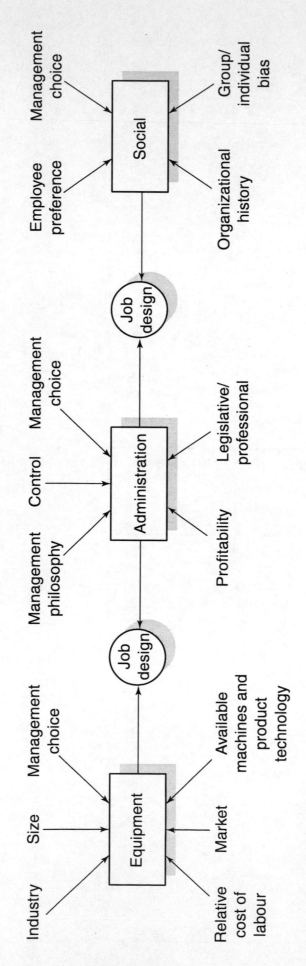

Figure 12.5   Technological influences on job design.

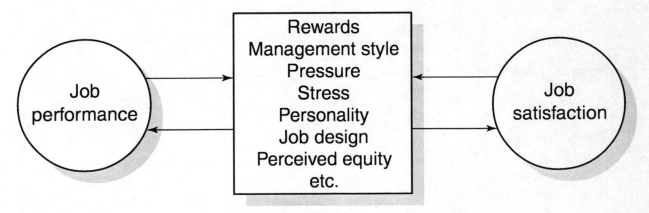

Figure 12.7 Relationship between performance and satisfaction.

Figure 12.8 Factors influencing job design.

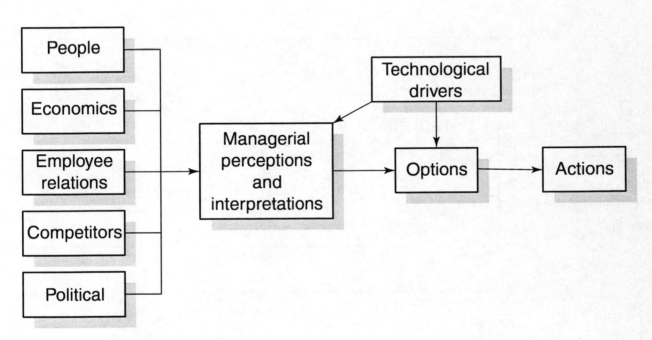

Figure 13.1 Technological choice and decision making.

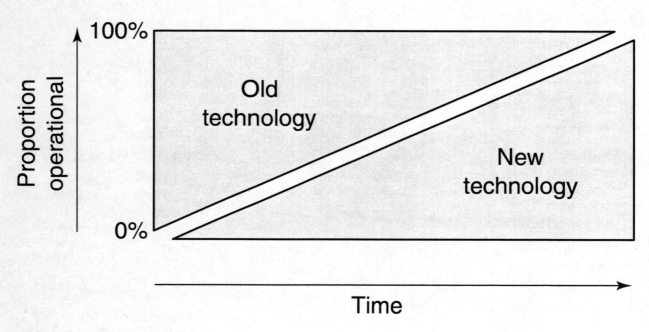

Figure 13.3 Technology transfer.

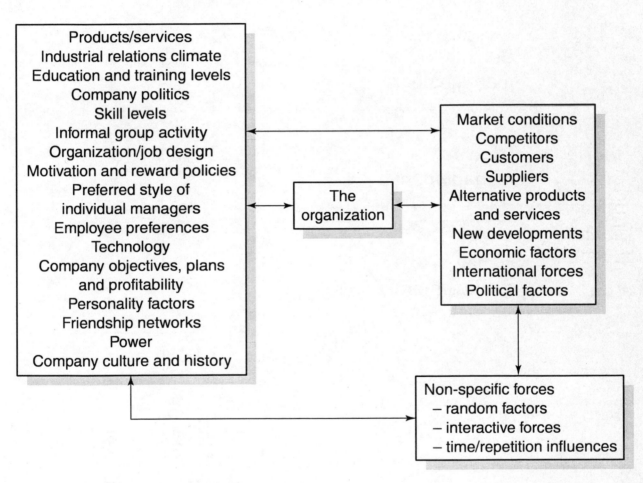

Figure 14.1 The complexity of the management environment.

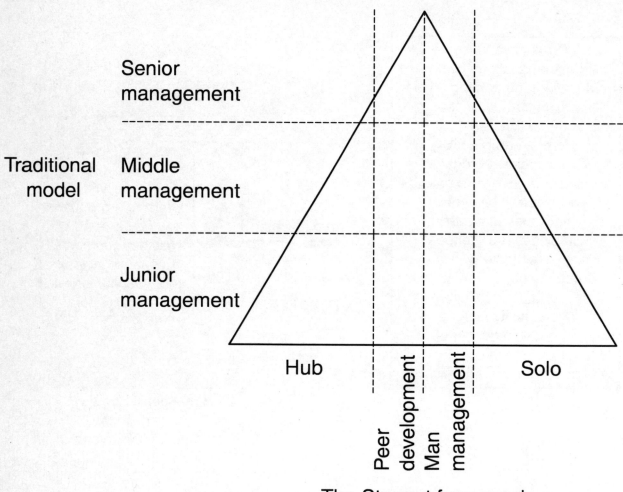

Figure 14.2 The management job matrix.

Leader/member relations	Good				Poor			
Task structure	Structured		Unstructured		Structured		Unstructured	
Position power	High	Low	High	Low	High	Low	High	Low
Situational favourableness	Very favourable			Moderately favourable			Very unfavourable	
Recommended leader behaviour	Task-oriented behaviour			Person-oriented behaviour			Task-oriented behaviour	

Figure 14.9 Fiedler's contingency model of leadership.

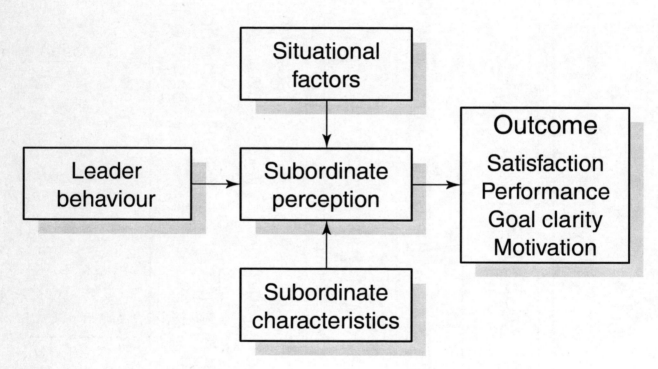

Figure 14.10 Path–goal model of leadership.

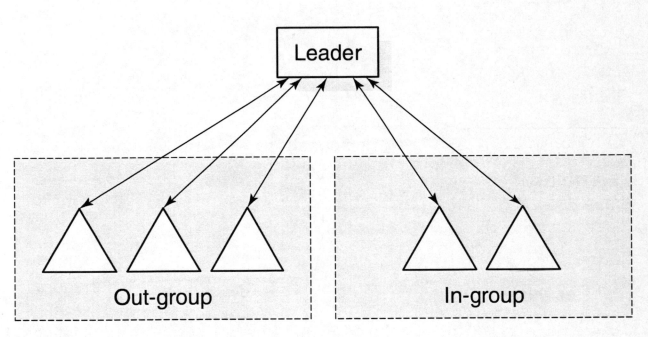

Figure 14.11 The vertical dyad model of leadership.

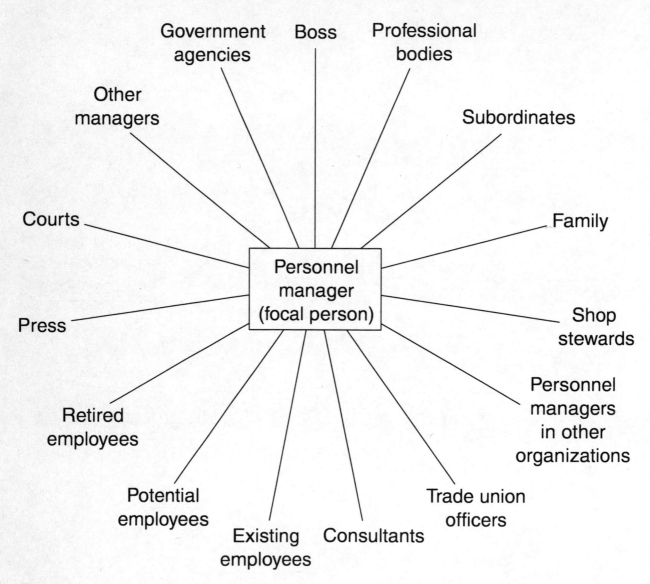

Figure 14.12 Role set of a personnel manager.

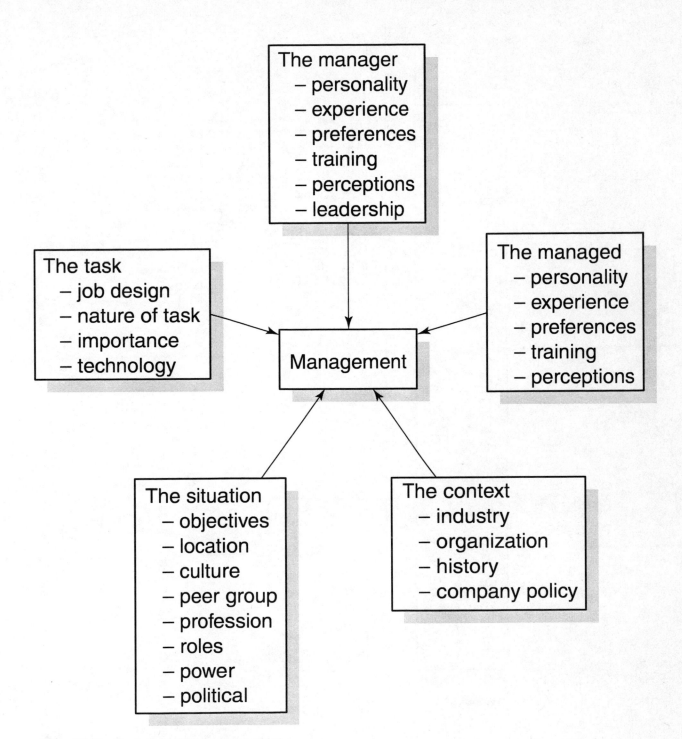

Figure 14.15 The factors influencing management.

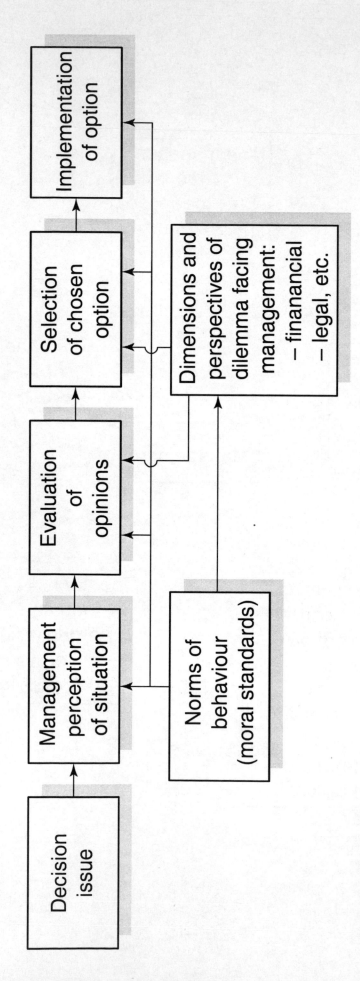

Figure 15.2 Hosmer's ethical model applied to a rational decision-making process.

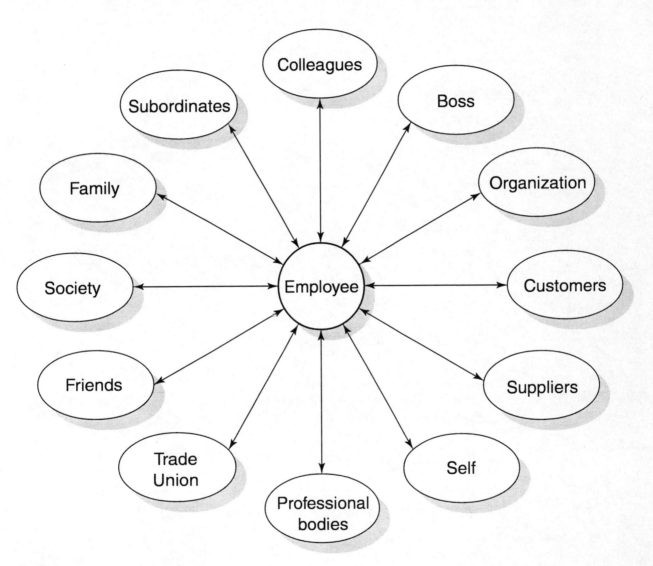

Figure 15.4 Employee obligation map.

Figure 15.5   The wheel of people role determinants within organizations.

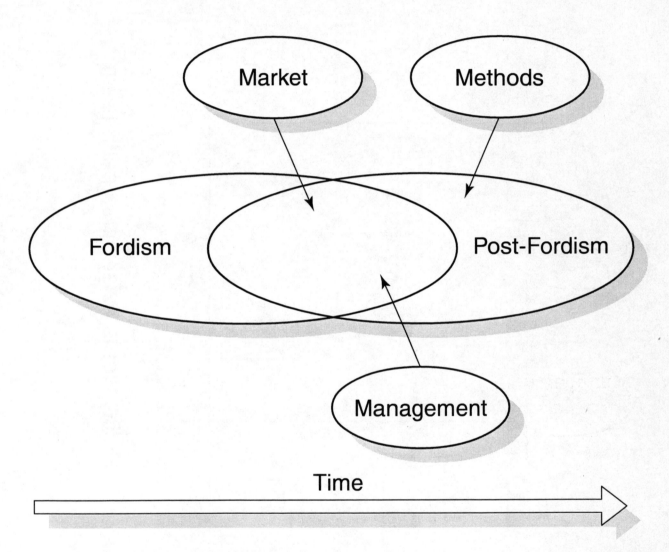

Figure 16.1 The evidence of post-Fordism.

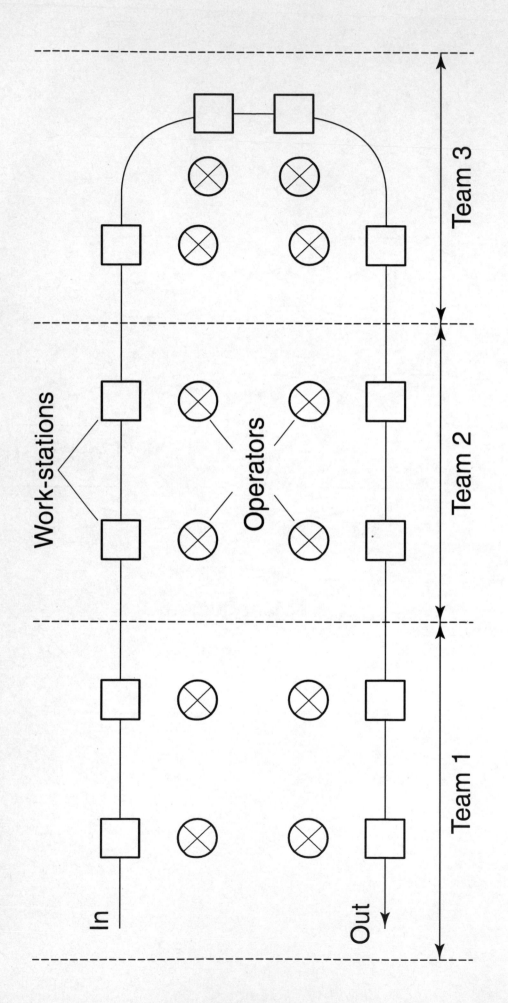

Figure 16.2 'U'-shaped assembly line production.

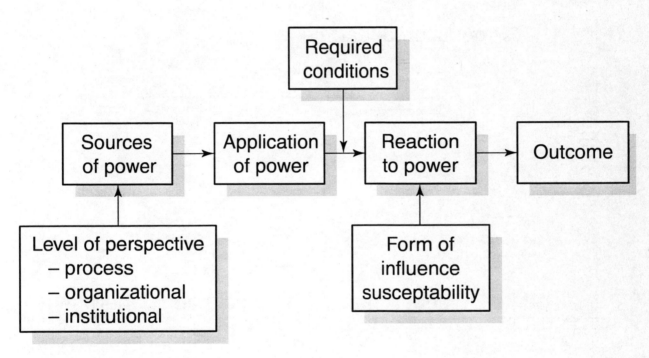

Figure 17.1 Contingency model of power.

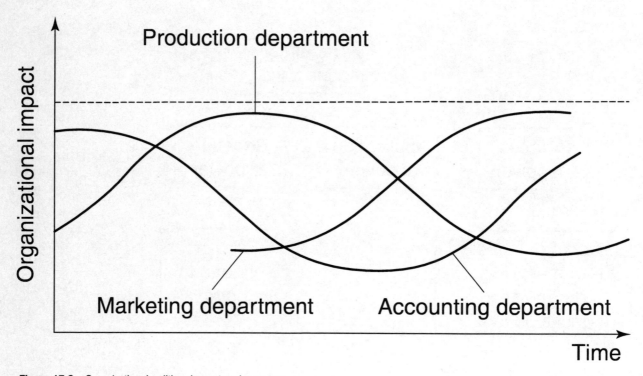

Figure 17.2 Organizational politics: impact and success.

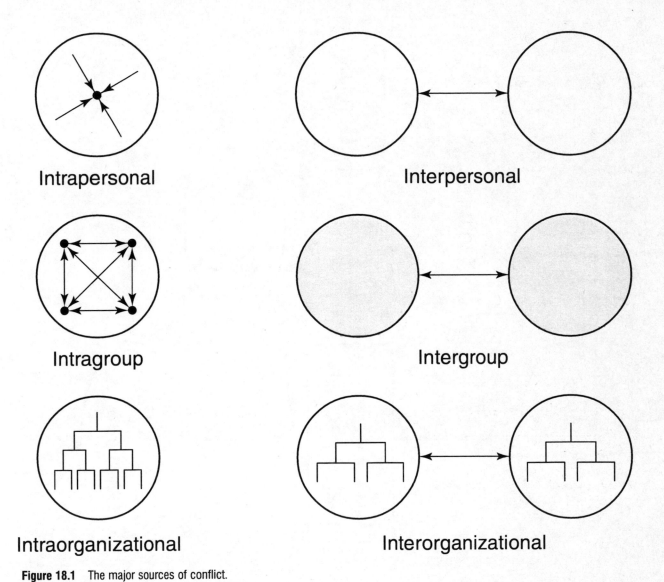

Figure 18.1 The major sources of conflict.

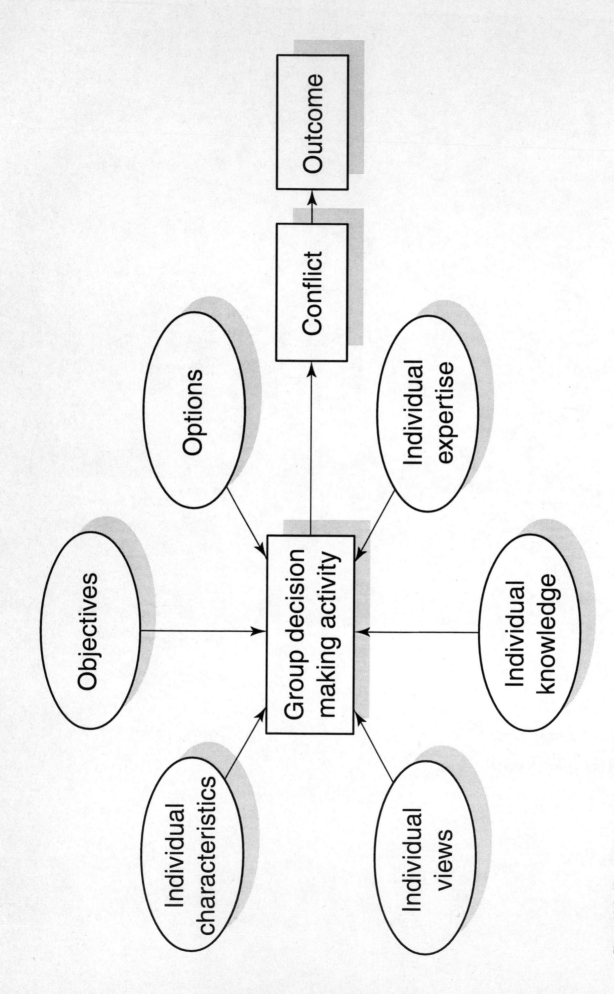

Figure 18.2 Group decision making and conflict.

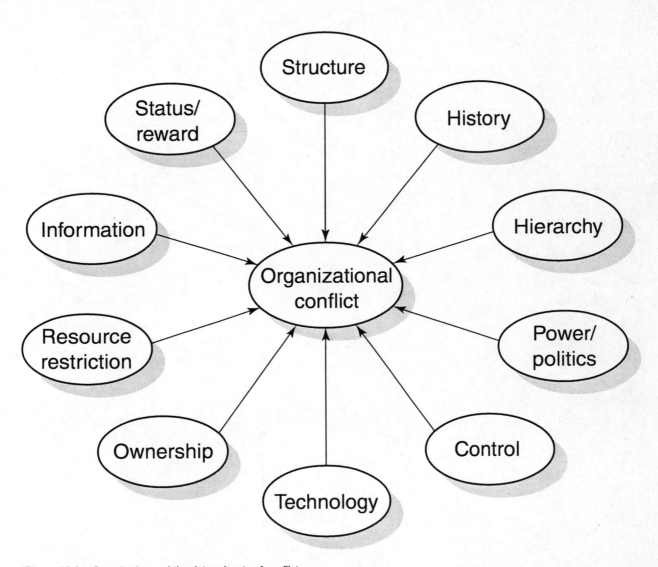

Figure 18.3 Organization and the determinants of conflict.

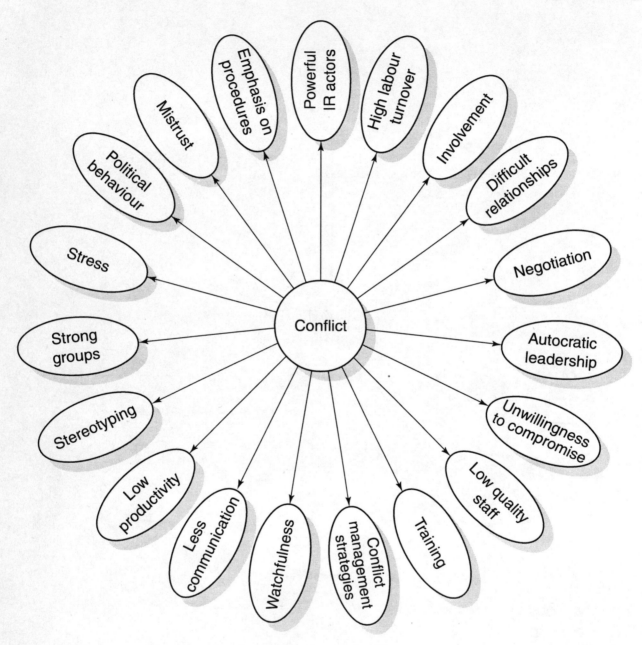

Figure 18.5   Some consequences of conflict.

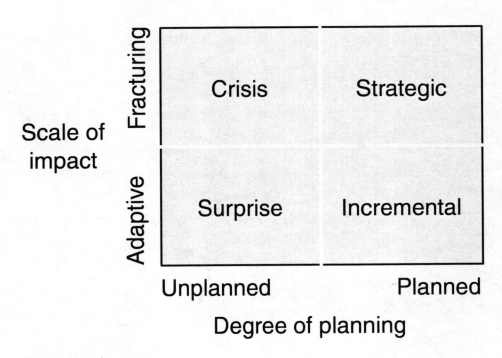

Figure 19.1 The change matrix.

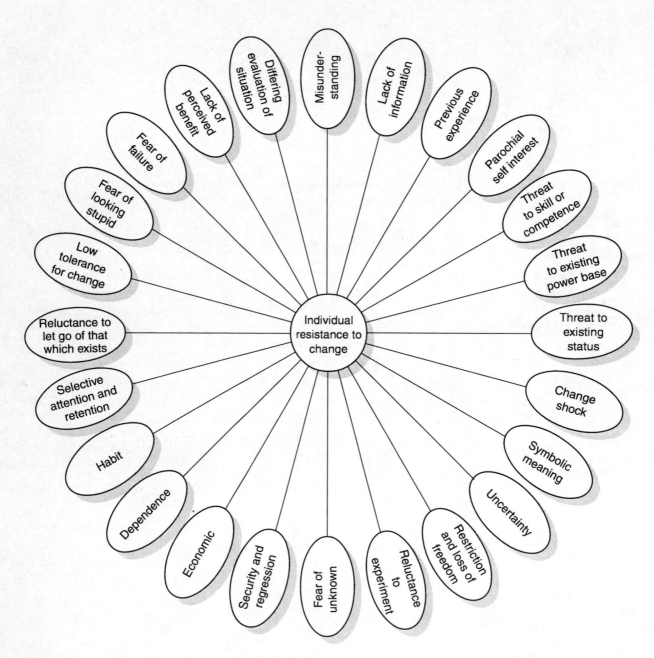

Figure 19.2 Individual reasons for resisting change.

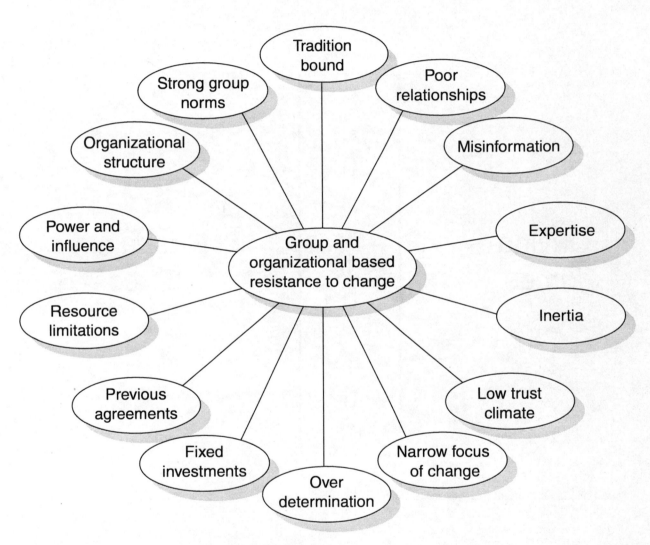

Figure 19.3 Group and organizational reasons for resisting change.

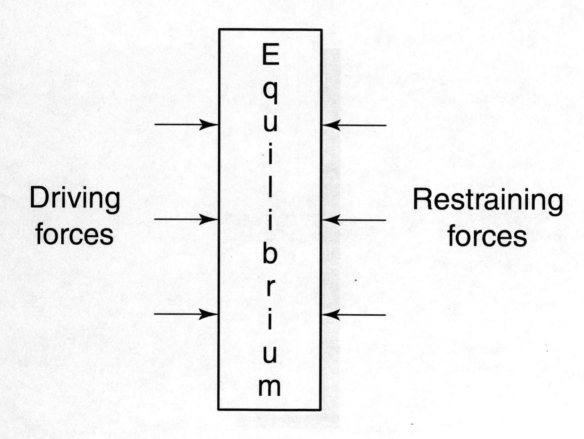

Figure 19.5   Lewin's forcefield analysis model.